THE WAGES OF SPIN

By the same author

Kill the Messenger
Yorkshire Millennium
Yorkshire Castles
Yorkshire Villages

THE WAGES OF SPIN

Bernard Ingham

JOHN MURRAY
Albemarle Street, London

A catalogue record for this book is available from the British Library

ISBN 0–7195–6481–6

Typeset in Monotype Bembo 12/13.5
by Servis Filmsetting Ltd, Manchester

Printed and bound in Great Britain by
Butler and Tanner Ltd
Frome and London

TO

*Charlotte and Tom who will, I hope, come to see this book
as a cautionary tale*

IN MEMORY OF

*The much abused Government Information Service, in
which I served*

Contents

Contents

Acknowledgements

This book is testament to the perseverance of my agent, Robert Kirby, of Peters, Fraser and Dunlop, who pressed, not to say pestered, me over the 1990s to write another book after *Kill the Messenger*, my memoirs as Margaret Thatcher's chief press secretary. My family also came to think that I ought to get off my chest my rising alarm and despair over the performance of the Blair government's unbalanced approach to presentation and the remarkable activities of its 'spin doctors'.

I had long harboured the idea of writing a history of the Government Information Service (GIS) I once led. So I was eventually moved to start putting the new governmental obsession with presentational command and control in the context of its relations with what is now called the media. In the course of this eventful journey I have had much help from former GIS colleagues and journalists whom I served as a press secretary. I would like to acknowledge their contributions by name but it would perhaps be better for them if I did not do so, given the circumstances.

I can, however, say I am indebted to John Desborough, former political correspondent the *Daily Mirror* and past chairman of both the Parliamentary Press Gallery and the Parliamentary Lobby Journalists, for his many constructive criticisms and his reminiscences. My son John, a journalist, much improved the text before it reached Matthew Taylor, my editor at John Murray. I would also like to thank Caroline Knox, of John Murray, for her sustained enthusiasm and Catherine Cameron, Robert Kirby's colleague, for her cheerful help.

I also extend a heartfelt acknowledgement to my daughter-in-law Christine, who immediately unearthed Paul Margey, a computer consultant in nearby Kenley, to rescue the text from my computer when it comprehensively crashed just when I had finished editing it.

Finally, turning to sources, I owe much to the following authors for permission to quote from their books: Don Macintyre, Peter Oborne, Andrew Rawnsley, John Rentoul, Professor Philip Schlesinger, Lord Lawson of Blaby, Nicholas Jones and Chris Moncrieff. The last two named also gave me valuable advice. I also appreciate the agreement of HarperCollins for me to quote from my book *Kill the Messenger,* and of *PR Week* for me to quote from my own and Charlie Whelan's columns in that newspaper.

I benefited much from reading the work of a range of authors, including Baroness Thatcher of Kesteven, Lord Howe of Aberavon, Lord Heseltine of Thenford, Tony Benn, Professor Peter Hennessy (who also offered useful advice), John Cole, Marlin Fitzwater, Robert Harris, Kenneth Harris, Doon Campbell, Joe Haines, Sir Harold Evans, James Margach, Lord (Francis) Williams, Marjorie Ogilvy-Webb, Sir Fife Clark, Graham Cawthorne, Alan Clark and Viscount Kemsley. I am grateful to all of them, living or dead, for their insights. Any failure to mention any other author who might recognize his or her contribution to my thinking on the issue of spin doctors and press secretaries is inadvertent, and my publisher and I would be ready to acknowledge their work.

I

Joy confined

THE DAY dawned bright but chilly on the Labour Party's triumph. On 8 June 2001 they achieved their overriding objective – a second term of office with a majority to guarantee them a full Parliament. For the first time in their 101 year's existence they viewed the satisfying prospect of a long run at governing Britain. Now they could really fashion the nation in their own image. The new Jerusalem was at hand.

Joy should have been unconfined, but the weather accurately set the tone. The bright sun fell on cold stones and on the chilled television crews littering the south bank of the Thames beside the ultimate political scene-setter, the Palace of Westminster.

The Prime Minister, Tony Blair, was remarkably subdued in the immediate aftermath of his historic victory. In his speech on winning the Sedgefield constituency in Co. Durham, albeit with a reduced majority, he spoke of 'a different mood' from the elated expectation that had greeted his first landslide victory in 1997 and of a 'a more reasoned judgement . . . based on a record of office'. On the pre-dawn flight from Teesside to London he confessed to being both happy and relieved. But he was manifestly not exuberant. He made it clear he wanted to see joy very much confined.

Television cameras were excluded – and prevented by window coverings – from filming the victory party at Labour's headquarters in the Millbank Tower. The party activists were not dispatched, as they had been in 1997, to wave their flags and exult in Downing

Street as Blair re-entered No. 10. Humility was the order of the day. Not even the breakfast-time resignation of the Conservative leader, William Hague, lifted the curious state of self-effacing sobriety into which Labour politicians seemed to have been plunged, though it gave the chattering classes something else to chatter about.

As my teeth chattered with the rest of them in the shivery, tented TV studios on the South Bank, I wondered whether the restrained emotion and cautious utterances were just another example of the 'spin-doctoring' that had come to brand the first term of New Labour, another demonstration of their remarkable ability to project the prescribed image. I have grown fascinated with this new profession which has come to dominate our society – and not merely the body politic – not least because I am widely accused of having provided the model and excuse for it.

The cynic in me shouted that Labour judged their interests would be better served by appearing humble on receiving their endorsement, that they thought it would look better if they went back to work without self-congratulation and adulation of their gloriously remarkable leader. Over a year later I have not the slightest doubt that Blair and his image-obsessed managers were indeed motivated, at least in part, by such concerns. But among Blair's portfolio of reputations is his ability to respond to the mood of the nation, which, in the moment of his own constituency victory, he acknowledged was different from four years earlier. That mood was not just a feeling. It was borne out by statistics that provided the justification – and excuse – for any pre-victory decision by Blair to seek public relations advantage by playing down his expected success.

Those statistics conveyed one message to him: 'OK, you're back with a huge majority of 167 – only 12 fewer than your record-breaking 179 in 1997 – but the punters aren't very happy.' In front of the black door of No. 10, which in another age had so often opened to me, he acknowledged the voters' 'very clear instruction to deliver'. In other words, Blair saw that he had chalked up another first by being the first British prime minister to find himself back in office with a landslide and yet on probation.

However vast his majority, he had commanded only 40.7% of

the votes polled, less than Margaret Thatcher had managed in her two landslides in the 1980s. But this time only 59.3% of the electorate had bothered to vote. This was by far the worst turn-out since the advent of universal adult suffrage in 1928, and 12 percentage points lower than in 1997. Just over 40% of the voters refused to go to the polls. More accurately, since roughly a quarter of those qualified to vote never exercise their right anyway, up to a fifth of those who would normally have made the effort stayed at home.

This meant that, chillingly – as Blair must have sensed as he played pianissimo in a minor key to the gallery – he was back with the full-hearted consent of only 24.1% of the British public. President Clinton did marginally better than that in securing his second term in 1996. True, the Conservatives obtained only 18.7% of the nation's support and the Liberal Democrats a mere 10.8%. But those figures just rubbed it in. Despite William Hague's skilful performances in the House of Commons, the Conservatives had never established themselves as a credible Opposition and the Liberal Democrats had become mere poodles of New Labour in the vain hope of securing proportional representation – a hope now buried under another landslide. One thing was for sure: it was not a triumph for the 'spin-doctoring' that had come to dominate his first term of office.

Yet Blair had one formidable achievement to his credit: he had not dissipated his golden economic legacy from John Major and Kenneth Clarke, the former Conservative Prime Minister and Chancellor of the Exchequer. These two Tories get next to no credit for eventually rescuing Margaret Thatcher's transformation of our economic fortunes from two disasters propagated in Brussels, or for setting a responsible Labour government up for at least two terms by their good works.

There are those tinder-dry Conservatives who have long argued vehemently that Labour's Chancellor, Gordon Brown, is steadily wasting that legacy by his propensity to tax, especially by stealth, and spend, even if he is inclined to exaggerate his redistributive largesse. But the fundamentals looked to be just what the doctor ordered for an election in the spring of 2001. Inflation, interest rates and unemployment were at their lowest levels for three decades and, even more electorally promising in a property-owning democracy, house prices were merrily buoyant. Public finances seemed to be under control. People felt good and had precious little incentive to change their government.

It is true – as Blair acknowledged outside No. 10 in taking the voters' instructions 'to deliver' – that Labour had not much else to show for four years of endless initiatives on education, the National Health Service, welfare reform, crime and that sick joke called transport. But there must be something seriously wrong if you can get only three out of five electors to the polls when the economy is in good nick and Her Majesty's Loyal Opposition is hardly worthy of the name.

Blair knew that he could not just dismiss the appalling turn-out as political apathy. He had to explain why that apathy existed. Certainly, his election campaign had done little to galvanize the voters. Labour took their watchword, like so many of their methods, from ex-President Clinton: 'It's the economy, stupid.' So they kept the temperature down, suppressed controversy, hid away from public view 'liabilities' such as Robin Cook, Clare Short, Keith Vaz and Geoffrey Robinson, ignored – and, worse still, were allowed to ignore – whole areas of public policy, including Europe and the looming crisis in Northern Ireland, and let the blessed state of prosperity speak for itself. Not even Hague's attempt to turn the election into a referendum on the euro discomfited Blair's strategy of burying inconvenient issues.

So the style of the campaign goes some way to explaining the apathy. But there was something else at work, too. The people were developing an antipathy to politics. Could it be, I wondered, that this stemmed from Blair's approach to government, which in turn stemmed from his approach to politics?

At this point I should make a confession. In the immediate after-math of Neil Kinnock's resignation as Labour leader, following his 1992 defeat, I urged the Labour Party through the *Daily Express* column I was then writing to choose Tony Blair rather than John Smith as his successor. I did not feel very comfortable doing this. I had worked for and liked John Smith when he was Minister of State in the Department of Energy in the late 1970s. Indeed, I probably retained my job as director of information in that department because of his wise advice.

My secretary of state, Tony Benn, arrived in a straight swap with Eric Varley from the Department of Trade and Industry. He was hurt, sore and resentful at what was effectively a demotion. After closeting himself away for weeks with his two political advisers, Francis Cripps and Frances Morrell, he eventually turned to mischief. One item took the form of seeking to make a ministerial broadcast on the newly gushing North Sea oil without right of Opposition reply, which the rules permitted in certain defined circumstances.

I told him it was not on because the issue was controversial. I was proved right when both No. 10 and the BBC rejected the idea when it was put to them with my proposed script, as amended by Benn. I was foolish enough to say that I agreed with them when I conveyed their rejection to him. Overnight he effectively gave me the sack by telling my permanent secretary, Sir Jack Rampton, that he didn't want me to accompany him on a forthcoming visit to Washington DC.

I consulted John Smith about my plight. He told me to go and have a row with Benn. 'Wedgie doesn't like rows', he said wickedly. I asked for a private meeting with Benn and, with a list of points to get over on my knee, I told him that of all the 1,300 people in the department I had a vested interest in his success since I had to try to clear up the mess of any failure with the press. Wedgie did not like rows – or signs of them. He immediately said he had treated me very badly and that it wouldn't happen again. We went on to forge a good working relationship.

That was one reason why I did not like advising the Labour Party to prefer Blair to Smith, not that it would have taken the slightest notice of me. But I thought Blair looked fresher, more attractive, more flexible and more likely to shake up Labour than the orthodox, archetypal 'Old Labour' John Smith, as he would now be called, had he not died tragically young as leader of the Opposition. His ideologically correct approach to taxation was partly blamed for costing Labour the election in 1992.

My judgement of Blair was subsequently vindicated when he became Labour's leader in 1994. He ditched Clause 4 of the party's constitution, which demanded the public ownership of production, distribution and exchange, distanced himself from the unions, which had demonstrated their propensity for abusing power, and committed the party to prudently managing the nation's finances. For good measure he also proclaimed he would contain inflation, a pledge for which my colleagues in Hill and Knowlton, the PR company of which I was a non-executive director for eleven years, like to give me the credit. During a lunch at their offices Alastair Campbell, Blair's press secretary, asked me directly what more they should do to make themselves electable. I replied, 'Promise to contain inflation.' They duly promised.

John Smith, as Labour leader, had taken the fear out of electing a Labour government, as Conservatives confided to me in his lifetime. Blair not only killed off any residual fear but also made Labour electable by changing the product on offer to the voters and vigorously marketing it. But that formidable achievement after their tragic irrelevance in the 1980s did not give New Labour a higher purpose than winning and holding office. And office itself brought no hint of a higher purpose when the declared objective from the start was to win a second full term.

I am sure Blair wants to make Britain 'a beacon for the world', to use one of his sound bites, through its quality of life, its 'modernization' (whatever that means), its economic performance and its leadership in Europe and the world, its education, health care, welfare, law and order and transport systems and through its community relations. But I don't think he has much of a clue how to light the beacon. And I am absolutely certain that he has no overarching philosophy other than pragmatism. He wants Labour to become the natural party of government and believes that the best way to perpetuate its dominance is to dispense with dogma, political principles and the baggage of belief.

This approach seems to have served him admirably for a remarkably long time. But it contains seeds of its own destruction because it conditions how you approach the business of government. If you don't believe in anything much apart from office, you will do everything you can to safeguard office because that is the be-all and end-all of your existence. Central control becomes an absolute requirement, especially given the Labour Party's history of dissent. You only move when you know how the public will take it. Clintonesque government by focus group becomes *de rigueur*.

This risks turning the government into followers rather than leaders of opinion. Admittedly, if it develops sharp antennae for the public mood, it can sometimes seize the moment, as Blair did when Diana, Princess of Wales, was killed and over Kosovo and the appalling terrorist attacks on New York and Washington in September 2001. But this form of government strains every sinew to present its governance in the most positive light. It becomes preoccupied with what it looks like because there is not much else to detain it.

My experience of working as a press secretary for the governments of four prime ministers, Labour and Tory, over twenty-four years through most of seven parliaments teaches me that even the most ideologically driven seeks a measure of control, to keep the public onside and to be seen to advantage through newspapers and the broadcasters. It also teaches me that post-war Britain has never had a less ideological government than Blair's and has never seen such obsession in government with issue and message control, public opinion and the management of press, radio and television.

It was the unprecedented intensity of Blair's obsession which bred the antipathy reflected in the 2001 election turn-out. Long before that election Labour voices could be heard condemning the Government as being 'all spin and no substance'. Government, it seemed, had been reduced under Blair to a mere game of media and, with their help, manipulation of the public.

I began to ask myself why the world of media management I had known professionally for nearly a quarter of a century had changed so abruptly overnight on 1 May 1997. Why had the landscape of Government–media relations, which had developed with geological slowness over the centuries, suddenly become transformed by an eruption of 'spin'? Why, given the constitutional responsibilities of Parliament and top civil servants as accounting officers for their departments and the collective nature of Cabinet's remit, was it allowed to happen? Why did it continue when it became clear that the upheaval which swept aside rules and conventions was damaging the Government that produced it, when it was clearly generating antipathy in a democracy that had hitherto taken its politics rather seriously? Why did the sea green incorruptibles of the press I had known, loved and fought become so easily spun?

In short, how on earth did we come to this pretty pass and where is it leading? This book seeks to find some answers to these questions in tracing the history of the development of what is now called spin-doctoring. What were the pressures that brought it about? Where does 'conventional' Government media management end and spin-doctoring begin? What, indeed, is a spin doctor? I fear my explanations in this book reflect credit on no one, not on Parliament, politicians, Civil Servants or journalists. It is a tale of woe that has been long in the making. It starts with the burning of books.

2

Repression and farce

CHAO CHENG Shih Huang-ti, the man who linked fortresses to form the Great Wall of China around 200 BC, is as good a chap as any to start with in the search for an explanation of the spin doctor's trade. His reputation has suffered from them, if you regard historians as the earliest surviving form of spin doctor. The traditional view of this Chinese emperor is that he was inhuman, crude and superstitious, but he united China, and the bureaucratic and administrative structure he laid down endured. In modern China he is seen as an outstanding personality who civilized barbarians and facilitated progress. In our own history Richard III, that glorious son of York, and Henry VIII, for example, have similarly blurred images.

Although history has eventually been kind to Shih Huang-ti, to give Cheng his posthumous name, he was condemned by Confucian scholars at the time as a charlatan because of his abiding interest in magic and alchemy. In his search for immortality he repeatedly summoned magicians to his court, and some 460 learned Confucians who opposed this practice are said to have been executed for their temerity. He also ordered a famous burning of the books, in which every tome outside the Imperial library not dealing with agriculture, medicine and prognostication or historical records of the Ch'in dynasty was consigned to the flames in 213 BC. He has had many followers, the Nazis not least among them.

Cheng's book-burning provides an early exhibition of the pre-occupation of rulers and governing cliques down the ages with controlling their environment and of their abiding difficulty with uncongenial views and those who express them. He may not have the image spin doctors would prescribe for their heraldic device, but he is part of the explanation for their existence. The issues of control and message have always been at the heart of governments' relations with publishers. And those liaising with the media – spin doctors, as they are now called – have always been ground between the upper and nether millstones of politicians' and journalists' interests.

Moving on sixteen centuries, the tensions between governors and governed – and especially the governed who comment on their governance – reappear in fifteenth-century England, which William Caxton was helping to revolutionize with his introduction of the printing press. At first both state and church, with Bibles pouring from the presses, welcomed this technological development. Richard III and his successor, Henry VII, the first Tudor king, actually encouraged the book trade before Henry VIII protected native stationers with a series of measures and eventually prohibited the free importation of books.

This may have been a commercial response to the arrival of printing, but from then on there were regular censorious proclamations against books considered to be heretical or seditious, culminating with a requirement to secure a Privy Council licence for the printing and distribution of books in English. By 1557 commercial advantage and censorship in Elizabethan England had been institutionalized under the Stationers' Company, at whose premises near St Paul's Cathedral journalists these days ironically hold their most prestigious events. The company thereby acquired a monopoly which it operated with what has been described as a 'self-interested subservience to authority' while at the same time establishing the rudiments of copyright. Thirty years later it was given powers, which it zealously exercised, to inspect printing offices and seize and destroy offending presses or material.

Things did not improve in the seventeenth century. With the Puritans in full flush, the Star Chamber clamped down further in 1637 by laying down licensing procedures, reducing the number of authorized printers and, of course, prescribing severe penalties for offences. The Parliamentarians soon ended the brief taste of freedom after the Star Chamber was abolished four years later by restoring licensing and the powers of the Stationers' Company.

Their measure of 1643 stimulated one of the most celebrated compositions in pursuit of religious and civil freedom: John Milton's *Areopagitica*, which sought to demolish every argument in favour of censorship. The battle over the freedom of the press was joined but not won. Licensing was restored with the Restoration and was operated more or less rigorously until it lapsed in 1679. James II revived it in 1685 but Parliament refused to renew it in 1694. Freedom of the press from licensing, if not from attempts to control it by other means such as libel actions, had arrived.

So too had adult literacy. Technological innovation brought social change, and with it an increasing number of people able to read and hungry for material. In fact, the first newspapers – that is, reasonably regular publications containing topical information – arrived in Britain in 1621. They were called 'corantos' (currents of news). The first were unauthorized, so their pioneer publisher, Thomas Archer, ended up in gaol. For the next twenty years licensed corantos were mostly English translations of foreign news, highly dependent on the arrival of ships, combined with domestic trivia because of censorship.

Even foreign news got the publishers into trouble, notably for their anti-imperialist reporting of the Thirty Years' War, and all 'news books', as the corantos were called, were banned for six years, until the end of 1638. Like books, these early newspapers had their ups and downs for the next fifty years, from the abolition of the Star Chamber to the demise of licensing. But one thing was clear: both books and newspapers flourished and proliferated in freedom.

In the more relaxed atmosphere after the Glorious Revolution of 1688, and as packet and post systems improved, newspapers spread to the provinces and to Scotland and began to specialize in such things as trade, politics, entertainment and culture. The *Worcestershire Post Man*, the *Edinburgh Gazette*, *Lloyd's News* (the forerunner of *Lloyd's List*), Daniel Defoe's political *Review* and the *Tatler* and the *Spectator* were the leaders. But it was a perilous existence. You might not have been required to have a licence, but, by

Jove, you had to watch your step. Within a year *Lloyd's News* had succeeded in offending the House of Lords and, rather than aplogize, John Lloyd shut it down for nigh on thirty years. In 1702 Defoe was only one of many to be imprisoned and pilloried for, in his case, an offending pamphlet on dissent.

Governments have always had a variety of ways of applying pressure if they choose to use them. One of them is taxation. So in 1712 the British Government tried to curb the embryonic power of the press by introducing the Stamp Act, imposing a halfpenny tax on every two-page and a penny tax on every four-page newspaper, as well as a duty on advertisements. This package of measures had for the Government the satisfactory, if only temporary, effect of killing off many newspapers, including the *Spectator*. But another way to kill a cat, or at least to make it harmless, is to stuff it with cream. Subsidies to preferred client organs and hand-outs to journalists by both Whigs and Tories were rife in the eighteenth century and beyond – some people claim right up to the Reform Act of 1832.

So was repression, which, in terms of law, reached its high-water mark in the early nineteenth century, in the wake of the bloody French Revolution. Nine years after William Cobbett, journalist and tribune of the poor, was fined and imprisoned in 1810 for denouncing flogging in the army, came the panicky response by Lord Liverpool's government to the Peterloo massacre in Manchester. Liverpool's Six Acts of 1819 equated demands for Parliamentary reform with treason, prohibited meetings of more than fifty people, extended the summary powers of justices of the peace, increased stamp duties on newspapers and made the publication of blasphemous and seditious libels a transportable offence. Dissident journalists were clearly earmarked as suitable for transportation.

Yet the battle to report Parliament had been won nearly fifty years earlier. MPs threw in that towel in 1771, when they tacitly conceded they had gone far too far in asserting their authority. In the process they crossed swords with the City of London and caused a riot outside the Palace of Westminster. When a member complained that a City printer had reported his speech, the Speaker ordered the Serjeant-at-Arms to arrest the offender on his warrant. This infuriated the City Corporation, which claimed independent jurisdiction over its territory. It arrested Parliament's messenger for assault on the printer and Lord Mayor Crosby incarcerated him in prison.

The Commons promptly summoned the Lord Mayor and aldermen to attend at the bar of the House to answer for this offence to their sovereign authority. The City dignitaries processed there down the Strand and Whitehall, accompanied by a host of City tradesmen and shopkeepers who were in a foul mood. They unceremoniously dragged MPs out of their carriages and the Prime Minister, Lord North, was struck by a baton as he stepped from his conveyance. He is reported to have cried: 'Gentlemen, do you call this liberty?' 'Yes', cried the mob, 'and a great liberty, too.'

The farce continued in the House. The Lord Mayor, suffering from gout, was allowed to address MPs seated instead of kneeling, as required for those summoned for censure. Mr Speaker duly admonished him and he went to cool off in the Tower of London for six weeks until the end of the session. After this excess Parliament retained its powers to punish offenders but never seriously disputed the principle that it might be reported.

The powers were still available in 1949, when an MP complained he had been misrepresented by a newspaper. The Committee of Privileges solemnly examined the evidence and three months later reported: 'By the resolution of the House of 3rd March 1762 any publication of reports of speeches of honourable Members is a breach of privilege. Therefore the publication of a report . . . of the speech by the honourable Member was technically a breach of the privileges of this House.' Wisely, it recommended no action. Given the resolution of 1762, it had no option but to find for the MP, but there were those who saw the majesty of the whole episode as a bit of a joke.

The City and Corporation of London may have been instrumental in forcing the issue, but the heroes in the long battle for the right to publish accounts of Parliament's proceedings are the guerrilla army of reporters who employed every wile to get their way, from downright duplicity to massive invention and coruscating pens. It was inevitable that the reporting of Parliament should be a fraught issue. The reasons for it were also as complex as they were emotive. MPs – and not just governments – were initially opposed to a word being printed about their debates. Publication of anything beyond the bare votes was regarded as privileged. Any report of Parliament was condemned as a misrepresentation and any publication was declared libellous, however accurate. The greater the truth, the greater the libel.

The MPs' objective was to keep their business from the monarch, or to confine it to what they thought fit to tell him about through their representative, the Speaker. This was the origin of the Parliamentary tradition, now more honoured in the breach than the observance, forbidding the reading of speeches. Until relatively recently, while Parliament had some life in it, MPs would bawl 'Reading, reading' at a back-bencher, as distinct from a minister at the dispatch box, who resorted, however briefly, to a script. No notes, no leaks to the Palace, seemed to be the theory. So note-taking was also forbidden in the Strangers' Gallery and still is, although an experiment in 1993 briefly allowed it in an 'informal' way for 'personal purposes'. Back in the seventeenth century MPs reckoned without Charles I, who had a number of their colleagues in his pay to keep him informed.

From trying to keep their debates secret from the king it was but a short step for MPs to justify keeping the people they represented in the dark. Of course, however convenient it may have been to them to debate the nation's affairs in private and unreported, it was futile to expect this cosy state of affairs to continue in an increasingly literate society demanding greater rights. But the battle for those rights took a long time – well over a century, in fact, discounting a brief relaxation under Cromwell.

In taking their time, MPs occasionally made themselves look as ridiculous as they eventually appeared in their confrontation with the City in 1771 as they consigned their colleagues to the Tower of London, or had their texts publicly burned by the common hangman for publishing their own speeches. Others were hauled before the Bar of the House to apologize – on their knees, of course – for their gross intrusion in publicizing its proceedings. But the more Parliament tried to keep its deliberations under wraps, the more people tried to expose them to the public gaze and the more their reports became commercial.

Samuel Johnson kept himself financially afloat from 1741 to 1744 reporting speeches for the coffee-house newspapers on the basis of second-hand information and invention. His intelligence, such as it was, came from runners who bribed their way into the Strangers' Gallery. The bare bones of their tales were more than enough for Johnson, and no doubt some MPs preferred his speech to their own and basked in the glory of his journalism. 'Memory men' in the pay of printers were also sent to the Strangers' Gallery and they too provided Johnson, and others, with material. William 'Memory' Woodfall, editor and printer of the *Morning Chronicle*, stationed himself there for twenty years, repairing to his office when he had heard enough to report the speeches verbatim, or so it was claimed. Others were reputed to go straight to the printers and dictate speeches word for word to the typesetters. They remind me of my first editor, Will Ashworth, who never wrote a word on paper after council meetings in Hebden Bridge, West Yorkshire; instead he just set them in type at his linotype machine from the shorthand in his notebook.

According to Boswell, Johnson's particular memory man was a chap called Guthrie, with a 'very quick and tenacious' memory, who sent his notes to Johnson for revision and publication in the *Gentleman's Magazine*. Johnson reported Parliament under a pseudonym, 'The Senate of Lilliput', and used easily deciphered anagrams of their names to identify MPs. His speeches were so good that Voltaire claimed 'The oratory of Greece and Rome is revived in the British senate'. Eventually, however, Johnson was stricken by his conscience and stopped 'reporting' Parliament, according to Boswell, because 'he would not be an accessory to the propagation of falsehood'.

All this may have been endearingly British, not to say Ruritanian, but it could not go on with 'that devil Wilkes' around. John Wilkes, journalist and politician, was a curious champion of the freedom of the press. He was extremely ugly, with a hideous squint but cartloads of charm, and was a profligate reprobate, often deep in debt and as frequently on the run as he was expelled from Parliament. But his ready wit and hard-hitting, vituperative pen, notably in the pages of the political newspaper *North Briton*, helped to extend the liberty of the press in two ways. Wilkes established through the courts the illegality of general warrants, which did not name the persons to be arrested. Government then used them against the press to such excess that forty-eight persons were once seized in the search for evidence before they apprehended Wilkes. He also effectively destroyed the power of Parliament to exact retribution for the reporting of its debates by exploiting around the time of the City's great bust-up with Parliament in 1771 the judicial privileges of the City of London to prevent the arrest of its printers.

The early history of newspaper journalism in Britain has left its mark down the centuries on journalistic attitudes to government and politicians and all who exercise authority. It contributes to the turbulence of the frontier between government and media that spin doctors, as they are now called, are required to patrol. It conditions – or should condition – their approach.

3

Grudging – and inaudible

IT WAS one thing for journalists to win the right, if only tacitly, to report Parliament; it was another for them to secure MPs' acceptance of their role. The winning of that long battle is the story of the nineteenth century. Indeed victory was not really secured until 16 July 1971, when the Commons overturned a resolution of 3 March 1762 defining any publication of reports of speeches by MPs as a breach of privilege. It then resolved not to entertain any complaint of contempt of the House or breach of privilege for the publication of its debates or proceedings, provided they were not conducted 'with closed doors or in private or when such publication shall have been expressly prohibited by the House'. Nine years later, on 31 October 1980, it made the reporting of evidence at public sittings of select committees legitimate.

These victories went largely unnoticed since the March 1762 resolution had long since fallen into dusty disuse. In fact, there was no great pressure for it to be overturned; those journalists who were aware that there were still constitutional limits to their activities preferred simply to let sleeping dogs lie. They feared that any liberating resolution might complicate matters by making their acceptance conditional on such subjective requirements as 'fairness' or 'accuracy' or, heaven forfend, 'balance'.

Graham Cawthorne, chairman of the Parliamentary Press Gallery in 1949–50, dated the beginning of tolerated, though not officially recognized, parliamentary reporting at Westminster to

1803. That is rather later than Boswell put it. Boswell claimed in his *Life of Johnson*, published in 1791, that 'in our time the press has acquired an unrestrained freedom, so that the people in all parts of the kingdom have a fair, open and exact report of all the proceedings of their representatives and legislators which in our constitution is highly to be valued'.

The event on which Cawthorne based his claim was a speech by William Pitt on the war against Bonaparte. Two years before Trafalgar every seat was taken in the public gallery to hear Pitt's speech about the imminent threat of invasion. People swarmed into seats normally occupied by reporters, no doubt bribing their way in, for the attendants made a fat living out of the 'sale' of seats. The result was that Pitt went unreported. *The Times* wailed, 'We cannot contend with impossibilities'. The following day the Speaker ordered the back row of the Strangers' Gallery to be reserved for journalists, and the Parliamentary Press Gallery was born. The reporters were allowed to take notes, using their knees as desks.

This milestone in the development of an open Parliamentary democracy was not calculated to please the 'publish-and-be-damned' Duke of Wellington, who went to his death in 1852 bitterly resenting the reporting of Parliament's proceedings. It would be unwise to make too much of 1803, but at least by then journalists had a foothold – or more precisely a place for their bottoms – in Parliament. And by 1828 Macaulay was moved to coin that most famous phrase about the power of the press: 'The gallery in which the reporters sit has become a fourth estate of the realm.'

It is far from clear that this was how the early gallery saw itself. Charles Dickens, the most distinguished gallery reporter Parliament has known, spent four years in it from 1831 and left some idea of the appalling conditions in which he performed his task. Having learned Gurney's shorthand in three months and practised as a reporter in the law courts, Dickens became an independent shorthand writer looking for full-time work in the Commons, like his uncle John Henry Barrow before him. It was Barrow who eventually took Dickens on to report for the *Mirror of Parliament*, a well-respected weekly account of the proceedings of the Commons and the Lords, for the handsome sum of £5 a week. The Lords, always more progressive than the Commons, reserved a gallery for the press in the year he arrived, though it was a mere 'pen' in which they had to stand. On his back-row bench in the Commons Dickens found it hard to hear what was taking place below on the floor of the House, dark and 'so ill-ventilated that few constitutions could long bear the unwholesome atmosphere'. Personal hygiene was not what it is today. He later moaned: 'I have worn my knees by writing on them on the old back row of the old gallery of the old House of Commons, and I have worn my feet out by standing to write in the preposterous pen in the old House of Lords, where we used to be huddled together like so many sheep – kept in waiting, say, until the Woolsack might want re-stuffing.'

After his shift of 45–60 minutes' note-taking, this 'rapidest and most accurate shorthand writer in the gallery' emerged stifled, with numbed wrists and aching back, and deeply unimpressed. He departed the Commons with contempt for it, in spite of his coverage of the passage of the Reform Bill of 1832. Its remoteness from life as it was lived by the masses possibly inspired him to begin writing *The Pickwick Papers* and *Oliver Twist* while he was labouring there.

Well before this, the poet Samuel Taylor Coleridge and the essayist William Hazlitt tried their hand at reporting. Coleridge retired hurt and in 1815 Hazlitt, finding the work very laborious, was advised on medical grounds to leave the gallery (and never again to touch alcohol). Coleridge, in the early part of his immensely troubled life, went to work in Westminster without shorthand and, perhaps inevitably, did not earn himself a reputation for accurate reportage. Once, when his report was questioned, he tried to excuse himself on account of stress, as it would now be described, having had to queue for a place from 7 a.m., many hours before proceedings began, and having repeatedly fallen asleep during a 25-hour stint. 'I shall give up this newspaper business,' he told a friend, 'it is too fatiguing.' He returned, fortunately, to poetry.

Being a Parliamentary reporter was no picnic. Nor did it improve when the Commons burned down in 1835. The Lords graciously gave up their more or less surviving chamber to the

Commons, who, with unwonted liberality, maintained the press 'pen' – with all its 'standing room only' deficiencies. That was the origin of a separate Commons press gallery. When Sir Charles Barry, assisted by A.W.N. Pugin, designed the new Gothic revival Palace of Westminster, reporters hoped for improvements, especially when Queen Victoria opened the new session in a new House in 1850. But their hopes were immediately dashed when the acoustics in the magnificent chamber with its lofty roof proved so bad that nobody could hear a word spoken. It had been designed for anything but debating or the reporting of those debates. *The Times* complained that its reporters would go deaf if they did not die first of rheumatism from the draughts and the constant dripping from the new gas lamps above their heads.

The Prime Minister, Lord John Russell, pronounced conditions impossible when he himself conducted an audition in the Press Gallery. He cannot have been surprised because MPs could not hear each other in debate. The member for Montrose demanded Barry be hauled before the Bar and tried, presumably for incompetence. 'Any schoolboy would be flogged for such a design. The nation [has] spent £1 million on the education of Mr Barry as a medieval architect.'

The campaign for the right to report Parliament, having been succeeded by a sixty-year campaign for, first, a seat from which to report it and then for a seat in the press's very own gallery, now gave way to an even longer campaign for the right to hear what was being said in the name of the nation. Even allowing for Dr Johnson's supreme ability to report speeches without having heard a word of them, it is in many ways the most comic of the glacially slow-moving episodes in the history of relations between politicians and journalists. It is also part of the compost from which spin doctors emerged.

Before they knew where they were, Parliamentary reporters were back in the Lords' inaudible chamber while Barry put in a false ceiling, which from 1852 made Commons reporting just about feasible, once reporters had adjusted to its acoustics. The Lords remained more or less unintelligible to listeners for another seventy-five years – further evidence of the leisurely pace at which Parliament's media relations evolved. In that time they made only one concession: they brought the reporters of *Hansard* down from the gallery to sit on the actual floor of the House, close to the action, not out of compassion but because they were fed up with the inevitable inaccuracy of the official report.

It was not until 1925 that Reuters persuaded the Lords to conduct an experiment with amplification by placing a microphone on the floor, connected to headphones in the gallery. They did so with much misgiving because they feared the reporters would overhear and, worse still, report backchat. Their fears were justified on the very first day. When an Opposition peer expressed the hope that he would reply to a debate, Lord Birkenhead was heard to mutter 'You bet I will', or words to that effect. The microphones became accepted practice, however, after reporters had been put on their honour to concentrate on debate and cut out eavesdropping. This was a bonus for those peers who had hitherto been unheard and so under-reported and under-estimated. Among them, it is recorded, was little, wizened, old Lord Haldane, whose splendid copy brought him more newspaper coverage in the last two years of his life than during his previous fourteen in the Upper House.

The Commons remained impervious to the seductive benefits of being easily heard as well as seen. Every effort over the fifteen years up to the Second World War to get microphones into their chamber was summarily rejected. The MPs were supported by a combination of gallery reporters who took inordinate professional pride in having overcome the bad acoustics and those who feared they would be out of a job in Parliament because their organs would pipe the debates to their offices.

With war looming, William Barkley, the celebrated Parliamentary reporter of the *Daily Express*, resorted to Latin. In a letter setting out the problem to the First Commissioner of Works, a man rejoicing in the name of Herwald Ramsbotham (later Lord Soulbury), he extended an invitation that he found irresistible. 'Quare non venis nos videre aliquando ut ait Maia Occidentalis', wrote Barkley, 'Why don't you come up and see us some time, as Mae West would say?' With the war three weeks old, Ramsbotham agreed to try sitting in the gallery, where he admitted he could hear nothing. He reported later that Mr Speaker had agreed to experiments.

The Press Gallery were then informed that an experiment, conducted in their absence, had confirmed the view that amplification was impossible. They reckoned it had been rejected by ministers for fear that back-benchers would pick up their impromptu reactions and embarrassing asides. And then in 1941 the roof fell in on the Commons, in two ways. First it was bombed and then it took over the Lords' chamber, where the Press Gallery was wired for sound. And so the reporters eventually had their way, and both Houses of Parliament have been more or less audible ever since.

Nothing better illustrates the evolutionary nature of British history than the grudging pace of its development into a more or less open democracy. It took 247 years from the end of licensing of publications for reporters to be admitted to Parliament and then to acquire such fundamental facilities as the ability to hear debates within normal earshot. Over those centuries nothing was given away by the Commons. Most of the concessions had to be forced, like rhubarb, by events ranging from farce to fire and bombs. Journalism has absorbed that history into its psyche. That is why political journalists need handling carefully, a fact that spin doctors, as they are called, should never forget.

4

The age of deference

THE PRESS gallery's hundred-year hearing problem speaks
volumes for Parliament's reluctance to accept reporters in its
midst. It also testifies to the ambivalence of government towards
the news media and to the care with which journalism approached
its political masters. Even in 'the best club in London', as Dickens
described the Commons in *Our Mutual Friend*, journalists working
in very difficult conditions were remarkably slow to come together
institutionally. In fact, it took 110 years from the time Parliament
tacitly accepted reporters for them to form the Parliamentary Press
Gallery.

The date scarcely rates a mention in the gallery's booklet on its
development. But its centenary was celebrated in 1981 at a gallery
dinner in the Caledonian Club in London which I attended with
the Prime Minister, Margaret Thatcher, their chief guest. Parliament was then in crisis, just as it had been in 1771. There were
rioters in the streets of an unnaturally quiet London and my driver,
Tom Savage, gave Brixton a wide berth when he drove my wife
and me home to Purley in Surrey afterwards. I had spent the
dinner keeping in touch with No. 10 about the state of rioting,
and by the time we reached Purley I was very worried about Tom
getting home safely. Not surprisingly, the Prime Minister made
her theme freedom and responsibility – and the responsibility of
the 'oldest and most distinguished press gallery in the world' for
guarding that freedom.

Before we got anywhere near the Caledonian Club that evening Mrs Thatcher put on a bravura performance which has enabled me to describe her as 'the fastest dresser in the west'. She had the ability not only to look like a star but also to achieve the effect in next to no time. I cleared her speech with her at the last minute and dictated the changes as I was getting into my dinner jacket. I then had to get it in the right order and when I dashed into the hall of No. 10 I found the Prime Minister impatiently tapping her foot and asking what had taken so long. Come to think of it, it was a pertinent question to ask the press gallery. After the uneasy acceptance of journalists in 1771 and the acquisition of their back-row perch in 1803, why was it not until 1881 that the gallery was formed?

The only rational explanation is the slowness with which MPs adapted to the concept of an open democracy, let alone one with full adult suffrage, and the care with which journalists proceeded amid the latent hostility. But there was also another reason: filthy lucre.

The date 1881 really marks the opening up of the Press Gallery to provincial journalists. Until then it had been a monopoly of the London papers. The provincial newspapers had to make do with reports from the London men after they had written their copy. This was a lucrative trade for these monopolists. The owners of the sharpest ears in London and the otherwise robust constitutions needed to cope with their testing working conditions were immensely rich. Their earnings were put at £3,000 a year at a time when the working man generally scraped by on a few shillings per week. They owned, it is claimed, some of the best shoots in Scotland. Such vested interests are not easily overcome, but a phys-ical extension of the Press Gallery in 1881 did for them and their monopoly.

Uncharacteristically, in this tale of stately progress towards Parliamentary acceptance, the next move came only three years later. In 1884 a body of Parliamentary Lobby journalists – or the Lobby, as it is now known – was formed, for the benefit of what may be termed newspapers' political intelligence agents, as distinct from mere reporters of what is said in Parliament. Its formation almost certainly owed more to the needs of security against the activities of the Irish Fenians than to any desire on the part of politicians for the public to be better informed about their activities. The Lobby gets its name from the privilege its members are accorded. They reach the parts of the Palace of Westminster which other journalists are denied – namely, the Members' Lobby of the Commons, where they have ready access to ministers and MPs. Their registered membership is the means by which the Serjeant-at-Arms controls access to this inner sanctum.

The Lobby was until relatively recently a minor subsidiary of the Press Gallery, to which its members also belong. Now the Lobby is numerically dominant since reporting of proceedings has largely gone by the board. Its members are the political editors and correspondents who cover the war between the parties and assess and interpret the significance of events in Whitehall and Westminster.

Mr Speaker Peel sanctioned the idea of a Lobby just as General Gordon was going to his doom in Khartoum and the French were protesting – as they still do from time to time – about the adoption of Greenwich at the Prime Meridian Conference as the home of universal time. Peel was nothing if not cautious in his innovation. Initially, only one 'gentleman' of the press was accorded this mould-breaking concession. And nobody is now certain of the identity of the pioneer who took up his lonely station, wearing the regulation silk top hat that was the required mode of dress until 1939, with a break from protocol during the First World War. The Lobby's entire records were destroyed in the fire caused by the bombing that wrecked the Commons in 1941 and no one survived, or bothered, to recall the past for posterity. Some think the first of the many to follow was Sir Henry Lucy, who wrote a distinguished column for *Punch* as 'Toby MP'.

What is clear is that he was expected to behave like a child and on no account to speak to MPs before he was spoken to. When I joined the Government Information Service as a press secretary in 1967 I was similarly given to understand that it was better to be seen than heard. Perhaps that is why an Irish correspondent, so legend has it, was once seen wearing a mustard tweed suit beneath the black topper: he wanted to be noticed. *The Press Gallery at Westminster* records that for a long time the privilege 'went no further than the right to talk to any member who was so good as to stop and pass the time of day with the phenomenon'. He and his successors had to content themselves 'with writing their carefully phrased pieces and with being as inconspicuous as possible'.

But the genie was out of the bottle. The privilege was steadily extended and a select crowd of 'seven or eight round the table talking to the Prime Minister' was soon noticed, as well as their lengthy third-person pontifications on the political situation identified by initials such as APN (A.P. Nicholson) and EJ (Edward James).

Like their gallery colleagues, they were concerned to preserve their privilege and to allow it to evolve. From the first they were preoccupied with discretion and restraint, in an age of deference that survived until the 1960s. Yet decades before the Lobby was formed, sources close to the Cabinet regularly leaked 'secrets' to John Delane, the editor of *The Times*, for whom disclosure was an article of journalistic faith. He built up a formidable reputation in the mid-nineteenth century for regularly and accurately publishing Cabinet decisions very soon after they had been reached. He would not, of course, have received these leaks and been able to practise the disclosure he preached if he had identified his sources.

Nor would the Lobby have later had the chance to evolve if its members had spent their time revealing where they had got their stories from and attributing quotes to their informants. Speaker Peel's innovation would soon have collapsed, had the earliest journalists to be allowed into, as distinct from let loose in, the Members' Lobby supplied the source of the inspiration for their lengthy 'think-pieces', as such articles came to be called. Journalistic self-interest required a certain discretion and their rules came to reflect it.

They still reflected it in the 1969 edition of *Lobby Practice*, a little, maroon 4½″×2½″ pocket book that I acquired as Chief Information Officer working for Barbara Castle in the Department of Employment and Productivity. And the 'little maroon book' technically still governs Lobby behaviour, since it has never been withdrawn, though, to be fair, it has not been reissued with amendments resulting from 'the Great Lobby Revolt', as I describe it, in which I was intimately involved in the 1980s.

First, the booklet is at pains to teach individual members their personal and collective responsibilities: 'He [the Lobby member] has complete freedom to get his own stories in his own way', it says.

> There are no restrictions of any kind on personal initiative. But he also owes a duty to the Lobby as a whole, in that he should do nothing to prejudice the communal life of the Lobby or its relations with the two Houses and the authorities. This is in the Lobby journalist's own interest and that of his office, as well as in the general interest of the Lobby. It is a responsibility which should always be kept in mind.

Clause 2 denies the Lobby's existence as an 'association' but adds that 'in our common interests we act collectively as the Parliamentary Lobby Journalists'. Over fourteen paragraphs the document then goes on to explain how a member should behave operating alone or in concert with other Lobby members. Because these rules governed my operations with them as well as their relations with my ministers for much of my twenty-four years as a Government press officer from 1967, I set out the text below to show just how carefully Lobby journalists were expected to conduct themselves in pursuing their rough trade.

Individual Lobbying

3. The work of a Lobby journalist brings him into close daily touch with ministers and Members of Parliament of all parties and imposes on him a very high standard of responsibility and discretion in making use of the special facilities given him for writing about political affairs. The cardinal rule of the Lobby is never to identify its informant without specific permission. In any case, members of the Lobby must always take personal responsibility for their stories and their facts.

4. Great care must be taken not to reveal anything, even indirectly, which could lead to identification of informants. There are, of course, numerous instances when an informant is perfectly willing to be identified. This is in order as long as the journalist has obtained his permission.

5. The Lobby regularly receives advance copies of official documents to facilitate its work. All embargoes on such documents, and on all information given orally or operationally in advance for the Lobby's convenience, must be strictly observed.

Collective Lobbying

6. The Lobby frequently invites ministers and others to meet it collectively to give information and answer questions. Members are under an obligation to keep secret the fact that such meetings are held and to avoid revealing the sources of their information.

7. It is recognized, however, that a correspondent has a special responsibility to his editor. The following resolution was therefore passed by the Lobby in July 1955:

'That it is consistent with Lobby practice that members of the Lobby may tell their editors, or acting editors, the sources of their information at Lobby meetings on the rare occasions that this must be vital, but must, on every occasion that such information is passed on, explain to their editors, or acting editors, that the source is strictly confidential.'

8. DON'T TALK ABOUT LOBBY MEETINGS BEFORE OR AFTER THEY ARE HELD, especially in the presence of those not entitled to attend them. If outsiders appear to know something of the arrangements made by the Lobby, do not confirm their conjectures or assume that as they appear to know so much they may safely be told the rest.

9. The Lobby correspondent should bear in mind that the purpose of a meeting is to elicit information, not to score political or debating points.

10. It is a point of honour to stay to the end of a meeting. If there is some compelling reason for a correspondent to leave, he is under an obligation to obtain the permission of the chairman to do so and, if released, is under an equal obligation not to make use of anything that has been said at the meeting before it ends.

11. When meetings are arranged on the Lobby's behalf, every correspondent should endeavour to attend. The Lobby works most effectively when the courtesy and co-operation shown by ministers and others are reciprocated in this way.

General Hints

12. Do not 'see' anything in the Members' Lobby or any of the private rooms or corridors of the Palace of Westminster. It is the rule that incidents, pleasant or otherwise, should be treated as private if they happen in those parts of the building to which Lobby correspondents have access solely because their names are on the Lobby list.

13. Do not run after a minister or Member. It is nearly always possible to place oneself in a position to avoid this.

14. When a member of the Lobby is in conversation with a minister, MP or peer, another member of the Lobby should not join in the conversation unless invited to do so. Nor should the Lobby activities of any colleagues ever be the subject of published comment.

15. Do not crowd together in the Lobby so as to be conspicuous. Do not crowd round the Vote Office when an important document is expected. Never use a notebook in the Lobby. Should it be necessary to make a note of anything, care should be taken to do so discreetly and unobtrusively – e.g., on the back of an order paper.

16. NEVER IN ANY CIRCUMSTANCES MAKE USE of anything accidentally overheard in any part of the Palace of Westminster.

The document ends with comments on the rules governing Parliamentary privilege, and an admonition, in capitals, to members to ensure that any deputy acting in their absence understands Lobby practice.

By 1984, when the Lobby celebrated its centenary, some of these rules were being disregarded. Margaret Thatcher, the chief guest at their celebratory lunch, had much fun with them. She said it was 'the first time the Fourth Estate had avowed its Secret Service. Today the organization that never was, is . . . Today in the Savoy the Lobby is made flesh. I for one rejoice in your fleeting identity – in your being let out, as it were – for it simplifies my task of proposing the health of an organization which otherwise would not exist and would never meet.' She also made clear that 'Celestial Blue is on the record'. That was what she would have been called by old Lobby hands when speaking among themselves in code about a meeting with the Tory prime minister. Their code for a Labour prime minister was apparently 'Sunrise Red'. 'Red Mantle' and 'Blue Mantle' were code for the Leader of the House and Leader of the Opposition, who saw the Lobby regularly on Thursday afternoons after the statement on the following week's Commons' business.

The Lobby's rules, though technically still operating, are now regarded as a relic of a bygone age of preposterous secrecy, freemasonry and subservience. Some erstwhile journalists, such as Professor Peter Hennessy, who found themselves in the Lobby, came rather to despise them. There was also tension between Lobby journalists and especially labour and industrial correspondents, of which I used to be one, since labour correspondents tended to cover economics, politics and strikes when industrial disputes were rife and they were a power in journalism. Sir Trevor Evans, the celebrated *Daily Express* industrial correspondent, dismissed the Lobby as 'the hand-out hussars', as if they existed on a diet of Government press releases. The Lobby retaliated by describing labour and industrial correspondents as 'The Marquess of Granby's Own' after the pub outside the Transport and General Workers' Union's HQ, where they gathered.

More recently journalists such as Peter Riddell, of *The Times*, say the rules were designed to elevate the importance of the Lobby (now political) editor in newspaper hierarchies, even though their men in the Lobby were always going to be kingpins. The critics miss the point. The rules accurately reflect the atmosphere and environment into which the Lobby was born and its need to preserve its privilege of access to the Members' Lobby if it was ever painstakingly to win acceptance. They also recognize a contemporary professional reality: since their brand of journalism is driven by background information rather than the reportage of events, stories will be more easily come by if a certain discretion prevails. They put in perspective all the preposterous contemporary piety about the need for journalists to quote informants when many – and perhaps even most – political stories owe far more to a quiet 'secret' chat or tip-off than to open, volunteered quotes.

It became one of the perks of members of the Lobby to have twice-daily briefings from the Prime Minister's press secretary, though under the arrangement they were technically always called by the Lobby itself. The Lobby has also become a major and perhaps the most important channel of communication for specialist government departments. Its members do daily battle with the Government's spin doctors, as press officers have come to be called. They are also partly why we acquired spin doctors. Members of the Lobby have much to answer for.

5

Random and piecemeal

I F THIS history teaches us anything, it is that our democracy
evolved with painful slowness in roughly 100-year cycles. It
took a little longer than that to get rid of the Tudors' licensing of
book (and later newspaper) production in 1694. Virtually another
eighty years elapsed before Parliament tacitly accepted in 1771 the
inevitability of its proceedings being reported. While the back
row of the Strangers' Gallery was reserved for reporters from 1803,
it was not until 1850 that the press got their very own gallery in
the Commons and it was nearly another 100 years after that before
they acquired one from which they could adequately hear the
proceedings. And, as we have just seen, it was no less than 110
years after Parliament caved in to reportage that journalists were
moved to form their own institution – the Parliamentary Press
Gallery.

It may be argued that journalists, competing fiercely with each
other, are not very clubbable. Certainly some are lone wolves, but
generally they hunt in packs. Yet even those of a solitary disposition must have seen possibilities in a larger gallery-size pack of persuading politicians to deliver more by way of facilities as well as
stories. The Press Gallery came to provide a happy hunting ground
for all in its regular lunches, which gave – and continue to give –
politicians news-making opportunities. I conclude that the notion
that journalists are resistant to clubs does not wash. They are generally as gregarious as deer.

They are also by nature demanding and sceptical towards authority. Yet the Government took nearly seventy years from the formation of the Press Gallery and the Lobby to establish a branch of the Civil Service to manage relations with them. It was not until 1949 that the Spin Doctors' Surgery, as it would now be called, was established. The brave new post-war world ushered in the Government Information Service (GIS), or the Government Information and Communication Service (GICS), as it has been known since 1998.

The tortoise-like pace of progress from one milestone to another in the evolution of politicians' relations with journalists demonstrates an inescapable truth: the politicians treated the press with a circumspection akin to handling nitro-glycerine and journalists trod carefully because, for the most part after that eighteenth-century rake Wilkes, they reflected an age of deference that extended well beyond the Second World War.

Spin doctors, as they are now called, were as long in gestation as members of the Press Gallery. They were first sighted in rudimentary form in the British Government's service in 1809, in the Treasury, of all places. The Treasury's lead owed less to its forthcoming nature than to its having acquired responsibility for speaking to the press on overseas policy. Like all spokesmen, it needed facts and lines to take. So it made a Christmas appeal to the departments of War, Foreign Affairs and the Admiralty, which read, somewhat languidly:

> As long as the Newspapers shall continue to be considered as important as they now are, some person in each of the three Departments ought to read the principal Newspapers every morning and send to the Treasury . . . either a correct statement of the Facts if Facts are to be stated, or a Hint of the Line which it is wished should be taken.

I heard echoes of this authentically bored voice of the bureaucrat bestirring himself when confronted with the need to do something about the tiresome press reverberating down the corridors of power in the late twentieth century.

It will come as no surprise that the first Government department to enter the business of publicity, as distinct from handling the press, was an organization directly serving the public: the Post Office. From its very first annual report in 1854 it saw the need to publicize its services. The Postmaster-General, in the embellished indirect style of the day, wrote: 'It could not be otherwise than satisfactory to Parliament if by means of a periodical report the general scope and extent of the progress made by the department were brought under its notice.' Roughly translated by those called spin doctors today, it means, 'We're sure you're dying to hear what we've been up to'.

It was fortunately much more direct in its report, with its 'Suggestions to the public': post early in the day; write the address legibly; and equip your house with a suitable letter box. The Post Office was also the first to embark on a mass advertising campaign, when in 1876 its staff distributed a million handbills 'setting forth in clear and simple language the advantages offered by the Government system of Savings Banks, Life Insurance and Annuities'.

The Insurance Commission was the first to recruit specialists for publicity work when in 1912, under the instructions of Lloyd George, then Chancellor of the Exchequer, it sent a corps of lecturers out into the country to explain the historic 1911 Insurance Act to employers and workers. Just as public services needed to explain to the people how they could make best use of them, so Government recognized it had an obligation to tell them how they were affected by its legislation.

This concept of information as a service to consumers had been developed earlier, with the launching of the *Board of Trade Journal* in 1886 and the *Ministry of Labour Gazette* in 1893, both of which supplied factual information and statistics to businessmen. But before this information could be communicated to the people it had to be collected. And this 'intelligence' role was rather dramatically recognized in 1895 by the formation of the first specialized information unit in government within the Board of Education. It followed a report on secondary education showing the need for accurate and up-to-date information about the national situation.

A minister, commenting on circumstances as they then existed, was reported as saying:

There is a large number of matters affecting education as to which the Department lives merely from hand to mouth, failing to record the knowledge it obtains for future use, and unable to obtain information as to what is being done elsewhere, whether at home or abroad, in an efficient manner. There is now such a waste of power through this deficiency [that] the appointment of an officer with a limited amount of help whose duty it shall be to collect and supply information and to make occasional reports in special matters . . . has become essential if the Education department . . . is to do its work efficiently.

The unit produced a stream of reports on, for example, modern language teaching abroad and school hygiene, and was partly credited with laying the foundations for a national education system.

All these jobs – managing relations with journalists, publicizing services, advertising rights and obligations, leavening discussion with facts and performing an intelligence role – were originally performed by 'amateur' Civil Servants. Later they were brought together in the person of what is now derisively described as the spin doctor. But Government's approach to these various tasks before the First World War was random and piecemeal. There was certainly no overall commitment or purpose, even though mass-circulation newspapers in a new age of adult literacy were now, with the invention of the telegraph, bringing up-to-the-minute news to the people.

It is a depressingly sad fact – demonstrated by events since 11 September 2001 – that nothing more concentrates most ruling politicians' minds about the dissemination of information than hostilities. Sometimes military campaigns bring a leap forward, for example following the widespread criticism of arrangements for handling the media during the Falklands conflict. The First World War, however, produced scarcely a ruffle.

It is true that in September 1914 the Government, faced with a German propaganda machine through its embassies and legations abroad, made the Chancellor of the Duchy of Lancaster director of propaganda, with the aim of influencing the Empire and allied and neutral countries. But it kept quiet about it for two years until it began to recognize that it might have a problem with morale at home because of the carnage on the Somme and elsewhere. The response was classical: it formed a committee. Indeed, it formed not one committee but two: a Home Office Information Bureau, to advise on the dissemination of news on the progress of the war and the maintenance of public morale at home, and later in the year an Information Advisory Committee, consisting of leading journalists and newspaper proprietors.

Eventually, in 1917, Britain acquired a department of information, responsible partly to the Prime Minister (Lloyd George) and partly to the Foreign Secretary, to co-ordinate and extend the work of the Home Office Information and War Propaganda bureaux. It was raised to the status of a ministry under a press baron, Lord Beaverbrook, less than nine months before the Armistice. The progressive upgrading of the publicity effort from Lord Kitchener's 'Your Country Needs You' poster into a fairly substantial programme reflected three imperatives: to maintain public morale in the face of the appalling losses on the Western Front and in the Atlantic; to explain policies such as conscription and food rationing; and to prosecute the propaganda war against enemy and neutral countries.

The Government may have been slow to discover all these needs but it was very quick to break up the entire apparatus once peace was declared. A government with the central machinery and staff to inform, explain and advise the people in peacetime – and possibly to abuse its position – was seen in 1918 as not British, as simply not done. But the wholesale dismantling of this branch of the war effort did not, of course, abolish a free press. Some parts of the Government at least saw that journalists needed to be catered for and so, piecemeal as ever, press officers – the people now called spin doctors – began to appear. Haltingly, Government relations with the press stuttered forward into the 1920s.

The Foreign Office retained a news department in London and a few press attachés in the most important embassies abroad. The Air Ministry had a press officer from its inception in 1919 and the other armed services departments followed its lead. The Ministry of Health instituted a Housing Information Office in the same year, and in 1921 the War Office press officer found himself still acting for Winston Churchill, at his request, when the future war leader moved to the Colonial Office, which was then the subject of close press interest. In later life Churchill was less inclined to use professional information services.

While the flappers flapped their way through the giddy 1920s, Government information services marked time. Not much happened to disturb the even tenor of Whitehall's ways apart from the General Strike in 1926, during which the Government produced its own emergency newspaper, *The British Gazette*, when the independent press ceased to function. Once again official Britain discovered a need for communication with the public at a time of crisis.

Marjorie Ogilvy-Webb, in her account of the development of the Government's information services *The Government Explains*, identified five factors in the 1930s that accelerated the pace of public information development: inquiries from journalists determined to make the arcane works of government and Parliament relevant to Mr and Mrs Smith; film and broadcasting technology; a new social awareness by Government of its responsibility to the governed; the success of the Continental dictatorships' propaganda machines; and the approach of the Second World War.

Ramsay MacDonald was the first Prime Minister to acquire a chief press liaison officer, in 1929. He had professional experience of the press and felt the need for assistance after his buffeting during his earlier brief period of office. He shared George Steward with the Treasury and the arrangement between the two departments continued until the end of the Second World War. The dual manning and the inclusion of 'liaison' in his title suggest a relatively mechanical range of duties. The Home Office appointed a press officer soon afterwards, and social departments in daily contact with the public, such as the Post Office and Health (operating jointly with the Board of Education and Ministry of Labour) were also in the van. Wider public relations divisions grew out of the initial press liaison role and by the outbreak of war all bar the Treasury and the Board of Trade had them. The latter did not even have a press officer until war broke out and clothes rationing had to be explained. The Treasury, even though it had led the move towards managing the media as early as 1809, did not acquire a fully fledged information division until 1947.

Slowly, very slowly, the concept of a Government publicity function was becoming respectable. The potential was unlocked by Sir Stephen Tallents in the form of the Empire Marketing Board, set up in 1926 to publicize the Empire's resources through films, posters and exhibitions. Tallents, an administrative Civil Servant, seized the opportunity to exploit the potential of new techniques to inform and educate the public. He had a flair for recruiting creative artists and publicists, including such pioneers of documentary film as John Grierson, Robert Flaherty and Alberto Cavalcanti. When the Empire Marketing Board was disbanded in 1933, Tallents formed the first comprehensive Government departmental information division, at the Post Office. Among his contributions to British life were the Central Film Library, the Crown Film Unit and a Post Office publicity film known across the world – *Night Mail*, produced by Grierson, and with a commentary written by W.H. Auden to music by Benjamin Britten.

Tallents's gifts to communications were bestowed on Britain in an increasingly hostile world. British interests were under attack, especially in the Middle East and Latin America, by Italian, German and Communist propaganda. This led to the formation in 1934 of the British Council to promote British culture and the English language abroad. Similarly, the BBC was asked to build on its service in English to Commonwealth countries. The first foreign language service in 1938 was in Arabic. Spanish and Portuguese services aimed at Latin America soon followed, and after Munich came the first European services, in French, German and Italian. The Government found the cash and prescribed not only the languages to be broadcast but also the time each should be on the air. The BBC controlled programme content. The BBC World Service was born.

After 350 years the Government was slowly coming to terms with the press and its development in the form of radio. It was also gearing up for another war, which this time would bring a typically cautious yet decisive step towards what is now seen as the age of the spin doctor.

6

Forcing agent

IF WAR is a great force for change, the Second World War had
much to force in terms of attitudes to public information, even
if by its outbreak most Government departments had public relations divisions. Press officers, as distinct from Sir Stephen Tallents's
informative entertainers, tended to exist on sufferance. They were
seen to be there in a defensive rather than a positive role and, being
executive second-class citizens, with a mechanical role as paper
shifters and parroters of basic information to relieve pressure on
ministers and senior officials.

This remained the case even though the Home Office provides an
example in 1936 of the appointment of a press officer by popular
external demand. Journalists dealing with that department complained that they were not getting the information required in time
to meet their deadlines. Lord Reith, founder Director-General of
the BBC, who became a wartime Minister of Transport after a brief
and unsuccessful spell as head of the Ministry of Information, provides evidence of internal pressure for a more positive approach to
media relations. In his autobiography he reports finding his new
department suffering from a lack of proper public explanation. His
Permanent Secretary, the official head of the department, argued
that there was no work for a public relations or press officer. Reith
none the less had his way and when, on being moved to the Ministry
of Works, he tried to take his press officer with him, the Ministry of
Transport flatly refused. He was, they said, 'much too valuable'.

In this haphazard way different bits of Government discovered a need for at least some rudimentary form of information services. But one lesson of the First World War had been learned. Whatever doubts might remain about a Government information machine in peacetime – and they were substantial – there were few about the need for it in war. This time the politicians did not procrastinate until hostilities were nearly at an end before introducing a Ministry of Information. Its formation had been planned as an essential part of wartime administrative machinery to present the Allied case abroad, meet the needs of press and public at home and provide a censorship machine. It was established only a few days after the declaration of war in 1939. That was when the foundations of the present GICS, the umbrella under which 'spin doctors' now operate, were laid.

The wartime Ministry of Information is now generally seen as a source of mild amusement, with its injunctions to 'Dig for Victory', its warnings that 'Careless Talk Costs Lives' and that little ditty out of *Food Facts*:

> Those who have the will to win
> Eat potatoes in their skin
> Knowing that the sight of peelings
> Deeply hurts Lord Woolton's feelings.

(Lord Woolton was the Minister of Food and the wartime face of rationing.) At its peak, though, the ministry had 2,950 staff working in Britain and another 3,600 overseas, not counting those employed on postal censorship. By 1944 another 1,700 were engaged on information work in individual Government departments, of whom 1,000 were in the three military service departments. By the end of the war information was a bigger employer than it ever had been before or has been since.

For all the rush and centralizing nature of war, the responsibilities of the Ministry of Information, as they emerged, show politicians' fear of its potential power. While its political head had to answer to Parliament for general government information policy, departmental ministers retained control over their own. The Minister of Information was responsible only for press and broadcasting relations which went beyond the interests of any one department, though his ministry was the centre to which news-paper and broadcasting journalists submitted their copy to depart-mental censors. He was king only for the nature and execution of Government publicity overseas outside enemy and enemy-occupied countries. His overseas planning committee devised and operated a unified political warfare plan for that purpose. He also provided a common professional publicity and materials procure-ment service which was the forerunner of today's Central Office of Information (COI).

At home the ministry was in the business of mobilizing the pop-ulation behind the war effort by information and explanation, the bedrock of all press officers' work. In the days long before televi-sion and universal radio, the people had to be informed of the need for them to join the Home Guard, the National Fire Service and the Women's Land Army, to become ARP wardens or bus conductors, staff the war factories, dig for victory, save waste paper, hand in old aluminium pans, avoid making any unnecessary journeys, steer clear of the black market and avoid bathing in more than five inches of water (if they were among those toffs with a bathroom – for most it was a tin bath in front of the fire on Friday night and more than five inches of water in it would have flooded the hearth when the bather climbed in).

There was also the massive task of explaining Government measures such as rationing (which moved the Board of Trade, as we have seen, to acquire a press officer) as well as price control, conscription, welfare services, taxation (as the number of payers trebled to 12 million), and the whole panoply of regulations insep-arable from war. People had to be informed of their rights and their obligations, including those they were never going to like. With Sir Kingsley Wood as Chancellor of the Exchequer – perhaps the minister of the era with the keenest interest in public-ity – the Board of Inland Revenue appointed a public relations officer with the Sisyphean task of making income tax 'under-standed of the people'.

The complaint against Government measures that 'however well intentioned [they] simply do not fit the habits of common life', as *The Social Use of Sample Surveys* put it in 1946, is eternal. Too often wartime regulations were found to be incomprehensible or unfair and had to be modified in the light of experience. This was perhaps inevitable because the Government had no idea how many houses were without bathrooms, indoor sanitation, gas and electricity. It had no idea of what the average wardrobe consisted of or the extent of the demand and availability of, for example, razor blades, wedding rings, matches or teats for babies' bottles. How could it make sensible decisions about rationing if it hadn't a clue what people needed, how much they purchased or the state of supplies?

War therefore gave a tremendous impetus to consumer surveys (which have now partly evolved into focus groups), first tested somewhat sensitively between the wars. In fact, there was nothing new even before the First World War in the Government's seeking to find out people's circumstances. In 1904 the Board of Trade had begun compiling a cost-of-living index based on the spending habits of working-class families, and the ministries of Labour and Agriculture and the Post Office went on to employ survey techniques between the wars. But the Second World War left Britain much better informed about itself as a nation as a result of ownership surveys of domestic appliances and facilities, clothing, food, property and health. It even became apparent that in those buttoned-up times the people would not mind publicity about venereal diseases. There were also regular attempts to assess the state of public morale and the effect of government publicity on it.

Marjorie Ogilvy-Webb, in *The Government Explains*, claims that one direct result of this 'passion for administrative detail reminiscent of the Elizabethan state', as historians of the war put it, was that the people came out of the experience in 1945 better fed and clothed and with far better maternity and child welfare services and industrial health and safety standards. Indeed one of the deficiency diseases of the British working class, rickets, disappeared during the war. Press officers are not normally shrinking violets, but I have yet to hear one of them claim responsibility for such a remarkable improvement in social conditions.

The contribution of what would now be called the Ministry of Spin was certainly not generally appreciated at the time. The wartime spirit by no means prevented MPs from criticizing both the ministry's theoretical basis and its practical results. It had tremendous problems finding its feet under a succession of ministers who lasted only a few months. Other departments saw it as a threat when it sought to assume special responsibility for domestic morale and Government publicity as a whole, and members of the Cabinet felt their authority as departmental ministers was in danger of being usurped. They soon saw off the intruder by establishing themselves as supreme on their own fiefdom's policy and publicity and ensuring that the Minister for Information had to work in consultation with other ministers, or groups of them, in prosecuting the Government's war aims. This reaffirmed the principle that departmental information officers owe their first duty and loyalty to their own Cabinet minister and not to the Prime Minister, still less to the Prime Minister's chief press secretary.

Another challenge that came early in the Ministry of Information's life was from MPs jealous of Parliament's position. They identified a serious risk that a powerful Minister of Information, armed with professional publicists skilled in the arts of persuasion through publicity, might sew up public opinion before they had time to put in their own two pennyworth. After all, they argued, what were press officers for but to present the minister's proposals in the most favourable light? In other words, they thought the democratic playing field was perhaps being tilted to their disadvantage, undermining their authority and that of the Commons itself. To this constitutional point was added the fear that press officers, employed at the taxpayers' expense, might become personal public relations officers for their ministers. Lord Reith and others did nothing to calm this concern when they moved on and tried – and in some cases succeeded – to take their press officers and other officials with them to their new departments.

It is testimony to the success of the fourth Minister of Information, Brendan Bracken, founder of *The Banker* magazine, who bought *The Economist* and went on to become chairman of the *Financial Times*, that things eventually calmed down. An intimate of Winston Churchill, Bracken was on friendly terms with national, provincial and overseas journalists and their newspapers' proprietors. Under his guiding hand the Ministry of Information succeeded in testing out the principles on which a Government Information Service might be established. It also presided over the build-up of a cadre of publicity experts experienced in public information and explanatory techniques across a very wide range of media: advertising, posters, broadcasting, films, exhibitions, publications, conferences and public lectures, as well as market research.

The issue in 1945 was whether history would repeat itself. Would all this wartime machinery and expertise be dismantled and cast, redeployed, to the four corners of a Government silenced by peace, as more or less occurred after the First World War? Or would the Government bestow on itself an information and publicity arm and unwittingly embark on the long march to what is now called the age of the spin doctor?

7

Doubts and dispersal

B RENDAN BRACKEN was adamant. His wartime Ministry of Information should be 'instantly abolished with the coming of peace', as it was put by Sir Fife Clark, a leading pioneer of what has become the GICS. It was one thing to have an information and propaganda outfit in war but entirely another to arm a government with one in peacetime. But that did not dispose of the matter. Press offices and publicity teams had been growing in a haphazard way in government departments since before the Second World War, and commercial interests, allied to the need to promote British culture abroad and public services at home, had produced the Empire Marketing Board, the British Council and the Post Office's campaigns and pioneering films.

The coalition government recognized in 1944 that it could not just leave a vacuum. A review reached the conclusion that there would be a continuing need in peacetime both for British information services overseas and, more hesitantly, for government information and publicity services at home. There were two provisos: they should be on a reduced scale compared with the wartime effort and, especially in the case of domestic services, they should be 'subject to vigilance against abuse by the Government of the day', in the words of Sir Fife. This conclusion was generally supported by a specialist group of the independent body Political and Economic Planning (PEP), which made its views known through a bulletin early in 1945.

Awaiting Clement Attlee, when he came to office as Prime Minister in July 1945, was a series of recommendations designed to balance supply with control and prevention of an abuse of power. The general view that the wartime Ministry of Information should be disbanded carried the day, although, as is the wont with bureaucracies, the Ministry of Information, under a new minister, made a late but doomed bid to continue.

As at the beginning of the war, the recommendation had been that individual ministers should assume responsibility for policy and its presentation in their own jurisdictions. Their public relations and information divisions, with limited staffs, should be the primary instruments for departmental publicity and keeping ministers in touch with public opinion. With an eye on economy, there should be a central body to provide technical and production facilities as a common service to government departments in the same way that HM Stationery Office was responsible for government printing. It would be uneconomical for each individual department to employ all the specialists required for such things as film-making and the production of radio programmes, advertising and posters. There should also be machinery to co-ordinate both overseas and home publicity but without an overlord.

With the war over, the power of the individual Cabinet minister for publicity and its execution was to continue to be paramount. Economy was the other watchword. Attlee was thus left to define who would be responsible for co-ordination without having total command. Curiously, he appointed Herbert Morrison (later Lord Morrison of Lambeth) Peter Mandelson's grandfather, who had threatened to challenge Attlee for the leadership in 1945, to design the machinery and make it to work in a wary Whitehall and Westminster.

Some sense of the atmosphere of suspicion and doubt can be gathered from Attlee's words when he arose in the Commons on 17 December 1945 to present the nation with a Government Information Service, as it was called. He was at pains to justify the move:

The Government . . . are satisfied that . . . these services . . . have an important and permanent part in the machinery of

Government under modern conditions. It is essential to good administration under a democratic system that the public shall be adequately informed about the many matters in which Government action directly impinges on their daily lives and it is, in particular, important that a true and adequate picture of British institutions and the British way of life shall be presented overseas.

Attlee put responsibility for information policy firmly on individual ministers and foreshadowed the formation of what became the COI, 'performing certain common technical and production functions and making specialist services available to departments for both home and overseas purposes'. Morrison, the Lord President of the Council, like his grandson not usually at ease with his Cabinet colleagues, began to work out the details. The Ministry of Information was disbanded in March 1946 and the COI, as the first element of the eventual GIS, was born on 1 April. No doubt the sceptics saw some significance in the date. There are many in the GIS who have felt that it was handicapped by its propagandist war parentage, just as others claim that the nuclear power industry has a burdensome cross to bear in its ancestry in atomic weapons.

The extent to which both the COI and departmental information divisions grew out of the Ministry of Information was shown by Attlee in another statement to the Commons on 7 March 1946. The COI, he said, would 'take over most of the common services duties now carried out by the Ministry of Information and in the first instance it will be mainly staffed from existing officers of the ministry. Provision will be made for the interchange of staff between the office and departmental information branches, both at home and abroad.' For the purposes of pay and rations the COI, as a non-ministerial body, was made to report to the Treasury and a junior minister there had the job of answering for it in Parliament – not on information policy, which rested with departments, but on its staffing, methods and efficiency.

So each member of the Cabinet was responsible for his or her own publicity policies and their execution. In the interests of economy, they were generally required to use the specialist services of the COI, which took its policy direction from them but had its resources controlled by the Treasury. And a senior minister (Morrison) had to try to make the system work without treading on the toes of his Cabinet colleagues. Management experts would be appalled at these arrangements, so typically British in their dispersal and therefore curbing of power.

The COI was not born a lusty child, even if it started with a staff of 1,500. Nor was it a happy baby. Its director-general, Robert (later Sir Robert) Fraser, reported on its first six months thus:

> It had lost almost all its wartime leaders . . . These losses, plus the exodus of many key technicians at lower levels, had sapped its powers. Its internal self-confidence was shaken by the prolonged anxiety about its future . . . Happily, a number of officers of talent had taken the decision that they would accept the personal risk of remaining on a ship with its decks awash. They had formed a genuine liking for public information work and a belief in its value to the democratic process; and they had a sense of loyalty which was moving.

But mighty oaks can grow from tiny acorns.

Attlee's great reforming government, however, marked time over the future of information officers. The war had produced an administrative mess that went far wider than information, publicity and propaganda. The haphazard growth of government public relations work before the war and the recruitment of staff for the wartime Ministry of Information had left tidy-minded administrators struggling in their wake. Some people allocated to information and publicity work were members of the executive class of Civil Servant – the middle tier in the hierarchy between policy-making administrators and clerks – while others had been brought in for their media expertise as temporary Civil Servants on an 'unestablished' basis (that is, without entitlement to pensions). Putting it at its most urgent, how was the COI to attract and retain good information and publicity staff if people did not know where they stood in terms of pay, conditions and a career? The same applied to government departments who had recruited information, public relations or press officers, as they were variously described.

It took the Government three years to sort this out, while the COI strove to establish itself and fairly rudimentary departmental information divisions tried to find their feet, sometimes playing into the hands of critics by failing to demonstrate their political impartiality. Fortunately for them, for part of the time that committed communicator Francis Williams was at the centre, trying to make something of the unworldly Attlee, at least in media matters.

Kenneth Harris, in his biography *Attlee*, records how Williams was summoned to No. 10 in the small hours after a leak of Hugh Dalton's budget in 1947 had appeared in *The Star*. 'What's all this about?' demanded Attlee, fully aware that something of the budget had got out. Williams, without enthusiasm but knowing all the facts, replied, 'It seems that the Chancellor talked to the press'. 'Talked to the press', said Attlee in a tone of incredulity. 'Why on earth did he want to talk to the press?' Attlee was astounded, Williams explained some years later, not so much because his Chancellor had been indiscreet 'but because anybody in his senses had chosen to talk to a journalist'.

Attlee could not be expected to appreciate indiscretion in his Chancellor, leading to a budget leak, but his dismissive approach to journalists gives some indication of the stony soil in which the GIS struggled to establish itself. The first post-war prime minister scarcely endeared himself to government communicators any more than to journalists. All too often he was, at best, monosyllabic.

This was, however, only a minor part of the problem. The country had been bled white by the war. There was continued rationing, a general shortage of dollars to pay for imports and recurring balance of payments crises requiring a tremendous export drive while, at the same time, the Labour government was implementing highly controversial reforms, notably in nationalizing industry and introducing the welfare state. As a government, it was far more positive about communicating with the people than might have been supposed from its Prime Minister's approach to the press, and it felt the need for an extensive public education programme on the economic realities of life, as it saw them. On the other hand, the Conservatives and their supporters in the press saw the Government's policies as compounding these post-war problems and, not surprisingly, given the suspicions about the whole idea of peacetime Government information services, they were inclined to see anything that these services produced as Labour propaganda, suppressing anything unfavourable to it.

In retrospect, the wonder is not that a public education programme got off the ground but that the COI and eventually a GIS became an established feature of post-war government. On behalf of departments, the COI was called upon to help explain economic problems and the details of the new social security measures, to encourage exports and to boost confidence in Britain's heritage. In 1947–8 alone it produced eighty-eight films for home and overseas audiences, covering such diverse subjects as the British coal, shipbuilding and scientific instruments industries; our dependence on imports; agricultural and industrial techniques; the spiritual and physical care of children (for parents and teachers); and international food problems and our colonial stewardship of Malaya. The COI's publications division was similarly busy on pamphlets for the Board of Trade, ranging from the importance of exports to post-war national achievements. Among them was a 32-page family guide on National Insurance, delivered to 14 million homes, asking every citizen to choose his or her NHS doctor.

At the same time Morrison, as the co-ordinating minister, filled a vacuum. In the exceptionally severe winter of 1946–7, with its coal crisis and 2.5 million unemployed, there was a demand from MPs, press and public to be told why the country was running into trouble when industry was supposed to have been revitalized by an increasing supply of manpower as servicemen were demobbed. And what was all the talk of 'too much money chasing too few goods' about? Since no single government department was responsible for economic policy – the Treasury was narrowly financial – no information machinery existed to answer such questions. Morrison established a Central Economic Planning staff and in June 1947 an Economic Information Unit (EIU) associated with it. Within six months both had been absorbed into the Treasury.

The EIU set the nation a tremendous example of dynamism. Its output was positively Stakhanovite, backed by an enthusiastic new, austerity-minded Chancellor in Sir Stafford Cripps. He urged the Treasury's staff to think of information work as not just 'a hobby or

a frill to smooth and protect the administration' but 'as a fundamental part of our great experiment upon which a considerable
part of its success or failure will depend'. If those words show he
had to persuade his department to take public information work
seriously, he also revealed the extent to which the EIU was shaking
staider minds. He saw its mission to explain as 'an almost indecent
economic striptease performance . . . which may probably make a
few of the older inhabitants of Treasury Chambers shudder . . .
bringing out into the open a great deal of material that hitherto
was considered most secret and confidential'.

The EIU took hold of official papers, committee minutes,
memoranda, statistics, reports on economic and financial issues –
virtually anything that, suitably translated, might educate the
people – and boiled them down into informative material in the
form of speeches, bulletins, film scripts, leaflets and advertisements. Its women's section set out to explain to housewives how
the nation's economic problems were affected by their behaviour.
Its innovations included a system of regular press conferences on
economic affairs and a popular version of the annual *Economic
Survey*, which looked at economic issues from the point of view of
the ordinary citizen.

All this helped to convert the Treasury from a narrow financial
department into one responsible for the management of the
economy. It also raised the Opposition's blood pressure. The EIU
was the focus for many of the attacks on the Government's information output in the immediate post-war period. In 1950 a select
committee called for the EIU to be disbanded, wrongly believing
that the COI, as a common service organization implementing
departmental policies, could do the EIU's highly specialized work.
The response, worthy of an episode of *Yes, Minister*, was that the
EIU carried on regardless under another name. It became, with
the Treasury's press office, that department's information division.

By this time the status of information officers, including press
officers, had been sorted out by James (later Sir James) Crombie.
He was appointed by the Treasury in 1946 as part of the post-war
reconstruction of the Civil Service to rationalize and unify various
groups of specialists that had developed with the growth of departments. Crombie's job, with a team of officials, was to consider 'the

recruitment, remuneration and conditions of service of departmental Information Officers' and 'the organization and staffing of Information Divisions in departments'. His team included Robert Fraser, Director-General of the COI, and Francis Williams.

They recommended in July 1947 a new class of Civil Servant engaged on information work in home departments as distinct from the Foreign Office, which has always expected its diplomats to be information officers and has generally staffed its London headquarters press office (its news department) with career diplomats. Crombie said the information divisions they formed should 'for the purposes only of recruitment, transfer and promotion . . . be regarded with the COI as one information service and their salary scales should be linked to the executive class'.

Two years later, in August 1949, the GIS was inaugurated by Treasury minute. Sixty-eight years after the formation of the Parliamentary Press Gallery the Government had acquired its own recognized corps for handling relations with these and other journalists. The Spin Doctors' Service, as it would now be called, had finally been established. But how would a Conservative party in government, rather than opposition, see the work of the EIU, COI and departmental press officers?

8

OK – but economize

ONE OF the cardinal failings of a press officer is to become the
story. In the days before television, press officers were fined if
they were careless enough to get their photograph in a newspaper.
I took this culture of anonymity so seriously when I became
Margaret Thatcher's chief press secretary in 1979 that my friends
used to rib me when I was caught dodging out of the sight of TV
cameras. Yet the infant GIS was all too often the story in the
immediate post-war world.

The Labour Government was pushing through vast – and
vastly controversial – social and industrial reforms and there was a
Government machine issuing popular explanations of their proclaimed benefits. Not surprisingly in those early days, the Conservative opposition and the anti-Labour press saw Government
information services as both propagandizing on behalf of the
Government and suppressing matter that was unfavourable to it.
They had other objections too. One was to the COI and the
other to the cost. The COI was described by a Conservative
critic as 'a vast machine of Government information which can
with difficulty be distinguished from political propaganda'. Why
should this expensive and unnecessary outfit, as the Tories saw it,
spend public money on advertising, whether encouraging immu-
nization against diphtheria or explaining the need for higher productivity when the free media – that is, newspapers and radio
– could do the job for nothing through their reportage? And

wasn't it always going to present the Government in a favourable light?

The truth is that, quite apart from being a dangerous novelty, the GIS was caught up in an ideological battle between state leadership and individual freedom and public spending and private provision. The Government argued that if the public were to play a full part in the nation's post-war recovery, they must be helped to understand the situation confronting Britain. The Opposition was adamant that the Government's policies and performance were the cause of the economic difficulties. Worse still, it thundered, the Government machine and taxpayers' money were being used to promote its viewpoint, leading to the 'sapping away of individual judgement and the substitution of the state machine'.

Attlee's six years as Prime Minister from 1945 to 1951 saw a sustained Opposition attack in Parliament on the concept and operations of the GIS. Four major debates were held, and each year brought an average of twenty critical references. Mistakes were also made which invited and justified criticism as ministers and information officers stumbled along 'like the raw recruit and the unbroken horse – they had to learn together', as Marjorie Ogilvy-Webb put it in *The Government Explains*. Some information officers went with their ministers to party conferences, which was not exactly a convincing display of political impartiality. (I never went anywhere near a party conference or my ministers' constituencies after joining the GIS: I was on holiday at Thornbury Castle, near Bristol, when the IRA blew up the Grand Hotel with Margaret Thatcher and her Cabinet in it in 1984.)

On another occasion COI speakers were caught out being briefed from a Labour Party headquarters hand-out. Worse still, the script of a Government film entitled *Ours is the Land*, about new housing schemes, said: 'They promised us new houses in 1935 . . . Now we are at last beginning to get new houses.' This was not calculated to please the Conservatives, who had led a coalition government in 1935, and only reinforced their conviction that this newfangled GIS was nothing but Labour's propaganda apparatus. On the face of it, the GIS's days were numbered as Labour struggled and finally succumbed in the 1951 election.

This seemed to be a racing certainty when one of the fiercest critics of the GIS concept and its operations, John (later Lord) Boyd-Carpenter, was given special responsibility for information services on Winston Churchill's return as Prime Minister. 'Spring-heel Jack', as Boyd-Carpenter was called because of his gait, later became Margaret Thatcher's boss when she joined his (and her first) department, the Ministry of Pensions and National Insurance, as a junior minister in 1961.

Yet far from wielding the axe, Boyd-Carpenter left well – or, evidently, not too bad – alone. Nothing was fundamentally changed. The cynic would say that the only thing to which Boyd-Carpenter and the Tories objected was that the GIS had been in Labour hands, and that they were not going to forgo the advantage of having it on their side when they took office. It is a shade more complicated than that.

While the Conservatives had seen the GIS in ideological terms, as an instrument of the state versus the individual, they could not deny that modern government had an obligation to explain to the public their rights, entitlements and responsibilities arising from legislation and other measures. There was also manifestly a need to promote Britain and its products and culture abroad. To do that effectively, they needed professional help. They could have bought it in, but nowhere at that time was there a more experienced professional machine than that working inside their own organization. In the end, it was probably not much of a contest.

In any case Sir Stafford Cripps, the Labour Chancellor, had handed the Tories a gift. In 1948 he had asked Sir Henry French, who had wide experience of public relations at the Ministry of Food, to inquire into the cost of the home information services. A member of *The Times* was in his team as an outside voice. French reached four basic conclusions, which still affected my approach during my twenty-four years in the GIS. He advocated not only economy – indeed, a cut – in spending but also, more specifically, the use of paid publicity – advertising, films etc. – as a last resort. He also proclaimed the need, when that last resort was exercised, to be able to justify the choice of the right medium to get over the message effectively. In doing so, it could be argued that he promoted the use of 'spin' since he advocated the much greater use of the free media to get over the Government's messages. Persuading press and radio to do the work that might otherwise have been done by advertising – the source of a newspaper's profits – puts a premium on press officers' ingenuity. They are up against journalists who much prefer to hand out free biffs than free puffs.

Spending on the home information services was not just cut from the £5 million budgeted for 1950 for the COI, Stationery Office and departmental information divisions; in the early 1950s it was slashed by more than half, to about £2 million. The COI, which had been spending £2.5 million on advertising, films and publications fell back to a measly £750,000. What is more, spending did not rise to its pre-French figure of around £5 million for a good twelve years and by then, thanks to inflation, it fell far short (by about £3.5 million) in terms of value.

In the GIS, the new Conservative Government in 1951 had a ready-made publicity machine, but one that was required by a Labour-instigated report to do what the Tories had advocated in opposition: minimize the cost and maximize the free publicity. The service was thus preserved virtually intact, but left strapped for cash and resources. It was also set to work to win publicity rather than pay for it. In doing so, it excited much less *angst* in the Labour opposition than it had in the Tory opposition of its earliest years. In the first six years of Tory government it provoked not a single major debate and produced an average of only five or so references a year in *Hansard*. The year 1951 marked the beginning of the acceptance, at least by our politicians, of a suitably economical and properly behaved GIS. It was the year that 'spin', as they would loosely describe it today, was institutionalized.

One other factor facilitated this. That was the internal Treasury inquiry known in the trade as Crombie. The adoption of Sir James's report in 1949 meant that the GIS had become part of the system and had had nearly two years to bed in by the time the Conservatives came to office. All this may help to explain why they accepted it after their regular sniping it at between 1945 and 1951, but it does not give many clues as to why expressions of concern about its impartiality largely evaporated in the 1950s and did not seriously re-emerge until after Tony Blair took office in 1997.

In my judgement there are four reasons for this: the nature of the GIS as an arm of the Civil Service; a willingness by politicians and Civil Servants alike to learn from their early mistakes, especially in making sure press officers not only were politically impartial but were also seen to be so; professionalism on the part of GIS staff; and the maturity of our politicians who, when in government, recognized the restraints and limits under which the GIS must operate and, when in opposition, made sure they were observed. The most important of these is the Civil Servant status of the GIS officer, something highly relevant to the current concerns about the politicization of the GIS.

Crombie identified four functions for the GIS: first, to create and maintain an informed public opinion about the subjects with which a department deals; second, to use suitable methods of publicity to help a department achieve its publicity objectives; third, to advise on matters bearing on relations between the department and the public, including, of course, the media; and fourth, to advise on the reaction, or likely reaction, to existing or contemplated policies. But he did not pontificate on how the service should do its job. Instead, he merely required heads of information divisions to have 'the attributes which make a good Civil Servant'.

In doing so, he performed a signal service for British democracy and ensured the GIS's survival, provided it met the requirements of political impartiality, honesty and self-effacing restraint. These requirements were not set in tablets of stone when the GIS was established, but they came to be detailed in later guidance. They came with Civil Servant status and until 1997 were generally interpreted by the GIS with common sense and sensitivity. The attributes that make 'a good Civil Servant' separate the genuine press officer from the spin doctor.

9

Rules of the game

On 2 May 1967 I became a temporary Civil Servant. As a *Guardian* labour reporter, I accepted an offer from Aubrey Jones, chairman of the National Board for Prices and Incomes (NBPI), to become the board's press and public relations adviser. It seemed the sensible thing to do since it gave me an opportunity to find out what government was like, if not from the inside, certainly from the periphery. The argument for branching out of Fleet Street was put to me by Eric Jacobs, who had left *The Guardian* a couple of years earlier at the NBPI's inception to take the press and PR job. I had followed him on to the labour staff at *The Guardian* and was covering the endless round of strikes when he tried to persuade me, on Jones's behalf, to succeed him again. Jacobs was joining the *Sunday Times* and felt I would be a better journalist, as he clearly thought himself to be, for having worked on the 'inside' for a time. The NBPI also paid far better than *The Guardian*.

My detractors on *The Guardian* claim that I left because I was not going to be promoted to labour correspondent, the top man covering trade union, Labour Party and industrial issues. It is true that I did not expect to be promoted, but that was not why I took the plunge outside. If it had been, I would not have made myself so unpopular with the newspaper's management by trying, unsuccessfully, to persuade them to freeze my pension until I returned. This was in the days before transferable pensions. It was the prospect of becoming a better, more informed journalist through having some experience of how government operated that motivated me to leave for a limited period.

I joined up on a short-term 'unestablished' contract. Twenty-four years later, in 1991, after Mrs Thatcher's resignation and my 'retirement', I returned to journalism and began writing a weekly column for the *Daily Express*. By then Fleet Street was no longer the home of newspapers. They had been cast by a commercial and technological diaspora to diverse parts of London from Canary Wharf to High Street, Kensington, and were printed all over the country at the touch of a button. They had also been changed by the competitive power of broadcasting (especially television) and by the increasing control of accountants, who find news-gathering extremely expensive, from a breaker of news into more interpretative, commentative journals, giving the story behind the story. Parliament was even being televised. And the term 'spin doctor' was just beginning to creep into everyday use.

It was in the different, declining and increasingly anarchic Britain of May 1967 that I first walked into the NBPI's headquarters in Kingsgate House in London's Victoria Street. The NBPI had been invented, in the eyes of the unions, to hold down wages. Its chairman, Aubrey Jones, saw it as an agent of change to remove one of the obstacles to faster growth: low productivity. As a result, the board came to be seen by such conservative elements as bankers and brewers as a meddler in matters it did not understand. I conceived my task as being to try to present it positively, through its reports, as a modernizing force.

I am not sure many others in the NBPI saw my role in that way, apart from the chairman and its secretary, Alex (later Sir Alex) Jarratt. Most people seemed to see me primarily – and many of them principally – as the person responsible for keeping press, radio and television journalists under control and at bay. They even chased me around Paris by telephone while I was on a family holiday, after a *Daily Telegraph* journalist got loose in the board's corridors and interviewed members of the staff. They assumed that, since I was a journalist, I knew how to handle my fellow beasts and should do so at every opportunity, even while I was on leave.

Generally, I was seen far more as a defender and protector of the NBPI's and chairman's interests than as a promoter of its ideas. My first week's experience seemed to confirm that I was not expected to be innovative. Indeed, I began to wonder whether I had made a serious mistake in swapping the hurly-burly of national daily journalism for the board's cloistered calm. And then the penny dropped: I could make of the job whatever I chose.

If I chose to wait for media trouble to come to me, concentrating on defence, my life would be easier but a lot more boring, so I chose to attack, and tried to carry the board's ideas for doing things differently to the public through the media. Among other things, I began to write a series of popular guides, based on board reports, on such subjects as productivity bargaining and 'payment by results' schemes.

It may be that I was in a privileged position as a temporary Civil Servant brought in from outside and that greater efforts would have been made to control me had I been a 'regular' press officer. Yet, far from looking back on the experience as frustrating, I have no impression of being discouraged from being an activist, still less obstructed, though I suspect I was a source of amusement to some administrators who had learned to pace themselves and to bring an air of studied deliberation to their work. No doubt, they thought I would calm down with experience or return whence I came, never more to disturb the even tenor of their ways.

I now look on my year at the NBPI as my university. I learned a great deal very quickly. But nobody taught me how, over and above the expertise for which I had been hired, to do my job. Nobody presented me with a set of rules and conventions that I should observe. Nobody gave me a manual of GIS good practice to read and digest. It is true that, as a labour reporter, I was familiar with the essentials of Government–media relations, but I was an innocent on the details of reconciling political and journalistic interests with parliamentary privilege when, for example, the Government called on the board to issue several related reports quickly over a weekend. I learned by experience and by receiving unsolicited guidance from No. 10 when they felt I needed keeping on the path of constitutional propriety. My position reminded me of all those girls in Hebden Bridge who began work in the ready-made clothing factories 'sitting by Nellie', the experienced hand, at her sewing machine.

Those who have created an industry out of personnel management may well consider my induction to a senior post in a quasi-governmental body as bordering on the negligent. I did, of course, sign the Official Secrets Act, but it was not presented to me as something that should weigh heavily on my shoulders – more as a necessary and natural rite of passage into the Civil Service. Far more important was my status as a Civil Servant, however temporary, working within the government machine. As one day followed another, I came to understand the ramifications of this status, not through pointed lectures, heavy-handed guidance or even light touches on my tiller, but from the very atmosphere. The ethos of the Civil Service provided all the guidance you needed and you behaved accordingly. Where you were doubtful, you consulted the oracle for guidance or precedents; and there was no shortage of oracles in No. 10 or departmental press offices.

As a Civil Servant, you are required to be a civil servant of the Queen and, through her, of her ministers and officials and the public, who pay your wages. As such, you are required to be politically impartial. If the voters so decree, you may have to serve a government of a different political complexion tomorrow. I worked personally for seven different Cabinet ministers: Labour's Barbara Castle, Eric Varley and Tony Benn and the Conservatives' Robert Carr, Maurice Macmillan, Lord Carrington and Margaret Thatcher. I moved overnight from the service of Benn to Thatcher and earlier from Castle to Carr and Carrington to Varley.

There is – or was – an accent on internal as well as external civility, an institutionalized determination to keep the temperature down in meetings and in the choice of language employed in minutes, as notes passing through the system are described. My robust nature and journalistic style were often felt to be 'a bit much'. In serving your minister you do not indulge in party political polemic. You present the facts in suitably flat and unemotive terms which no doubt seem dull and uninspired to professional PR agencies. For example, as her press secretary, I could not contemplate claiming that Margaret Thatcher was a miracle-worker on industrial relations after strikes virtually ceased following the year-long national miners' stoppage of 1984–5. Instead, if asked, all I could do was to present the statistics about the number of strikes and days lost through them for different specified periods and leave journalists and, through them, the public to draw their own conclusions.

You are allowed no role in party politics. I let my membership of the Labour Party lapse after joining the Civil Service, even though I expected to be back in journalism within two years, and I have not been a member of any party since. You do not as a general rule attend party conferences or party meetings (even with your minister), go to your minister's constituency, visit any party headquarters or attend any meeting called by a party official. Only a minister, or a more senior Civil Servant, can command your presence. You must not only be impartial but also be seen to be impartial. Another aspect of your impartiality, which loomed larger when I moved to a fully fledged Government department, is to ensure that public funds are not spent by the Government of the day for party political ends. All expenditure has to be justified on two counts: by the need to inform the public of how they are affected by Government measures; and by the necessity of using the chosen medium – for example, advertising – to reach the target audience.

You are also expected to give honest advice, however unwelcome, never to lie or mislead and to serve all citizens equally. In the light of experience I feel obliged to qualify the 'never lie or mislead' injunction with the word 'knowingly'. It is difficult to be accurate all the time, especially when you have to rely on informants who may not have a full grasp of the facts or keep some of them from you. But every effort must be made to ensure accuracy and to correct any mistakes. The public service notion of serving all citizens equally requires fair dealing with, among others, journalists. It rules out favouritism in the dissemination of news and therefore leaks.

So does Parliamentary privilege. You are – or were – required to respect Parliament's privilege to be informed first of all major developments in policy and to be given the first chance to question ministers on them. Of course, much depends on the definition of 'major' – that is, on the weight, sensitivity or controversial nature of the development. It is also true that Government advantage, media deadlines and Parliamentary privilege were often at odds because newspaper edition times were out of synch with Parliament's working hours. This pressure has eased somewhat recently, but when Parliament used to meet at 2.30 p.m. embargoes had to be used carefully if evening newspapers were to give a news service to their readers in their main editions without causing an unholy fuss on the floor of the Commons.

Finally, as a Civil Servant, I learned to avoid not only public controversy – unless your chairman (and later minister) was determined to court it – but also publicity for myself. It is the tradition of our Parliamentary democracy for ministers to be the front men and officials, such as press secretaries, the backroom boys. While it is difficult to remain anonymous in the television age, it is not impossible to keep away from the limelight. The Civil Servant should not become the story.

This catalogue of restraints which I learned in 1967 is not the result of a conscious and deliberate attempt to handicap the GIS in its operations. It stems fortuitously from the status of its members as Civil Servants. It is none the less a very necessary limitation for those who rightly see the GIS as a potentially powerful instrument in the hands of any government. It was enforced by a vigilant Parliament, which used to see to it that ministers, permanent secretaries, as the accounting officers for their departments, and their staffs trod the straight and narrow. Those who had responsibility for operating the GIS within this framework deserve credit for successfully squaring the circle of conflicting interests during the 1950s and 1960s. Not even the fraught circumstances of general elections brought serious allegations of abuse.

My generation of press secretaries inherited a system that had been shown over some twenty years to be successful in limiting the advantage that a government accrues from a GIS acting to stimulate and inform public debate. We also came to share the pride of our predecessors who had forged the instrument in the fact that it substantially avoided damaging controversy. Nothing changed after I retired in 1990. John Major's three press secretaries each felt bound by these rules. All of us felt that Parliament would be down on us like a pack of avenging wolves if we strayed from the established conventions of the herd. We also knew that any such fuss would not redound to the credit of the government we served.

The operational rules of the GIS effectively rule out spin-doctoring as we have come to know it since 1997. This raises the question of why spin-doctoring latterly came to dominate our governance and obsess our governors. What happened to bring so much emphasis on presentation to the exclusion of substance, even in the eyes of many Labour MPs? What precisely is spin? And where does professional presentation end and spin-doctoring begin?

10

Democracy's bovver boys

ALASTAIR CAMPBELL claims that the best spin doctors in the world are journalists. I have some sympathy with his point of view, although I am not sure he is the one to voice it, given his widely remarked propagandist performance on behalf of the Labour Party and its leaders as a political journalist with the *Daily Mirror* and *Today*. One friend of mine recalls from a long way back that his news editor on a provincial paper began virtually every sentence with: 'What we want him to say is this . . .'. The implication was that the reporter should try to manipulate the interviewee into saying what was required for the story. Journalism is one of the influences that have led over the past thirty years to the modern obsession with presentation.

Those of us who have been press secretaries are left with the indelible impression that there is very little difference between journalists and children. Most of them are demanding, jealous, petulant, cheeky and acutely sensitive to criticism; most cry a lot, or at least wail, like trying it on, are never responsible for anything and need keeping in order. Journalists are what they are partly because of their highly competitive trade and the nervous energy they expend in following it. Many also have an aggressive approach to government in its widest sense. They expect governments to behave more responsibly than newspapers, as Andrew Rawnsley put it in *The Observer* in June 2002, for they know that their own trade can be 'shameless, sensationalist, shallow, vain, vulgar, manipulative and duplicitous'. They would argue that all too often they are provoked by those in power. They are democracy's bovver boys and, to a greater or lesser extent, always have been.

They are also indispensable to a healthy democracy, as Thomas Jefferson implied in 1787: 'Were it left to me to decide whether we should have a government without newspapers or newspapers without a government, I should not hesitate a moment to prefer the latter.' Margaret Thatcher put it another way, though often, I thought, through clenched teeth: 'You can't have a free society without a free press.' The journalist's ability to ask the embarrassing question and to print or broadcast it with the embarrassing answer – or noting the awkward silence – is vital to our democracy, even if the journalists asking the embarrassing questions are no angels themselves.

In a healthy democracy the frontier between governmental authority and journalists is in a natural state of tension. Governments have come to see the need for someone to manage this tension and to prevent it from degenerating into open warfare, but they have been reluctant to recognize the value of the role. The way in which, before the Second World War, journalists cla-moured for a press officer at the Home Office so that they could get information in time to meet their deadlines was an early example of a threatened breakdown in relations. But the concept of the press secretary as a manager of relations with journalists was anything but specific in the Crombie report which led to the founding of the GIS in 1949.

As I have explained, Crombie laid down the prime functions of departmental information divisions as being 'to create and main-tain an informed public opinion about the subjects with which the department deals' and 'to use methods of publicity, where appro-priate, to achieve its purpose'. He came closer to acknowledging a management role in defining their duties as being 'to assist and advise on all matters bearing on relations between the department and the public with which it deals' and on 'the reaction of the public to a policy present or contemplated'. It may be that Crombie saw no need to differentiate between press and public, but it is curious that he made no reference to the principal medium by which the public were to be kept informed.

I was no more specific when in 1969 Sir Denis Barnes, Permanent Secretary at the Department of Employment and Productivity, asked me to write my own job description. Echoes of Crombie crept into my definition: 'To promote an informed press and public about the Government's policies and measures and to advise ministers and officials on their presentation'. Yet by then, two years into my Civil Service career, it was clear to me that effective management of relations with the press – and with radio and television – was crucial to the prime function of promoting an informed public. There are a lot more people responsible for external communications now called media managers. BBC PR, for example, has both a chief adviser and a manager of media relations, and the term is not unknown in government. The Department for Education and Skills calls its press office its 'media relations division'.

Whatever they call themselves, press officers are inevitably in the business of managing relations with a highly volatile, usually hostile, frequently mischievous and seemingly proliferating media mob. They have never been more necessary, provided they observe the rules and conventions I have described. Unless they are under such control, the frontier between Government in its widest sense and journalists would be in a more or less permanent state of conflagration. It follows that press officers themselves should exercise restraint in order to avoid pouring petrol on the glowing embers.

The new breed of spin doctors has done anything but that. It has forgotten, assuming it ever knew, that our pioneer journalists had to struggle to secure the right to ply their trade. Politicians and governments exacerbated an inevitably awkward relationship with journalists by their reluctance to open up their debates to reporters and their sensitivity to criticism. It was this attitude to the exercise of power and authority that prompted Lord Acton, the historian, to write to a bishop in 1887, warning that 'Power tends to corrupt and absolute power to corrupt absolutely'.

Thirty-five years earlier John Delane, editor of *The Times*, had set out in a leading article a clear exposition of the differences between government and press. It is worth quoting extensively:

The first duty of the press is to obtain the earliest and most correct intelligence of the events of the time, and instantly, by disclosing them, make them the common property of the nation. The statesman collects his information secretly and by secret means; he keeps back even the current intelligence of the day with ludicrous precautions.

The press lives by disclosure. The statesman's duty is precisely the reverse. He cautiously guards from the public eye the information by which his actions and opinions are regulated; he reserves judgement on passing events till the latest possible moment, and then records it in obscure or conventional language; and he concentrates in his own actions all that power which the press seeks to diffuse over the world . . .

It follows from this contract that the responsibilities of the two powers are as much at variance as their duties. For us, with whom publicity and truth are the air and light of existence, there can be no greater disgrace than to recoil from the frank and accurate disclosure of the facts as they are. We are bound to tell the truth as we find it, without fear of the consequences – to lend no convenient shelter to acts of injustice or oppression, but to consign them at once to the judgement of the world.

Similar views on relations between government and media are echoed daily in editorials throughout the country. Delane would have been on stronger ground in regarding government as secretive if he had not been privileged to receive from his 'reserved' and 'cautious' statesmen leak after leak of Cabinet decisions almost as they were taken. But he tells you what press officers have to cope with in managing relations with journalists who for centuries have found government generally secretive and believe they themselves are a 'power' in the land with a 'duty' to disclose what is going on.

The problem of managing relations with them is compounded by their commercialism. This is where Alastair Campbell has a point about journalists being the world's best 'spin doctors'. While editors are keen to suggest that they are in the business of Delane's truth and light, they are actually in the competitive business of selling newspapers or enhancing broadcast ratings. The more copies a newspaper sells, the more income it derives from sales and the more it can charge for advertising. Similarly, the higher the ratings of commercial radio and television programmes, the higher their tariff to advertisers filling the natural breaks in them. Nor is the BBC immune to the potentially corrupting forces of commercialism, since it has to compete with commercial radio and television.

Journalists do not achieve this commercial objective by being worthy, pedantic, obsessively accurate, dull and boring. Their job is to make the news interesting, compelling and preferably exciting and moving or entertaining, depending on the nature of the story. They aim to grip and hold the reader, listener and viewer. In the process they indulge in what is called journalistic licence – massaging, kneading, sculpting and arranging the facts to make them more interesting. This leads them to simplify, trivialize, interpret, select and sensationalize, sometimes suppressing inconvenient information and qualifications.

None of this came in with the 'spin doctor'. Journalists have always embellished stories – or 'spun' them, as they might say now – but not since Dr Johnson's day has the reporting of Parliament been so imaginatively colourful as it is now. In the 1980s Margaret Thatcher got so worked up about the press's treatment of the facts, as she perceived them, that I tried to calm her with these remarkably soothing words: 'I'm afraid, Prime Minister, you have to look at the British press rather as you would an oil painting. Close up, it looks like nothing on earth. Stand back and you get the drift.' And for all modern journalism's way with the facts, it does, by and large, give the drift of what is going on. In the circumstances, I am not sure we can expect much more.

One thing is clear: journalists are in no position to complain about others enlivening the facts, provided that interference does not give them the wrong end of the stick. Just as a journalist tries to give his story a 'lift' to secure its publication, so the press officer issuing a press notice or conducting a briefing seeks to capture the interest of the recipient journalist with an arresting headline and snappy first paragraph that command instant attention. He has to catch their eye and imagination as they dump press releases, measured in tree equivalents, into their wastepaper bins.

For those who take journalism seriously, the best journalists are those with the highest publication rate, with the most compelling stories, containing the least offence to the truth. Paradoxically, the best press officers are often those with the highest strike rate in preventing inaccurate stories from appearing. But does catering for the market or preventing fiction from being presented as fact amount to spin-doctoring?

It goes without saying that journalists value informants who can bring events vividly alive. They love being able to adorn their descriptions with any form of colourful detail. It is, after all, a nice touch to be able to report that the British Prime Minister entertained the French President in the state dining-room at No. 10 to English lamb under the enigmatic gazes of Wellington and Nelson. I was able to convey the atmosphere at Lech Walesa's lunch for Margaret Thatcher in St Bryggida's Presbytery in Gdansk in 1988, when she stopped her host in full conversational flight. 'Mr Walesa,' she cried, through an interpreter, 'this is wonderful stuff. It is music to my ears. Your Government should hear it.' Whereupon Walesa, pointing to the chandelier, replied: 'Oh, there's no problem about that. They're hearing every word.' Does such a report, colourfully conveying the atmosphere of that meeting, go beyond legitimate press officer briefing?

Another aspect of embellishment, though it also qualifies as simplification and dramatization, is the 'sound bite'. Whereas early government press officers sought the catchy headline to secure free newspaper publicity, every effort is now concentrated on producing a memorable sound bite for television, the public's main source of news. Superficially, it is a preposterous idea that even the essentials of a policy, fashioned out of a complex of circumstances, can be reduced to a few words, but the media never hesitate to coin their own sound bites to illustrate their own reports. So why should governments not try to summarize their own messages in a few dramatic words?

I am rather proud of one of mine. It emerged from a briefing Thatcher gave me after her very first meeting with Mikhail Gorbachev at her official country retreat at Chequers just before Christmas 1984, well before he became Soviet leader. The longer the conversation went on – and the pair came to love arguing with each other – the more Thatcher warmed to him and, it seems, the more Gorbachev respected her. By the time she had finished telling me about her meeting and the tone of the exchanges, I said, rather banteringly, 'It sounds to me that you think Mr Gorbachev is a man you can do business with'. She replied: 'Well, I do'. So, I said, 'Well, can I tell the world's press that when I meet them in an hour?' And she said, 'Yes'. So at my briefing in central London I produced my sound bite with a flourish: 'Mrs Thatcher thinks Mr Gorbachev is a man she can do business with.' She subsequently put it personally on the record.

In thirteen words I managed to convey an entirely new atmosphere in Anglo–Soviet relations and a feeling of hope for the future. More important, the sound bite reflected a reality that was to blossom into something approaching *détente*. But was this all in a press officer's day's work, or had I ventured into the world of the spin doctor?

If journalists live by colourful stories, enlivened by sound bites and background, they need them in time to meet their deadlines. Time waits for no editor in his effort to serve up 'the first rough draft of history', as Ben Bradlee, managing editor of the *Washington Post* during the Watergate scandal, described his craft. Time is of the essence in journalism. 'News', as one of my former colleagues on *The Guardian*, Harford Thomas, put it, 'has a short shelf life'. But if the journalist is up against a deadline, the press officer is up against the bureaucracy, which above all wants to be accurate.

On the face of it, this renders the journalist vulnerable to press officer delay. But if newspapers (and radio and television) are 'the best stab at the truth in the time available', in the words of Simon Jenkins, former editor of *The Times*, any delay in answering an embarrassing query, whether that delay is inevitable or deliberate, may achieve only an unwanted and inaccurate story. Procrastination in answering journalists' queries is thus a double-edged weapon. The timing of a story is another area where the press officer is in danger of becoming a spin doctor. Jo Moore's infamous e-mail of 11 September is a graphic illustration of this.

However, before attempting to establish the boundary between good press officer practice and spin-doctoring, I want to look at the question of how government, in its widest sense, manages its relations with the media. How is that relationship influenced by the way the media have developed and by the role played by politicians and senior Civil Servants as controllers of press officer operations?

I I

The catalysts: journalists

THE UNCIVILIZING of British journalism can be dated fairly accurately to around 1967, when I became a Government press officer. Much as I search my conscience, I cannot find a connection between the two events. I did not leave journalism because I thought it was becoming uncivilized. Nor can I recall anything in my behaviour towards journalists that might allow them to charge me with causing riotous conduct on their part.

Of course, before 1967 relations between Government and journalists did not take the form of a stately minuet of elaborate courtesy. While formalities were important, there was always something in them of the acid repartee that took place behind the fans and hands in a B-movie version of an eighteenth-century ballroom. The cartoonist Steve Bell, of *The Guardian*, has a respectable ancestry among artist–commentators preoccupied with the bodily functions of our governors. The earthy vulgarity, not to mention scatology, of, for example, James Gillray and William Dent, aimed at the likes of Edmund Burke, Charles Fox and William Pitt, enlivened the eighteenth century.

Another century on, Delane brought disclosure in *The Times*, via Cabinet leak, to a fine art and defined it as journalism's mission against 'secretive' statesmen. Seventy years after that, Stanley Baldwin learned the hard way about editors when he gave an unremarkable interview to *The People* before privately speaking his mind about his political colleagues over a cup of tea with its political correspondent, who had put away his notebook. James Margach, the long-deceased political editor of the *Sunday Times*, claims in his book *The Abuse of Power* that back in his office the interviewer mentioned Baldwin's frankness to his editor, who promptly commanded him to forget about the set interview and dish up the political dirt from memory. Baldwin, it is recorded, 'never again gave a formal interview or spoke to groups of journalists.

During the Second World War the *Daily Mirror* cartoonist Low incensed the Cabinet by showing a wrecked seaman in an advanced state of distress on a raft in a stormy sea over the caption: 'The price of petrol has been raised by a penny (official).' Winston Churchill felt this was meant to imply that seamen were risking their lives so that the oil companies could make bigger profits. For this cartoon, and for a blistering leader on army leadership, the Government threatened the newspaper with legal suppression under what was felt to be an abuse of the defence regulations. Only a decade later the Press Council was formed to bring some self-restraint to journalism, which was under political and public attack for, among other things, the glamorizing of crime. And just before I joined the Civil Service, Government relations with journalism had been thoroughly soured by the imprisonment of two journalists for refusing to disclose their sources in the Vassall spy affair.

In the Westminster closet governments no doubt felt it was just one darned thing after another with the scribes. But for all the press's battering on Government's door seeking rights and access, there was a certain civility, not to say deference, in the relationship between politicians and journalists in the front line, exemplified by the first Lobby member's being expected not to speak until he was spoken to. And notwithstanding the example of Baldwin, the 'gentlemen' owners of the newspapers kept the journalist players in order when they chose to do so. If not, how could it have been that a bishop rather than a newspaper blew the gaff on Edward VIII and precipitated the abdication crisis?

Members of the Parliamentary Press Gallery and Lobby were expected to do their duty in khaki in a special press platoon of the Parliamentary Home Guard from the outbreak of the Second World War. In that capacity they conducted the 'Guy Fawkes

Search' of the vaults of the Palace of Westminster, normally carried out by the Yeomen of the Guard, just before the arrival of the King and Queen for the opening of Parliament. They also provided a guard of honour for the monarch on several occasions. Not much evidence here of their perceived unreliability.

Reuters' Doon Campbell, who went in with the troops on D-Day, wrote in his book *Magic Mistress* that the firm 'set high professional standards and practised competent clean journalism. You felt proud to be in news. It taught you to approach issues without prejudice, with detachment and with proper scepticism; to check and challenge information; to quote named sources; to make sure of facts. Accuracy and speed, in that order, became a passion as well as a discipline.' And Viscount Kemsley, introducing his *Kemsley Manual of Journalism*, which I acquired on its publication in 1950, had no doubt

> of the desires and opinions of the general body of responsible journalists. They are professional men with professional standards and ideals. I have always taken the view that, apart from other considerations, the dignity of the journalist is reduced if he is asked to intrude into the private affairs, and in particular the private grief, of others or to twist his own honest view of a story to suit a political or any other angle.

I had become a junior reporter on a local paper – the *Hebden Bridge Times* in west Yorkshire – two years before the Kemsley manual appeared. From the very beginning – 18 October 1948 – I was taught that every single piece I wrote should be accurate, fair, balanced and complete in itself. If it wasn't, I could be sure I would at best be taken to one side in Market Street, or, at its embarrassing worst, bawled out wherever I happened conveniently to be for the aggrieved reader. I was also given to understand that I should be manifestly independent (I gave up my membership of the Labour League of Youth on joining the paper), protect my sources as I would my life and recognize that I had no rights over and above those of the ordinary citizen. I might be given such privileges as a seat in the council chamber or a ticket for a show because of the public service reporting or publicity I might provide, but I was on no account to demand any rights lest my newspaper might incur obligations it could not discharge.

Other journalists who were recruited in the immediate post-war years will testify that in joining the 'Brig Times'. I was not entering an unusually strict Baptist sect – even though the paper's offices were housed in the old Ebenezer Baptist Church, with its graveyard outside – but a pretty conventional newspaper office. Like Lord Kemsley, we thought we were doing a responsible job and should behave accordingly. I found no difference in ethos when in 1952 I moved eight miles down the valley to the Halifax district office of the *Yorkshire Post* and *Yorkshire Evening Post*, published in Leeds.

I did, however, see a difference between the attitude of my provincial colleagues and the style, approach and behaviour of the popular national daily journalists who invaded our territory on the larger or more outlandish stories. They were not burdened with working for journals of record. For them, in competition with their peers, the story was paramount, and they were invariably more cavalier with the facts and more creative in their writing. They were also more deeply attached to their beer than would have been seemly for a local reporter. I remain unclear whether this regular lubrication produced the celebrated 'Talking Dog of Drighlington' in the national press, but when I went to interview the phenomenon in a pub there, near Leeds, for the *Yorkshire Post*, the terrier was singularly uncommunicative. We never got on speaking terms. I think this merely demonstrated one of the iron laws of journalism: the closer the journalist lives to his readers, the more careful he is with his facts; the more distant his association, the more imaginative he becomes with them.

Yet a certain responsibility and civility reigned. For all the social mixing of the Second World War the age of deference and restraint lived on. People knew their place and remained in it for nearly another twenty years, even though Sir Hartley Shawcross, Labour attorney-general in the Attlee government of 1945–51, was reported as saying in 1946: 'We are the masters now'. Actually he said, 'We are the masters at the moment, and not only at the moment, but for a very long time to come.'

And then in the 1960s, on the back of the rising affluence of Harold Macmillan's 'Never had it so good' generation (he actually said, 'Most of our people have never had it so good') came a desire to break the bonds of deference and reticence that had held the nation, if not always its journalists, in check. The biting satire of the BBC's *That Was The Week That Was* glued the nation to its television sets on Saturday nights to see who would be savaged next, as if the events of the week did not advertise the victim, and how far they would dare to go. *TWTWTW* had a feast set before it by a government in its death throes. The imprisonment of 'Fireman' Reginald Foster (of the *Daily Sketch*), so nicknamed because he was sent on difficult stories, and Brendan Mulholland (*Daily Mail*) for three and six months respectively for refusing to disclose their sources to the Radcliffe tribunal on the Vassall spy affair was closely followed by further scandal when John Profumo, the Secretary of State for War, resigned for lying to the House over his association with Christine Keeler, who was also involved with the Russian naval attaché. But respect for politicians had not yet quite flown out of the window. The arrival of Harold Wilson, bent on forging Britain 'in the white heat of the technological revolution', was widely anticipated, even if he only narrowly managed to defeat Macmillan's successor, Sir Alec Douglas-Home. (Incidentally, Wilson actually said: 'We are re-stating our socialism in terms of the scientific revolution . . . the Britain that is going to be forged in the white heat of this revolution will be no place for restrictive practices and outdated methods on either side of industry.' More evidence of the press's penchant for sharpening up a quote.)

But the truth was that after heroically trying to reconcile full employment with low inflation in the post-war years, Britain was failing economically. It also had its application to join the Common Market rejected and its industry was too often in a state of anarchy. My job from 1968 to 1973 was to help conduct and choreograph the industrial theatre played out night after night, or more accurately early morning after early morning, on the door-step of the Department of Employment in 8 St James's Square as ministers and officials tried to find a way of ending successive national strikes with least offence to the economy. And all the while, a tired, staid old society was giving way to a new, perhaps less hypocritical, franker, more open culture in which deference and reticence gradually disappeared, along with the respect that had previously been accorded politicians.

In 1972 the Watergate scandal gave the US press its first presidential scalp in Richard Nixon. Even in Britain, for those who did not need much persuading, it confirmed that some institutions and politicians were not deserving of respect, and since then many politicians have poured oil on the raging fires of disrepect. At one stage it seemed that half the Italian political class was either on trial, in gaol, on the run or in exile. Willy Claes, former Secretary-General of NATO, resigned under a cloud and was later convicted of corruption. President Mitterrand, Chancellor Kohl and President Clinton have not brought unblemished distinction to the art of politics. Then, after the 1997 general election, conducted against a background of 'Tory sleaze', a series of scandals involving Labour Party benefactors such as Bernie Ecclestone, boss of Formula I motor racing, and leading Labour politicians such as Ron Davies, Geoffrey Robinson and Peter Mandelson (twice!) have not helped restore respect for a political class that has hardly been jealous of its reputation.

By the early 1980s journalism was increasingly driven by the conspiracy theory of government. My experience up to 1990 taught me that there is only one valid theory of British government: the cock-up theory. But that experience counted for nothing. The wary watchfulness with which journalists had always approached the exercise of power moved rapidly through scepticism to a consuming cynicism. Governments were felt to be up to no good. All a journalist had to do, they seemed to think, was to turn over the right stone in government in its widest sense and something unpleasant would sooner or later come slithering out to shatter the authorities and make the crusading journalist famous and, of course, rich. In my twice-daily briefings of the Lobby I began to encounter the built-in sneer instead of the good-humoured probing and knowing look when my interrogators thought they were on to something. Eventually the conspiracy theorists tried – and only narrowly failed – to break up the Lobby in the interests, as they presented it, of more wholesome government.

Journalists also rediscovered causes. Of course, crusading journalists were nothing new. W.T. Stead, editor of the *Pall Mall*

Gazette in the nineteenth century, is credited with not only introducing into Britain the American 'yellow journalism' – defined by Asa Briggs's *The Companion to British History* as journalism 'of a reckless and unscrupulously sensational character' – but also with raising the age of sexual consent to sixteen, through his exposure of child prostitution, in collaboration with the reformer Josephine Butler. His fame was burnished by the fact that he was imprisoned for the way he went about his crusade. A century on, editors seemed to acquire and abandon causes rather as some people acquire pets for the duration of the Christmas holiday.

When I was Director of Information at the Department of Energy, I myself was in at the birth of militant environmentalism. An operation conducted behind my back dubbed the publicly owned British Nuclear Fuels' Sellafield plant the world's 'nuclear dustbin'. My Secretary of State, Tony Benn, and his political adviser Frances Morrell combined with Bryn Jones, a labour affairs reporter I had known on the *Daily Mirror* and subsequently as an environmental campaigner, to hi-jack the front page of the *Mirror* to that effect. Since then Sellafield has known little respite from the environmentalists' wonderfully spin-doctored and often fact-free campaign to close it down with the help of journalists with whom they have formed a close working relationship.

Not surprisingly, pressure groups cottoned on to the publicity to be achieved through gullible journalists who knew their editors were suckers for a new crusade. Scares became two a penny as facts dispensed by Government press officers were summarily dismissed as 'spin'. I write as a consultant in my 'retirement' to BNFL. Pressure groups grinding their axes became the 'authorities' to be listened to, even after Greenpeace was shown to be spectacularly wrong with its claims in opposing Shell's plan to dump the redundant Brent Spar platform in the depths of the ocean. The internet has intensified the problem of coping with pressure groups peddling sensationalism, though it provides Government with an equally available counterpoint of fact.

Television fuelled both the rise in campaigning journalism and the conversion of essentially civil journalists into the truculent, demanding, rights-obsessed and often sneering horde I came to know before I retired. It became the medium by which most people heard the news. It therefore seduced politicians seeking to win friends and influence people as well as publicity. That in turn lent insistence to TV journalists' demands for an interview. It inflated their egos to the detriment of their manners, to such an extent that the late Sir Robin Day began to deplore the incivility of broadcasting interrogators who followed him. Television's sense of power generally increased journalism's self-confidence and self-esteem and made it an increasingly tricky handful to cope with.

Long before I went to No. 10 in 1979 most departmental press secretaries had ceased to trust a word uttered by producers of TV current affairs programmes. They no doubt believed that government was not to be trusted either. Press secretaries knew from experience never to take TV producers at face value. They regarded Government as fair game, and Government, as represented by press officers, was determined not to have its minister or department shot at dawn by them. It was often impossible to nail them down about the purpose of a proposed programme, which frequently seemed rather fluid. The very idea of allowing them an open-ended interview with your minister, later to be hacked about and inter-cut out of context, was tempting fate.

Television also greatly increased the pace of politics and government in a way that radio, with all the same advantages as television apart from images, had never quite achieved. Its ability to flash moving pictures of events as they happened across the world into your living-room perceptibly speeded up the chain reaction that constitutes most unfolding news. The implication when ministers failed to respond, with or without good cause, was either that they were not on top of their job or that they had something to hide.

Accompanying all these developments was a proliferation of the staff of the international communications industry, who now hunted in packs as reporters, photographers, cameramen and TV executives. The caravans of journalists and technicians that move across the globe from summit to summit are numbered in thousands. The posses who now dance attendance on celebrities in hospital, for example, are an absurd parody of the entire news business.

In politics the growth in the numbers of individuals pursuing a story presented me with a serious management problem in No. 10, and not solely because of the requirements of security as the IRA hunger-struck, bombed and shot its way through the 1980s. First, as the numbers of journalists pouring into the closed but none the less busy Downing Street rose alarmingly, we had to impose some sort of control in the interests of safety. So we required them to stay in a press pen formed of steel barriers. If it were a running story, with to all intents and purposes a 24-hour dog watch on No. 10, the floor of the pen soon became a litter-strewn mess.

Experience showed, however, that the pen was far from ideal. When I persuaded Mrs Thatcher to go out to inform the massed ranks of media about the progress of talks or the outcome of a summit, there was a fearful jostling for position, a menacing thrust of furry creatures enclosing mikes at the end of long poles and all too often an unflattering view of her left nostril on the TV news bulletins as cameramen did their best amid the press of bodies. So I ordered a lectern wired for sound, sited at a reasonable distance from the pen, so that every cameraman could get a decent picture and every sound-man a good-quality feed. I was not thanked. Instead I was accused of enabling the Prime Minister to dominate the proceedings and to break off the engagement as and when she judged advantageous (an argument that had little substance as she could seldom resist an argument or delivering a severe put-down). This just underlined how hard it had become to help journalists with impunity. Eventually for major news events such as summits I concluded that the only proper way to cater for the media's multiple needs was to convert the pen into a grandstand constructed out of scaffolding up against the wall of the Foreign and Commonwealth Office.

The memoirs of Francis Williams, press adviser to Clement Attlee, and of Harold Evans (later Sir Harold), Harold Macmillan's press secretary, present a stark contrast between the journalists of the 1940s and 1950s and those I came to experience. But I had also known the seriousness, decency, honour and civility that characterized most local, regional and national journalists, notwithstanding the competitive nature of their business, before the 1960s began to coarsen society. I could still testify to their existence in the 1990s, but I seldom expected to find them outside my generation.

This sad uncivilizing of Viscount Kemsley's profession would have required the invention of Government press officers if they had not existed, if only as a protection squad for ministers and departments. But before explaining in detail how the new incivility worked out in practice, I want to examine the influence of ministers and the Civil Service machine on the evolution of the 'spin doctor'.

12

The catalysts: politicians

WILLIAM EWART Gladstone liked publicity, at least for his interminable speeches. To this end he developed a close working relationship with Walter Hepburn, the first chief reporter of the Press Association, the national news agency formed in 1868. Chris Moncrieff, the PA's devoted and ultra-professional political editor when I was No. 10's chief press secretary, records in his history of the news agency *Living on a Deadline* that Hepburn, a dignified 20-stone giant, was cheerfully known as 'Mr Gladstone's Fat Reporter'.

Gladstone had Hepburn travel in his private coach on his famous Midlothian campaign in 1874. If the 'fat reporter' was not present, pencil poised, when he was about to begin one of his orations, Gladstone would cry 'Where's my reporter?' He would also wait before embarking on his speech until Hepburn was comfortably settled in the most advantageous seat at the press table. Gladstone wanted to be sure he would dominate the newspapers in those days when politicians were reported, and read, extensively. Politicians don't make speeches just for the hell of it.

They are only human. Most of them like good publicity which gets them talked about approvingly; some, it seems, will settle for any publicity. The likes of Robert Maxwell and Jeffrey Archer and, at a different level, Alan Clark and Peter Mandelson, seem to have acted like publicity junkies. Two of the seven Cabinet ministers I directly served – the Conservative Maurice Macmillan (later

Viscount Macmillan of Ovenden and son of Harold Macmillan) and Labour's Eric Varley, a former coalmining craftsman (now Lord Varley) – were the most self-effacing of men, ill suited to the histrionics of politics. They were nevertheless immensely rewarding to work for as a press officer. Three of the others – Robert Carr (now Lord Carr), Lord Carrington and Margaret Thatcher – were hardly publicity seekers, though it chased them. Barbara Castle and Tony Benn were more complex, but neither of them qualifies in my eyes as a publicity hound, avid for coverage. The only motive that would induce my seven Cabinet ministers to seek publicity was duty, and especially the need to explain, expound, defend and rescue their policies in the eyes of the voting public, or to promote and defend the collective interest of their Government. That could even sometimes be said for Benn, who frequently seemed to be waging a guerrilla war inside the administration of which he was a member. It is true that through the promotion of their policies they achieved personal publicity, but generally the motivating force was the advocacy or defence of policy.

It did not come easy to some of them. For Macmillan it was often a terrible trial. However delightful, intelligent and amusing a companion he may have made, stretched out, chain-smoking, on the sofa in his ministerial office at the Department of Employment, he fell apart on the floor of the House of Commons or when a microphone was thrust in front of him. He dug deep into his reserves of courage in and out of the Commons. So did Eric Varley, who was not a natural orator, still less a speech-writer. And Barbara Castle, that doughty fighter who died still battling for pensioners at ninety-one, once confessed to me that she felt the whole weight of the Government and the national interest on her shoulders when she rose at the dispatch box.

Robert Carr was as sure-footed as a mountain goat on the floor of the House and in front of a microphone when pursuing and then forlornly defending his Industrial Relations Act of 1971. He was the very antithesis of Maurice Macmillan, his successor at the Department of Employment, and in that respect a dream minister, never allowing his facility with the media to make him reckless. Lord Carrington would have been only too delighted to direct operations unseen in his headquarters if only that had been possible during those torrid two months I worked for him at the newly formed Department of Energy in the throes of coal, oil and political crises during the three-day week in early 1974.

As for Margaret Thatcher, she sparkled when she had to or could be induced to come out to play. She could put on a tremendous Dr Zhivago show, as in Russia in 1987, and exploit situations for her benefit, as for example when she cornered the runaway workforce in the Pallion shipyard in Sunderland until they just had to talk to 'that bloody hen' and found her astonishingly human, not to say flirtatious. She could not help generating publicity, admittedly of varying value, as she demonstrated when she breathlessly told the press outside Downing Street, 'We are a grandmother'. Margaret Thatcher is a very impulsive person, but she certainly was not and is not publicity-mad. Instead, she was and remains preoccupied with policy. All too often I had to explain the need for her (and not just me) to perform for the press in order to justify aspects of her policies.

Even Michael Heseltine (now Lord Heseltine), the high-flying Conservative troublemaker of the 1980s, thought twice about stunts as Secretary of State for Defence. I once heard him question me when he was fighting the Campaign for Nuclear Disarmament over the deployment of cruise missiles, 'You don't think that is too much even for me, do you?'

Of course, politicians need to keep themselves in the public eye. Lord Hattersley is credited with having the morbid thought that a sick politician is a dead politician. Unless you are a prime or leading minister, you are not making news in bed, provided it is your own. Junior ministers are inevitably keener to secure publicity because they are trying to make their way up the greasy pole. It was sometimes necessary to educate them as to how they could – and could not – secure it. They most certainly could not do so as a minister by putting out an Opposition-bashing press notice on departmental notepaper. Under governmental rules such a party political broadside would have to go out through their party headquarters. I tried to slake junior ministers' thirst for publicity by allocating them a personal press officer to work directly for them. For this I have been accused of promoting the concept of the spin doctor preoccupied with an individual minister's publicity, but it was good training for the press officer and it kept the minister in order, ensuring that if he promoted himself he did so through Government policies.

Back-benchers, from among whose ranks come the ministers of tomorrow, want to see their Government (or Opposition) scoring points. It does their morale good if their leader 'wins' the encounter at Prime Minister's Questions. They demand that their Prime Minister and Cabinet keep the initiative and they get uneasy when they lose it and, worse still, have a bad run and seem to get stuck in a rut. They then see their majorities melting away and their seats in peril. Being an MP is not the most secure form of employment. It is subject not only to the vicissitudes of Harold Macmillan's 'events, dear boy, events' but also to the strengths and weaknesses of policies and personalities, an uncertain loyalty to the cause among your colleagues and the redistribution of population and constituency boundaries. It breeds a paranoia that seldom blames policy – only its presentation. I wish I had a fiver for every time I have heard a politician say, 'Our problem is presentation'. That is why I entitled my memoirs *Kill the Messenger*.

While working for my seven Cabinet ministers, I never felt that my one overriding task was to get publicity for the boss. Sometimes ministers did not think I made enough of an opportunity, and sometimes they were right. Tony Benn undoubtedly had a case when he mildly complained I didn't get much publicity out of his trips to see his opposite number in Russia or to visit Sheikh Yamani, of OPEC, in Saudi Arabia. However, our job was not actively to promote our minister's image but to help him use every opportunity to get over his policy, with any political benefit accruing incidentally from a job well done.

The notion that Prime Ministers were, as a race, publicity hounds before it became a Blairite obsession is risible. It is true that David Lloyd George (1916–22) sprayed honours over the press barons he created, but for power rather than publicity. Stanley Baldwin, having had his fingers burned, never in his three terms as Prime Minister over the years 1923–37 courted Fleet Street. He treated those press barons who challenged him with crushing contempt, referring to their 'power without responsibility – the prerogative of the harlot throughout the ages'. Clement Attlee (1945–51) was, on the admission of his press adviser, Francis Williams, 'one of the most difficult men in the world to publicise and possesses fewer of the political arts of self-presentation than any public man I know'. He was the very devil to interview, answering with short, clipped sentences when he was not completely monosyllabic. Winston Churchill (1940–45 and 1951–5) devoured the newspapers but had no use for a press secretary, never met the Lobby and is thought to have given only one press conference. He believed in talking to the people either directly through speeches or indirectly through the Commons.

Anthony Eden (1955–7) had 'appallingly patchy press relations', according to a close observer, and lost his press secretary through resignation over the deceit of Suez. The gauche, awkward Edward Heath (1970–74) was simply not equipped for the media age or, perhaps, for living with fallible human beings. According to his Cabinet colleague Richard Crossman, Jim Callaghan (1976–9) was a 'virtuoso' performer in exploiting trade union contacts and the press, but it never seemed like that. Perhaps that was his skill. Margaret Thatcher (1979–90) came to office without a press secretary. Her approach to the media was that they were an uncertain means to a defined end who needed managing. John Major (1990–97) never quite acquired the self-confidence some Brixton boys would have instantly exhibited on entering No. 10 and the media soon found they could hurt him in his desperate concern with what they wrote about him.

I pass over Andrew Bonar Law (1922–3) and Sir Alec Douglas-Home (1963–4), who were only briefly in office. This leaves only Ramsay MacDonald, Neville Chamberlain, Harold Macmillan and Harold Wilson of our post-First World War Prime Ministers before we come to Tony Blair as a special case. MacDonald (1924 and 1929–35) was at home in the world of journalism, where he had earned his keep as a pundit and had a rapport with journalists, but he was hounded by the press barons with utter venom. Chamberlain (1937–40), with a strong connection with the Lobby before he became Prime Minister, tried to harness the press to his passion for the appeasement of the Nazis and Fascists and succeeded only too well with some before Parliament said, 'For God's sake, go'. Harold Macmillan (1957–63) became Supermac, the effortless, sophisticated thespian and communicator until he sank in messy panic at the end of what Labour described as 'the thirteen wasted Tory years'. Harold Wilson (1964–70 and 1974–6) was, like Blair, obsessed with the media and their control, with sad consequences.

Of course, all political careers end in failure but – and this should be a warning to Tony Blair – our Prime Ministers most at ease with the media or with the greatest passion for manipulating them seem to come off no better and conceivably rather worse as a result. It is perhaps as it should be.

The various approaches taken by our Prime Ministers over the years to the press, radio and television demonstrate what a curious lot press secretaries have had to cope with. Prime Ministers' relations with the media – and those of their Cabinet colleagues – are better seen not in terms of a thirst for publicity but as a quest for success and a buttressing of power. Francis Williams, in his book *Press, Parliament and People*, records lunching at the Commons with Hugh Dalton, subsequently a Labour Chancellor, shortly after he became editor of the *Daily Herald*. Looking around, Dalton said: 'You know, Francis, one thing you must remember is that all of us here are in one way or another prima donnas. We are all apt to get upset if we don't get what we regard as our fair share of the limelight.' But it isn't the limelight that really matters to them; it is, first what it is doing for their preferment and for the standing of their Government. Who's on his way up and who's on his way down is an abiding topic of conversation in Westminster – and not just among journalists. And they don't rise to the top just because they know how to attract publicity. Dalton was felled by a budget leak.

No press secretary can ignore this preoccupation with power and retaining control over its levers. It intensified over my twenty-four years in the Civil Service as the media became increasingly immediate, demanding, intrusive and conspiracy-driven, and as government became increasingly complex and difficult in a shrinking world populated by militant pressure groups with international networks and their own 'whistle blowers' and 'spin doctors'. It would be amazing if ministers had not sought some advice and protection for themselves in such a hostile world.

The three pressures that increasingly dominated my life as a press secretary – leaving aside the growing abrasiveness of journalists – were the increasing pace of the news business, ministers' desire to control as much as possible the timing of announcements and the forums in which they appeared publicly, and the problem of reconciling Parliament's requirements with Government interests. These clearly relate to the differences of interest between statesmen and journalists described by Delane in 1852. It is not the job of the media to run the country. They have not been elected to do so, even if they usually think they could do it better than the Government in office. Their job is to disclose, as Delane put it; to give the public the news as soon as they get it, without regard to the consequences.

For Governments the consequences matter. They have to handle them. Coping with news bulletin headlines every half-hour puts enormous pressure on the system while a lie, as Joe Haines, Harold Wilson's press secretary, put it, is half-way round the world before the truth has got its boots on. Retaining some semblance of control in these circumstances is difficult. Playing for time by saying 'No comment' can be disastrous: it is either taken as an embarrassing confirmation of the facts or as evidence of having something to hide. Going to ground convinces journalists that they are on to something. Margaret Thatcher developed a routine: 'When we have the facts we shall know what to say about them.' But we could not always hang about getting the facts and formulating a reply. If we did, the situation could run out of control. Time – and timing – is of the essence in news, politics and presentation.

This partly explains why every Cabinet is exercised by leaks, even if the odds against an inquiry finding the culprit are infinitesimal and despite the fact that most leaks are initiated, if not actually perpetrated, by ministers themselves. Except where they are the result of compulsive ministerial incontinence in the presence of journalists – and some ministers I have known seemed to be incapable of keeping things to themselves – leaks are, or were, usually designed to serve the narrow interest of the leaker against the wider interest of the Government as a whole. They used to be particularly rife at the time of public expenditure reviews, when ministers sought, by revealing their needs or proposals, to make it difficult through publicity for the Government as a whole to deny them. In other words, they can serve to rob the government of its control of the agenda. They are also damaging to the cohesion of a government because they undermine internal confidence in the honour and reliability of ministerial colleagues and Civil Servants, which used to be essential to the proper conduct of any organization until they all madly started drafting politically correct codes for whistle blowers. Yet governments have to take serious leaks seriously because they can impair co-operation, for example, with international allies. The USA, we were told, became careful about what it told the French after a leak during war crimes operations in the Balkans.

Under the Blair government 'trailing' – a polite word for leaking – has become endemic, indeed a way of governance. The substance of policy developments and initiatives is divulged to selected media outlets well in advance of their formal announcement. In this way Blair seeks by leaks to maximize control over presentation. It has become part of the armoury of the true spin doctor.

It seems inevitable that anyone suddenly acquiring the responsibilities of government would wish to secure as much control as possible over the forums in which they are expected to perform, including press briefings as well as Parliamentary appearances – in fact, anywhere where they can reasonably be expected to be making news. They would want to know as much as they could about the purpose and nature of the occasion, the audience and the interviewer and the likely problems as well as opportunities. They would certainly want to know, for example, what rules should govern the televising of the Commons, how to avoid being made to look foolish and how to prevent opponents from staging stunts to hi-jack their performance. I had much sympathy with the politicians when I was asked to advise John (later Lord) Wakeham on the preparation of the rules for televising the Commons in the late 1980s. The result, focusing the camera on the member speaking and away from extraneous events such as abseiling demonstrators, may not have made for compelling television but it did get the cameras into the Commons.

The privileges that Parliament has, of being the first to be briefed on important developments and of having the first opportunity to cross-examine the Government, have always been at odds with media requirements. Press secretaries have the problem of reconciling the two. Before Blair solved the problem by 'trailing' and by ignoring protests by successive Speakers of the Commons, ministers used to find their Parliamentary Private Secretaries – the MPs appointed to assist them – and later their special advisers useful in satisfying the media's needs and keeping Civil Service press secretaries pure. But when Parliament sat at 2.30 care had to be taken to prevent stories appearing in evening newspapers or afternoon bulletins before the House assembled or before it was clear that the reported business had been transacted.

The problem for press secretaries is now eased by Parliament's moving closer to normal working hours and by the Blair government's contempt for Parliamentary privileges, which it has consistently got away with for more than five years. Yet Parliament ought to be the forum where policies and measures are subjected to critical examination. If it is doing its job, it can be very damaging to a government and especially to a weak ministerial performer. That is no doubt why the Blair government, with its passion for control, has sought to move presentation out of the Parliament.

So the modern obsession with spin-doctoring is at least partly the result of the pressures of increasing pace, control of timing and Parliamentary privilege, compounded by the failure of the bureaucracy to adapt to a more open and urgent society. Something had to give.

13

The catalysts: bureaucrats

JAMES MARGACH, in his book *The Abuse of Power*, his eye witness story covering more than fifty years and twelve prime ministers, identified two overriding objectives in prime ministers: personal power and preservation of secrecy. He put it like this:

> With almost obsessional ruthlessness the majority sought to dominate and influence the press, TV and radio as the vital pre-condition to their domination of, Parliament, parties and public opinion. They desired to enrol and exploit the media as an arm of government. Two objectives possessed them: first, to establish and fortify their personal power; and secondly to reinforce the conspiracy of secrecy, to preserve the sanctity of Government behind the walls of Whitehall's forbidden city.

Margach's story began with Lloyd George and ended with Jim Callaghan, whose major sins seemed, in Margach's eyes, to be con-centrated on his tenure as Chancellor of the Exchequer. He would, no doubt, have had a field day with Margaret Thatcher and John Major, and certainly with Tony Blair. The only Prime Ministers who largely escaped his strictures were Baldwin, Attlee and Douglas-Home.

None is safe, however from allegations of secrecy, though Margach claimed that when he started as a journalist in the 1920s 'Ministers, Permanent Secretaries and ministers' private offices within departments were always accessible to political correspondents, ready to answer questions and explain policies'. That was, of course, in an era of relative respect, trust and honourable behaviour by the majority of political journalists, if not their editors and proprietors. Even so, access may well still have depended on the individual politician and whether it was worth his or her while. The modern journalist apparently lives in ignorance of or contempt for Aesop's fable in which the warmth of the sun works like a charm in persuading a man to remove his coat whereas the brute force of the wind achieves nothing.

I knew Margach, but had only limited dealings with him as a press officer. I assume he thought it was a mistake to invent the GIS since he complained in 1978 that 'a battalion of 1,500 press and information officers has been created to man the front-line trenches'. In fact, only a fraction of that number were in the press office front line, the rest being engaged on a variety of publicity projects. (It is an exaggeration that Joe Haines, Harold Wilson's press secretary, has been known to employ in his denigration of Government 'Public Relations Officers' since he ceased to be one of them.) Margach also ignored in his book the access that Lobby journalists have to ministers in the Commons Lobby, the links often forged between ministers and political correspondents, and the symbiotic relationship that exists between politicians and journalists.

Margach was fairer when he identified one other factor that undoubtedly helped to reinforce official secretiveness: the excesses of the media. First, Lord Rothermere and Lord Beaverbrook formed their own national political party in the 1930s to try to destroy Baldwin. Then in Attlee's time they instituted what Margach called 'an unbridled campaign of screaming irresponsibility, in my experience the worst period for the reputation and standards of journalism'. He did not, of course, witness their performance against John Major. In Macmillan's time the press was 'discredited' by the Radcliffe tribunal following the Vassal spy scandal. Radcliffe investigated more than 250 separate newspaper reports linked to the Vassal affair and found 'not a word of truth in any of them – not even after editors, news executives and reporters had been offered the protection of privilege under which to give evidence'. Margach's fourth example of media excess was the publication by the *Daily Mail* of a forged letter in its campaign against alleged bribery and corruption at British Leyland.

An impartial observer might say that politicians, faced with the piranhas of the press, radio and TV, whose teeth have been sharpened over the past twenty-five years, have much to be wary about. Every excess, failure, distortion, exhibition of prejudice or straightforward lie by the media, who are as fallibly human as politicians, reinforces the natural tendency of all bureaucracies to be secretive. Margach none the less has a point – as do the entire journalistic profession and the public – about official secretiveness. So do press secretaries, who have to fight it every moment of their working lives.

One of the myths of the journalistic profession is that press secretaries and their staffs spend their time hiding behind the Official Secrets Act. They still believe this, even though the act has been weakened by human rights legislation and will be undermined further by the Freedom of Information Act that Blair will bring in some time when it suits him, probably for after he is gone. The worst and most useless press officers may have sought refuge behind the act but neither I nor my senior colleagues in the GIS ever gave it a moment's thought in our operations. Of course, the act was a piece of background furniture and it may well have inhibited our Civil Servant informants. But our concern was to help journalists to get is as near right as we could, given all the pressures exerted on us by the machine and circumstances.

Henry James, briefly my predecessor at No. 10 after serving as deputy press secretary to several other Prime Ministers, used to argue that we were licensed not to leak but to break the Official Secrets Act by necessarily taking a judgement as to what we could and could not say. We then stood to be corrected after the event. I have calculated that I spoke subject to correction – that is, without clearing with the Prime Minister what I said on her behalf – for about 95% of the time in my relations with journalists. Lord Whitelaw recognized this when he once told me: 'You are the most exposed Civil Servant in the land and you have to be protected.' There were not many politicians like that.

With or without protection, speaking subject to correction is what press secretaries have done from the first. There is a wonderful tale of Francis Williams persuading the unworldly Clement Attlee, against the advice of his officials, to have an Exchange Telegraph news agency tape machine outside the Cabinet Room. Williams wanted to end his isolation from the world as a press secretary and did so with the seductive argument that it would enable the cricket-mad Prime Minister to keep up with the scores. Within a week Attlee found the ticker tape also chattering out Cabinet decisions. Williams patiently explained to him that he briefed political correspondents in broad terms on what was going on. 'OK, Francis,' Attlee is reported to have said, 'I'll leave the show to you. Good work.' Williams was thus authorized *post hoc*.

The issue is not the extent to which the Official Secrets Act – whether in No. 10 or Government departments – constrains press secretaries. It is when does Attlee's 'good work' become bad work in the eyes of ministers and officials? For there is a conflict of interests between politicians and senior officials. Generally ministers are much more relaxed about the disclosure of information, provided it does not unduly complicate their lives. They are, after all, the only people who can authorize disclosure, whether before or after the event, and they are not averse to publicity. They are positively enthusiastic about it when it serves their purpose. For them, as a bright girl put it at a talk I gave in 2001 at Kingston upon Thames Grammar School, 'It's all about advantage'. When there is no benefit to be gained from publicity, who can blame them for avoiding it, provided they are not engaged in a cover-up? Given the hostile world in which they live, it is only natural for politicians to want to protect themselves.

Despite my twenty-four years of trying to strike blood out of the official stone, I have to confess that I regard 'open government' as a contradiction in terms. The very notion that government can be conducted in a goldfish bowl is ludicrous. It is true that ministers of all parties deserve nothing less than being forced to live in a transparent environment for their endemic, freelance, partial leaking of Cabinet and other meetings. They have reduced the principle of collective responsibility to dust and thereby inhibited full and frank debate among themselves. Yet even if ministers have done much to destroy the confidentiality of collective discussion, which should be a condition of their contracts, there are whole catalogues of information that should be protected in the areas of defence, security, trade negotiations, finance, commerce and personal files. What is more, all bar the most exhibitionist of journalists would agree if his own personal file held, for example, by the NHS were made public.

I have always regarded the freedom of information campaign as monumentally hypocritical and its espousal by editors and our so-called liberal media élite as simply a means of putting themselves in a better position to run the country without the inconvenience of being elected. But the entire system of government could certainly be more open, to the benefit of government, politicians, officials, press and public, not to mention press secretaries. Secrecy, or a perception of it, utterly distorts the judgement of journalists. It used to be a joke in Whitehall that all you needed to do was to red stamp the most boring document in an entire day's governmental output with the words 'Top Secret', leave it in a Commons' photo-copier and it would automatically find its way on to a front page, accompanied by much speculation as to what it meant and whether it was written in code.

Unnecessary secrecy inhibits the proper explanation of the facts and situations and thereby perpetuates problems. At the same time, it reinforces scepticism by the media and the public about their governors. It is manifestly unnecessary when the bureaucrats clamp down on information already in the public domain through publication in looser regimes abroad, for example in the United States and Sweden. Yet more than once I found myself kicking the nearest wall because the obtuse official mind forbade disclosure of innocuous material freely available abroad, on the specious argu-ment that if we did not confirm its existence it somehow didn't exist. There is a distinction to be drawn here – one that would be roundly rejected by the self-serving media – between material rou-tinely disclosed abroad and security issues such as the *Spycatcher* affair. In the latter case a former public servant owed an obligation of confidentiality to the state because of his employment in the security services, and the Government understandably felt it nec-essary to demonstrate disapproval of his publication of his memoirs *pour encourager les autres*. In fact, far from encouraging anybody, some fifteen years later Stella Rimington, the former head of MI5, burst into print herself.

Partial secrecy is a more difficult concept but it can be damaging because, whether or not it is being practised deceitfully, the media's conspiracy theorists will inevitably conclude that it is. But there is a case to be made for it, given some journalists' determination to 'get' the Government. When, for example, I was asked a direct and precise question to which there was a precise answer, I saw no need to make life possibly more difficult for my minister by elaborating on the subject. Often the more intelligent and understanding journalists came up to me in private later and said rather ruefully' 'I didn't ask the right question, did I?' All this is now described as 'economy with the truth', as Lord Armstrong of Ilminster immortally put it when, as Cabinet Secretary, he was dispatched to Australia by Mrs Thatcher to intercede on the Government's behalf against the publication there of *Spycatcher*. Economy with the truth is a double-edged weapon in the hands of ministers and press officers. In the hands of journalists it has commercial value.

Whatever the need in some cases for secrecy and however naïve the calls for open government, the fact remains that throughout my time the system was far too buttoned up and that it may conceivably be even more so now because of the Blair government's often disastrous presentational operations and spurious openness. For a variety of reasons I often felt myself to be up against at best a grudging machine and at worst a brick wall. Most Civil Servants exhibit a common decency and courtesy, but they live under a 'need to know' regime that is inhibiting. They generally have a strong desire to protect their minister and to preserve his freedom of manoeuvre. They were brought up to respect Parliament and its privilege to be informed first of major developments. They live in an atmosphere poisoned by leaks, usually ministerially inspired, and naturally feel a need to protect their own careers against the charge of 'careless talk'. All these factors militate against entrusting information to 'representatives of the yellow press in Press Office'.

There are three other factors that, in my experience, made for closeness. First, there was a desire among a minority of senior officials to conduct their own press relations in their own interest, to the exclusion of the press office and certainly the minister's own press secretary. Occasionally this made for very serious difficulties, but I doubt, in the cases I experienced, whether it owed anything

to the mild resentment, which I also encountered, that a press secretary has such enviable access to a minister beyond his station.
Then there was downright intellectual snobbery on the part of
administrators who perhaps unconsciously regarded themselves as a
cut above the mechanics in the press office, whose job of managing
the media was unfortunately necessary (although the more honest
among them would confess they would rather I handled Denis
Thatcher's 'reptiles', as he described journalists, than they). There
was also a serious lack of understanding within the machine of the
role and *modus operandi* of press officers, which cannot have been
improved since by the antics of the Blair government. It is a legitimate criticism of the GIS's internal public relations – and one, as I
say, that I often made myself – that it has not overcome this ignorance after nearly sixty years. But that is to reckon without the institutional prejudice of the Civil Service against greater openness.

For most of my Civil Service career I was in a privileged position,
with a right of immediate access to and often close personal relations with my ministers. Similarly, I was blessed with Cabinet
Secretaries and mostly, if not exclusively, Departmental Permanent
Secretaries and No. 10 Principal Private Secretaries, who recognized I had a legitimate and necessary job to do. But throughout I
felt that at least part of the machine, though a decreasingly small part
of it, saw me as an institutional barrier between it and the media
rather than as a bridge reaching out to them. I never felt I had
enough access to meetings or information to enable me to do my
best. I thought those press secretaries who said they had no difficulty
in getting information either lived in another world or deluded
themselves. And sometimes I, as the senior information man in the
department or at No. 10, was deliberately kept in the dark.

Margaret Thatcher records in her memoirs *The Downing Street
Years* that in 1985, for example, the Government did not handle
Top Salaries Review Board recommendations very well. 'Fear of
leaks meant that those entrusted with explaining the rationale of
our policy simply did not know about it in time', she wrote. 'Even
Bernard Ingham had been kept in the dark, which, when he raised
the matter with me afterwards, I conceded was absurd.'

Such absurdities were nothing new. In my book *Kill the
Messenger* I reported that during the Falklands campaign

I was left to represent her [the Prime Minister's] interests with journalists, often feeling extremely exposed and ill-equipped and fearful, during the actual fighting, lest I put a foot wrong and compromise lives. . . . I had to take Clive Whitmore [the Prime Minister's principal private secretary] on one side and make arrangements to safeguard my position by improving the flow of information.

Those words rather gloss over the true picture. The fact is that I told Whitmore (now Sir Clive) that if there had not been a war on I should have resigned by then because I felt I was unable to do my job properly. That would have been ironic because Douglas Clark, Anthony Eden's chief press secretary, resigned during Suez, though for a different reason. He was protesting at the way the nation was being deceived. I would have been protesting about the way I was being left in ignorance.

Such absurdities did not end with Mrs Thatcher's condemnation of them in 1985. In March 1988 an even more restrictive regime forced me to bring matters to a head with the Prime Minister's Principal Private Secretary, Nigel Wicks (now Sir Nigel, chairman of the Commission on Standards in Public Life).

I set out my point in a note which first rehearsed my vow, after my Falklands' experience, to stay at No. 10 only so long as I felt I was doing a good job. I acknowledged that a chief press secretary had to find a balance in securing a flow of information and attending meetings, since he had other things to do. But I felt the balance was wrong and that my exclusion from meetings stemmed 'from a mistaken view of presentation'.

'You', I went on,

explicitly separate the formulation of policy and presentation. I explicitly reject that view. But again a balance has to be struck. . . . It would pay enormous dividends if I could attend more of those [meetings] where an issue is coming to a head and in which presentation is an important matter. This is where the narrow, mechanical view which you have fully exposed gets in the way, much (I may say) to the surprise of some Ministers who have assumed I would be at specific meetings.

The fact was, I added, that the press office in No. 10 was 'not now regarded as part of the team but as something standing a little apart from it'. If things did not improve soon, I would consider my future, having at that time been chief press secretary for nine years.

In fact, I stayed for another two years, until Mrs Thatcher's demise, and Wicks soon went on to higher things in the Treasury and elsewhere. My note perhaps tells you all you need to know about the problems of managing relations with the media within a secretive and élitist Civil Service. Wicks was partly reflecting the secretive nature of our Prime Minister. In spite of earlier evidence that she assumed I was being kept informed, she kept things very close to herself. I could cope because she was guided by a philoso-phy and firm purpose, knew what she was doing and did not change her mind. That firmness of purpose and constancy enabled me to brief with a power and authority that belied the system's secretiveness.

The moral of this tale is that no one should take a top job in the communications field without a written contract that entitles them to ready access to information and the boss without qualifi-cation. There is not much point working as the link between an organization and the media if the organization reposes no trust in your integrity and discretion.

There is one other problem that I have hinted at, which goes back to Crombie, the Treasury official whose report laid the administrative foundations of the GIS in July 1947. The report put the GIS very firmly in the executive class – the middle band between the clerical grade and the (top) administrative class. In a class-ridden system this put press officers (and chief press secretar-ies) below the salt. It made it harder for them to do their job. Yet, in defining the qualities to be sought in a chief press secretary, Crombie required 'the mental capacity to understand the full range of the work and the needs of the department and to discuss them with the highest officials'. The grading of the GIS reflected the 1947 view of the role of communications in government. That view proved remarkably persistent, but again sooner or later some-thing would have to give.

14

The catalysts: myself!

APART FROM the politicians, journalists and Civil Servants who have helped to shape the existence and operations of those whom we now call spin doctors, there is one other culprit, according to newspapers, politicians' memoirs and political folklore. It is, I am sorry to say, myself, though it may seem unduly immodest of me to mention it. I recognize that there are many who regard me as the first British spin doctor and I know, only too well, how the Labour Party has sought – and continues to seek – to excuse its spin excesses by citing my alleged behaviour as Margaret Thatcher's chief press secretary from 1979 to 1990. Who can blame them when members of the Thatcher Cabinet – or at least those who disagreed with her, notably over Europe – have assiduously cultivated the myth in their memoirs of a sort of malevolent guerrilla (or perhaps gorilla) at work in her No. 10 press office throughout her tenure? It is, of course, all bunkum and balderdash.

I should perhaps make clear that I do not rush to defend myself out of any concern for my reputation in the small print of the footnotes to history. Indeed, you could argue that I have a vested interest not merely in maintaining but also in cultivating my notorious reputation. It has made me a nice little earner in retirement, with scores of broadcasting opportunities and speaking engagements up and down the country and on ocean cruise liners every year for the last eleven years. My reputation has served me well and the least I can do is to record my thanks to all my inventive critics.

Those who should know better claim I have provided a model, and even set the tone, for how governments conduct themselves in the age of the spin doctor and thereby given Tony Blair *carte blanche*. This claim is partly reflected in the endless abuse that is still aimed at me and which I dine out on at every opportunity, as when I spoke at a dinner attended by Norman (now Lord) Lamont, the former Conservative Chancellor in his then constituency of Kingston upon Thames. Writers in *The Independent*, for example, have described me as 'a mound of poisoned suet' and the *Daily Mirror* referred to me as 'an obnoxious rentaspleen'. John Biffen, a member of Thatcher Cabinets, said I was 'the sewer but not the sewerage', presumably to indicate that I was the conduit for Thatcher's political sludge, and Sir Edward Heath, no less, said I was 'a menace to the constitution'.

The creative uses of the English language that I inspired in the service of our first woman Prime Minister would certainly divert the reader, but my purpose should be to dispel some of the misconceptions about my operations. I will therefore try to bring some perspective to my role as No. 10 chief press secretary. It is, in any case, necessary to do so if I am to draw a reasonably clear line between the traditional, mainstream and generally accepted operations of a press secretary and the spin-doctoring that now afflicts us.

When I joined the No. 10 staff at the beginning of October 1979, I had some knowledge of how the job of press secretary had been done because I had had direct experience of working, as a departmental head of information, to five No. 10 press secretaries: Sir Trevor Lloyd-Hughes and Joe Haines (Harold Wilson), Sir Donald Maitland and Sir Robin Haydon (Edward Heath), and Sir Tom McCaffrey (Jim Callaghan). As Director of Information at the Department of Employment, specializing in handling the conciliation of major national strikes, I had been called over to No. 10 to help with briefing between 1968 and 1974 at the invitation of Haines, Maitland and Haydon when disputes created political crises. I had also been in regular attendance over eleven years at Monday evening meetings, called MIOs (Meetings of Information Officers), at which departmental heads of information, under the chairmanship of the minister responsible for co-ordinating presentation across Government or the No. 10 chief press secretary, sought to work out the presentational week ahead in the context of the overall political situation, to review the results of presentation in the week gone by and to discuss operational issues in a professional context.

My concept of the work of the chief press secretary accorded him three roles: as a spokesman (of a peculiar kind) for and as an adviser to the Prime Minister and, as required, the Cabinet, and as a co-ordinator at official level of Government presentation overall. I considered myself bound, as my predecessors had been, by the Civil Service rules, which required us to maintain political impartiality, never to lie or mislead or indulge in favouritism in the dissemination of news, to respect confidences and Parliamentary privilege and to observe a backroom role, avoiding becoming the story. It is interesting to note that, in stark contrast to some special advisers since 1997, Joe Haines, as a politically aligned journalist, saw his role as chief press secretary restricted by his temporary Civil Servant status as an early special adviser.

I saw the Parliamentary Lobby journalists (the Lobby), as my predecessors had generally done and as my successors until recently did, twice a day: at 11 a.m. in my room in No. 10 and again at 4 p.m. in their eyrie in the upper reaches of the Commons' attics. That basic routine was supplemented by other Lobby briefings if events or crises demanded them. Then in 2002 the Lobby was banished from No. 10. The morning meeting was transferred to the Foreign Press Association across the Mall from a basement briefing room in No. 10 reached through a tradesmen's entrance instead of, as in my day, through the famous black door. The only other Government department that, again until recently, saw its specialist correspondents in the same formalized and regular way was the Foreign and Commonwealth Office (FCO).

Over and above that, I consistently met correspondents from abroad resident in Britain at the Foreign Press Association in Carlton House Terrace every Monday afternoon and the resident American correspondents in my room at No. 10 on Wednesdays at 12 noon. I also saw the British Sunday newspaper lobby at 4 p.m. on Fridays and in the later Thatcher years, at their request, a group of UK provincial political journalists on Tuesdays. From time to time Mrs Thatcher also invited in provincial editors for a personal briefing and reception. At the summits of the EU, G7 (now G8) and Commonwealth, I saw the international media, usually with the FCO spokesman, several times throughout the day and up to about 1 a.m. as events and their deadlines required. And, of course, journalists rang me or, in my absence, the No. 10 press office, at will to pursue their own interests or secure their own personal briefing or guidance.

In the course of the eleven years I calculate that I gave some 5,000 formal briefings and getting on for six times as many informal briefings. I had two objectives. The first was to set out the facts, as I understood them, and to guide journalists on the Prime Minister's views and, where Cabinet decisions had been taken, those of the Government. The second was to set out those facts as persuasively as I could in explaining the Prime Minister's or the Government's purpose and methods, and the likely benefits if those policies were successful, consistent with credibility. I knew the penalty for becoming an incredible informant: professional death through uselessness.

Such was Margaret Thatcher's newsworthiness that at summits I never wanted for a full house or for the stimulation of being baited by a Brussels, Commonwealth or British diplomatic press corps, all of whom had a remarkable penchant for 'going native'. They favoured anybody but Thatcher, the Eurosceptic and the opponent of sanctions against South African apartheid. The Lobby, widely derided for decades by its journalistic critics as lazy lap-dogs and poodles, were by comparison models of professional scepticism, independence and irreverence. As a group, they would try to bite anybody, any day at any time in pursuit of a story.

As in the departments I had worked for, I knew who paid my wages: the taxpayer. I knew to whom I owed my first loyalty: the Prime Minister and her office and the Government of the day. I knew to whom the Prime Minister answered: her Cabinet, for, as she often told me, if she could not get her policies through those among whom she was *primus inter pares* she was a prisoner. And I knew to whom she (and through her, I) was ultimately accountable: Parliament, a constitutional requirement that she observed meticulously.

I had also formed the firm conviction, which notably Joe Haines never seemed to accept, that I could serve neither the Prime Minister nor the Government properly unless I also sought to serve journalists and to be readily available to them. This did not mean that I felt I had to dance to their tune or do their every bidding. Far from it. But it did mean that I recognized that they had a legitimate role to perform in a free society, however much their particular performance might dismay or even disgust me, and that I had to be seen by the media as their voice at court, as it were. I sought to co-exist on a basis of mutual respect. I did so for eleven years, one month and five days – please note the precision – and was fêted and thanked when I left. Some also no doubt felt relief and Michael Brunson, ITN's former political editor, confessed it when he spoke at a farewell dinner I attended for John Major's first press secretary, Gus O'Donnell.

At the heart of this co-existence were my day-to-day relations with the Lobby, the people whose job it is, despite the decreasing coverage accorded to Parliamentary proceedings by press, radio and TV, to bring politics into the home by the written and spoken word. At the behest of their editors and proprietors they have been required progressively to personalize, trivialize and sensationalize politics into a good, intrusive gossip. The coverage of Parliament is redeemed only by some still distinguished commentators who try heroically to put the messy business into perspective and occasionally by sketch writers who treat it as a theatrical event. The general performance has not improved since I left the scene in 1990. John Major caught the worst of it, and nobody could reasonably fault the Labour Party, as the increasingly likely Government from the mid-1990s, for being concerned about its media relations if and when it came to office. Its experiences of the media were of bitter memory–and it was encouraging journalists to do their worst to the Conservatives.

For thirty-four years, from 1945 up to my being recruited to No. 10, press secretaries overall had, so far as I could see, shared my approach to the job and had at least set out to perform it broadly as I did. They were all peculiar spokesmen in the sense that they were neither seen nor heard, although it became impossible to remain unidentified in the television age or if you put a foot wrong. This invisibility, if not absolute anonymity, owed itself to our

Parliamentary system, where politicians, and not unelected officials, are supposed to be visible. In different systems where you have an executive president, as in the United States or Russia, or in what I would describe as more politicized democracies such as Germany, the press secretary is or can become one of the most visible TV personalities of the administration.

We do things differently in the UK. Until the end of 1990 Government spokesmen, both in No. 10 and departments, conducted their relations with the media on an unattributable or Lobby basis. This meant that what they said could be used but could not be attributed by name to the spokesman. In other words, journalists used the material either on their own responsibility or more likely, since editors increasingly wanted information to be sourced, by using such devices as quoting 'sources close to the Prime Minister' or 'a Government/Whitehall/departmental spokesman'. This was *homo sapiens* adapting to his Parliamentary environment. Then John Major sanctioned a slight relaxation to allow attribution to a No. 10 spokesman before Alastair Campbell became quotable as the Prime Minister's official spokesman – but not as Alastair Campbell – in order to preserve what was left of the self-effacing Civil Service convention.

The Lobby system sat increasingly ill at ease with journalism's growing attachment to the conspiracy theory of government and editors' increasing preoccupation not with the news itself but with the process by which it emerged. The dominant question became, who had talked to whom? This encouraged an increasing disinclination on the part of journalists to be bound by rules that they felt got in the way of a story and led in 1986 to an attempt by *The Guardian, The Independent* and *The Scotsman* to force me, as chief press secretary, to go on the record – that is, to be a fully quotable source – by 'withdrawing from the Lobby'. In fact, that was the last thing they were likely to do, because to have done so would have denied them access to the Members' Lobby in the House of Commons. Instead, they boycotted my briefings in Westminster for the next four years until I left. This did not starve them of the information I imparted. They could pick it up from the coverage given by the Press Association news agency. They also importuned those in the Lobby who felt disposed to help them for second-hand accounts of what I had said. They were not short of such informants because the Lobby was narrowly divided over the issue of whether the chief press secretary should be on the record. And they delighted in trying to come up with quotes to embarrass me. By and large all they missed was the day-to-day opportunity personally to assess the temper of the Government from my behaviour. They certainly did not forgo my briefings abroad or at summits held in the UK. Nor did they boycott briefings on Lobby terms held elsewhere in the Government. In fact, *The Guardian* welcomed at least one minister to its lunch table on exactly such terms. They were nothing if not inconsistent.

I refused to bow the knee to them because I knew that in the rebellious, if not entirely revolutionary, atmosphere of the time a concession would probably have brought an end to the post-war Lobby system. I anticipated an immediate demand from the broadcasters, once I agreed to go on the record, for the admission of cameras and microphones. Such an Americanization of the system would have either changed the conventional invisible position of officials or required the appointment of a press secretary with ministerial rank. I did not see my role in such constitution-busting terms.

I have set out the details of this episode in Government–media relations in my book *Kill the Messenger*. Suffice it to say here that the reasons given for trying to change the system were many and varied. They ranged from low commerce – seeking journalistic advantage – to high moral purpose – namely, preventing an alleged abuse of power by me by being able, under the cloak of anonymity, to say things I could not otherwise get away with. This was frankly preposterous because members of the Lobby, to the despair of their increasingly impotent officers, never hesitated to break their own rules against quoting me if it served their purpose or when I produced a colourful phrase. Sixteen years on, the justifications for 'The Great Lobby Revolt', as I describe it, remain as numerous as they were ill thought-out. In fact, the dominating objective of those leading the boycott was a perception that Margaret Thatcher, with a majority of 143, was too powerful and that her power might be curbed if they could stop me briefing with the authority that her clarity of purpose and constancy made possible.

Those who led the 1986 boycott have taken a long time to discover – if indeed they have – an excess of power in Mr Blair and his spin doctors, with majorities of 179 and 167. Perhaps they are not interested in power any more, only in being able to quote the Prime Minister's secretary at his official briefings. Apart from Nicholas Jones of the BBC, the broadcasters have also been astonishingly backward in coming forward with a request to film and record those briefings for broadcast.

Partly through operating under so-called Lobby cover, I have been charged with a catalogue of misdemeanours that, reduced to manageable proportions by citing the most significant, encompasses the following: promoting the centralization of power; leaking or at least engineering the leak that sparked the Westland affair; rubbishing Her Majesty's ministers; unduly personalizing Government in the form of the Prime Minister; creating what is now described as a presidential image; 'tabloidizing' Government, to coin a term; playing favourites, especially with Rupert Murdoch's *Sun*; generally manipulating the media; and being 'the real Deputy Prime Minister' in the influence I exercised over policy. This is what comes of spending eleven years with the 'wrong woman', as she is described, not least by some Tories who owed their careers to her.

15

Case for the defence

Two other charges made against me are of disloyalty to Margaret Thatcher and of politicizing the Civil Service. John Cole, the former political editor of the BBC, says in his memoirs, *As It Seemed to Me*, that my loyalty to the Prime Minister was not to be questioned, though he demonstrates that it was not a blind loyalty. He says I 'perspicaciously' observed at one stage that 'although she had earned great respect from her party for her abilities, there was not a lot of affection and this could be a weakness if things ever went wrong'. I actually put it more brutally in the context of her Parliamentary party: 'It will, I fear, end in tears.'

Those who wanted to topple Thatcher sought to oust me because they knew she could count on me to protect her, though Sir Geoffrey Howe (now Lord Howe) would put it differently. As his memoirs make clear, he wanted her to sack me in August 1986 for reflecting her views on further sanctions against South Africa rather than his (and, he claims, the Cabinet's) more wishy-washy version. He even said, 'I fear that the No. 10 press office, in its present style, is (and has been for some time) undermining our chances of securing a third term.' It was not my job or aim to get any party re-elected, and in spite of my alleged efforts to 'undermine' the Tories they were returned in 1987 with a majority of 101. Howe was not the only one who would have had me moved. According to John Cole, George Younger (Viscount Younger), no doubt among others, wanted me transferred from

No. 10 along with Charles Powell, Thatcher's foreign affairs private secretary.

On the politicization charge Nicholas Jones, in his book *Soundbites and Spindoctors*, reports John Redwood, once the head of Thatcher's policy unit, as saying, 'if there was anything overtly political to be done then Ingham always insisted on it being handled by the Prime Minister's political staff or Conservative Central Office'. Elsewhere in his book Jones, who has become the chronicler of Government–media relations, writes:

> Ingham never made any secret of the fact that his thought processes were much more those of a politician than of an official and he knew instinctively where the border lay between the work of government, for which civil servants have responsibility, and those matters which are strictly party issues. The clarity with which he could identify the boundaries of his public duties was a help, not a hindrance, because it enabled him, through the force of his personality, to assist Mrs Thatcher in asserting a clear, uniform line which could then be communicated both by the civil servants under his control and by the publicity staff at Conservative Central Office.

The final torrid months of the Thatcher years did test my political impartiality, not in the sense of keeping out of the inter-party battle but in the sense of being above the leadership fray being fought within her own party. As one approaching retirement and near the end of an amazingly privileged life, I was not of a mind to desert my leader. Nor do I think I would have been in different circumstances. I tried as best I could to keep a distance, but it was not easy and I was not entirely successful. For example, I recall joking in the autumn of 1990 with a weekend journalist-caller that Michael Heseltine, in writing a provocative open letter to his constituency party and then going abroad, was 'lighting the blue touch paper and retiring to a safe distance – to wit the Middle East – to see what happens'. It was, I fear, too good a quote not to break surface. I also once said in exasperation that Heseltine should either 'put up or shut up'. With an exaggerated sense of my powers he blames my remark for 'inspiring' a *Times* leader to that effect. I still do not think he would have stood against Thatcher without Howe's resignation speech in the Commons, which left him with no option.

The only accusation against me of leaking relates to the Westland affair and becomes ever more preposterous with the years and the Blair government's habitual incontinence. This was one of the earliest battles over Europe, the big issue that led to the downfalls of Thatcher and Major and will surely do for Blair eventually. Ironically, the two principal players were Europhiles: Michael Heseltine and Leon Brittan (now Lord Brittan). Heseltine wanted the relatively small and troubled helicopter firm Westland to be taken over by a European consortium which he did his level best to cobble together. Brittan and the Government generally felt that Westland should be left to find its own salvation, which it eventually did through the American company Sikorsky.

Essentially, a splendid tale of manoeuvre, intrigue and rank media hypocrisy boiled down to Heseltine (Defence) trying to keep open the European opportunity and Brittan (DTI), supported by an exasperated Thatcher, trying to keep open Westland's freedom of choice. Things went from bad to worse and eventually, while I was on holiday over the New Year, Heseltine wrote a letter to the *Times* which was felt to contain 'material inaccuracies'. The Solicitor-General, Sir Patrick Mayhew, was employed to write back to him pointing this out. I returned to work to be fully briefed on all this and to identify a pressing need for the Government robustly to defend its line of keeping open options, which I conveyed to the DTI.

While I was eating a sandwich at my desk, I was amazed to receive a telephone call from Colette Bowe, Brittan's press secretary, saying she had got her Secretary of State's permission to leak the Solicitor-General's letter. Moreover, the DTI wanted me to do the dirty deed – and immediately, through the Press Association news agency – because they needed it in the public domain before a Westland press conference at 4 p.m. This was the first I had heard of the idea. I refused to leak the letter point-blank, saying 'I have to keep the Prime Minister above this sort of thing'. I was, to say the least, extremely unhappy about the whole ploy but, to my regret, did not say that, if they had any sense, they should not leak the letter either. On that flimsy basis Brittan claimed No. 10 approval. A Cabinet Office inquiry followed. Mrs Thatcher, preparing to defend herself in the Commons, remarked with gallows humour that she might be out of office by 6 p.m. The media got into a state of superheated indignation over a leak, which is rather like Dracula complaining about being involved in a bloodbath. And then the whole furore fizzled out without me or, so far as I know, anybody else being reprimanded.

All this does not stop that unfastidious politician Gerald Kaufman from claiming to this day that 'Conservative members . . . are the party of Sir Bernard Ingham, who misused a letter from Law Officers against Michael Heseltine'. Kaufman is, of course, wrong in suggesting I am a member of the Conservative Party. I have not been a member of any political party since I left his on joining the Civil Service in 1967. He should also speak to Jim Wightman, formerly political editor of the *Daily Telegraph*, who came to No. 10 during the Westland affair to ask what on earth was going on. 'You have never leaked a single thing and certainly not to me since you went to No. 10', he said. 'Quite right', I replied, 'I've not and I'm not about to start.' Leaking was not my style.

Nor was rubbishing ministers. Yet that is the next charge laid against me by, among others, the precious Kaufman. An entire reputation for 'rubbishing' and 'undermining' ministers has been built on two quotes. First, I said of Francis Pym (now Lord Pym) in 1982 that 'It's being so cheerful as keeps him going', after Mona Lott, in Tommy Handley's wartime radio comedy. And four years later I said that John Biffen (now Lord Biffen) was 'that well-known semi-detached member of the Cabinet'. Pym was responsible at the material time for co-ordinating the presentation of Government policy and Biffen later did the same job. They were ministers to whom, in Pym's case, I worked at the time, or had worked. Nor was there anything hole-in-the-corner about either of my remarks. They were pummelled out of me at routine, collective Lobby briefings. The first was after Pym had made a very gloomy speech only days after the Chancellor, rightly as it turned out, had detected signs of economic recovery. The other was after Biffen had complained on TV that Thatcher was a liability to her party and should be replaced by a collective leadership.

Not surprisingly, the Lobby wanted to know how either could remain in office. It was a very good question, especially in the case of Biffen. I sought to fend off the journalists until, in some desperation, I fell back on the ministers' natures: Mr Pym's gloomy persona and Mr Biffen's remarkable ability as a commentator to be part of the Government yet to stand outside it. I regret the remarks because of the opening they have given the unscrupulous to hang the 'rubbisher' label round my neck. Some journalists claimed that I was accurately reflecting the Prime Minister's views of the two. They were wrong if by that they thought I had discussed them with her. Like Sir Donald Maitland with Edward Heath before me, I did not spend my time discussing Cabinet ministers with the Prime Minister. I was quite capable of identifying their natures myself. Honest journalists present at the briefing knew that I was seeking, in some desperation, to explain their actions. As it turned out, I also succeeded in defending them because I focused attention not on their 'offence' but on mine and got them off the hook. I still await 'Thank you' notes. As for undermining them, both remained in Cabinet for another twelve months, during which Pym went on to become Foreign Secretary during the Falklands conflict.

But that does not entirely dispense with the charge of undermining ministers. Geoffrey Howe clearly thinks that I undermined his appointment as Deputy Prime Minister when he was moved from the Foreign Office in 1989. I did no such thing and had no intention of doing so. Instead, I explained what Lord Whitelaw had done in a job with a courtesy title and no constitutional underpinning but which, with Whitelaw, was about as big as it ever would have got under Thatcher. I felt it necessary to do so in the interests of accuracy and possible future recriminations because Howe's acolytes had grossly over-egged his new role, investing it with a grandeur I simply did not recognize when it was retailed to me by Lobby correspondents. Howe should blame his devoted coterie for their over-enthusiasm and conceivably for the Thatcher-damaging revelation that he had first been offered the Home Office, a revelation that completely flummoxed me when I met the Lobby later that day. I had never heard of it.

That would be where my reputation as a 'rubbisher' of ministers would rest were it not for Tory memoirs and, of course, the use made of them by Labour opportunists. Lord Howe records that Peter Cropper, a former director of the Conservative Research Department, wrote to him a month before he was made Deputy Prime Minister, saying 'The Sunday papers seem to be fairly sure, no doubt on Bernard Ingham's advice, that you are going to be relieved of the Foreign Office and given a sinecure'. Give a dog a bad name . . . and you come a cropper. Lord Heseltine, who is no more likely to be objective about me than Lord Howe, writes in *Life in the Jungle* of 'the insidious undermining technique of Bernard Ingham', but again without providing any evidence for his assertion.

Robin Oakley, the former BBC political editor, said in an article in *The Times* that I was more 'sinned against than sinning' in respect of Patrick Jenkin and Peter Rees (now both ennobled). Their forecast departure from the Thatcher Cabinet left them 'twisting in the wind' for the entire summer of 1985 before they left in September. Again I played no role in that whatsoever, but the late Alan Clark, the insouciant diarist and former Tory MP, records discussing the September 1985 reshuffle with Robert Atkins, then MP for South Ribble and Parliamentary Private Secretary to Lord Young, as early as 24 April, five months before the event. Even then they listed Rees, among others, for the chop. Clark's morbid fascination with reshuffles was, in my experience, widely shared by politicians, who gossiped and then blamed me. This was bluntly my message to Archie Hamilton, former MP for Epsom, when he came into my room on his appointment as Thatcher's Parliamentary Private Secretary to say he did not want any more rubbishing of ministers during his watch. In a brief conversation he was given briskly to understand that there had never been any from my office and there would not be any at all, if only he could manage to get his own colleagues to shut up.

All too often politicians are like cushions, bearing the imprint of the last person who sat on them. John (now Sir John) Nott, Defence Secretary during the Falklands campaign, carried one imprint of me for eighteen years. During a Thatcher-fest at an astonishingly well-endowed Hofstra University on Long Island,

New York, in 2000, I was heckled by Nott when, in discussing my troubles with the Ministry of Defence during the Falklands campaign, I said they even wanted to shut me up. Nott shouted from the back, 'And quite right, too'. When I later bumped into him in the Gents, I told him I was appalled that he had been carrying around with him for eighteen years the lie that a media briefing of mine had anticipated the attack on Goose Green in which Colonel 'H' Jones lost his life. It was time he caught up with the fact that his department had apologized to me for the allegation.

As for the myth that I helped centralize power – so often the excuse for Alastair Campbell's 'control freakery' – my first act, in the month before I took up the chief press secretary's post at No. 10, was to see heads of departmental information divisions to urge them to be positive in communicating with the public through the media. I knew how Questions of Procedure for Ministers (QPM), the operational guidelines that John Major published for the first time, could be inhibiting in requiring departments to report to No. 10 first and act later. Perhaps I had felt it more acutely because of the nervousness within the Wilson and Callaghan administrations in the 1970s about my last minister, Tony Benn. But I had always felt it was ludicrous to expect autonomous departments whose Cabinet ministers were held personally responsible for policy in their bailiwicks to wait upon Downing Street.

I have set out in *Kill the Messenger* how I hoped to make the Thatcher regime different, with a looser, not a tighter, rein. My message to the departments was:

> You know your own subjects and journalists better than I do, and it is up to you to devise your own presentational programmes, within the familiar conventions and constraints affecting Government publicity. You will only find me nagging you if I feel you are not getting through to the public. My job is to try to drag the overall Government story together and to ensure that the communications orchestra follows the same score. I hope you will keep me informed of what you are up to so that I shall be in a position effectively to co-ordinate presentation and to ensure that the various elements of the orchestra come in on cue.

By that I meant they should let No. 10 know, as required by QPM, of planned broadcasts, articles, speeches and, of course, anything likely to be controversial so that we could eliminate clashes of activity, be forewarned and help get our message across.

It was intended to be a liberating regime. It also reflected the constitutional reality: I had no power, other than the power of persuasion, over departmental heads of information, who were answerable to their Cabinet ministers. Yet dissidents, whether for reasons of politics or personal animosity, presented an entirely different, Stalinist view of No. 10 and for the first three years consistently leaked to my intended disadvantage my Monday evening MIO co-ordinating meetings to *The Guardian*. This had no practical effect other than to stifle for a time the free discussion I had hoped for, because those attending felt they had a rat in their midst.

I plead guilty to trying, often vainly, to bring coherence to Government presentation by effective co-ordination. It is the greatest gift that a press secretary can bestow on any Government. But it can only be achieved by co-operation between colleagues, a lot of luck and a cohesive Government. Thatcher records in *The Downing Street Years* that 'The economic and public expenditure discussions of 1980 repeatedly found their way into the press; decisions came to be seen as victories by one side or the other and Bernard Ingham told me that it was proving quite impossible to convey a sense of unity and purpose in this climate.' You cannot co-ordinate an incredible product into a credible one.

The 'Real Deputy Prime Minister' jibe, which is aimed at Alastair Campbell with some justification, was part of the ogre-building by Tory and Labour MPs alike. But my difficulties with access to information during the Falklands campaign and my altercation with Nigel Wicks illustrate graphically the limits of my powers. All too often I felt that my existence was tolerated on sufferance by a disdainful system. The press secretary's job is to devise and prosecute a Government communication policy, not policy generally, though Joe Haines demonstrates in his memoirs that he, as a rather peculiar type of press secretary, had an early, commendable attempt at spreading home-ownership.

I am not conscious of ever having shaped Thatcher policy, even though John Redwood goes around suggesting otherwise. He recalled when I spoke for him in Llangollen in the mid-1990s that as head of the No. 10 Policy Unit he once charged me with inventing Government policy in a briefing. 'That isn't Government policy', he said he told me. To which, according to him, I replied–and I have no recollection of the incident–'Oh well, it is now'.

Press briefings can, of course, affect policy, if only temporarily. I demonstrated this once when I sent the pound crashing towards parity with the US dollar by unwisely stating that 'this Government will not throw good money after bad by defending the pound.' After all, Thatcher had often said 'you can't buck the market'. Treasury hands would say you should never give the markets a one-way bet. But my remarks confused the press, most of whom damagingly portrayed the Government as not caring about the level of sterling – which was nonsense – while a minority thought that this heralded a rise in interest rates. In fact, the Treasury was forced to raise interest rates, which it should have hoisted more decisively earlier.

There were few other instances of my presentational advice affecting policies. It is true that I was responsible, for presentational reasons, for forcing the Ministry of Defence to take journalists on the Falklands campaign. I also forced the MoD to reveal the loss of two Harriers during operations in the South Atlantic. I discovered that the Lobby was buzzing with rumours that the Government – and most people would inevitably have taken that to mean Mrs Thatcher – was holding the news back until the local government polling booths closed. I was not going to have the Prime Minister falsely tainted with a political 'scandal' when it became clear the defence interest justification for withholding news of the losses was pretty flimsy.

Somebody accurately leaked to *The Observer* that I prevented Michael Heseltine from being sacked as Defence Secretary during the Westland affair just before Christmas 1985. An august body assembled in the Prime Minister's study first wanted, in response to Leon Brittan's demand that he be sacked, to send him a warning letter, a kind of yellow card. My judgement of Heseltine, based partly on his record as a Thatcher-basher, was that he would call her bluff, and then where would she be? 'So, we'll have to sack him', she concluded. 'By all means do so,' I said, 'but, bearing in mind all I know of what is going on and his success so far with the media, that will only make him a martyr to the European cause. And do you want that?' Heseltine survived, only to resign later.

But in none of these examples did I have any influence on policy; my concern was tactics, which, leaving aside communication policy and strategy, is largely what press secretaries are engaged in.

The next charge is that I crafted Thatcher's image and made her the figurehead for all Government action, thereby providing a model for Blair's presidential style of government. But the reason for the increasing concentration on leaders is that technology has shrunk the world, eased travel and created a demand for leader to meet leader. This in turn has focused the camera's attention on leaders, and especially comely female leaders. In Thatcher's case the coverage was magnified by her position as Britain's first woman Prime Minister, her style and dominant personality and her eventual success in ending 'the British disease'. The world warmed to Maggie, or 'Madam Tatcha', handbagging a whole generation of statesmen and politicians.

At home the British press acquired the habit of attributing every initiative personally to her. Peter Hennessy recalls Douglas Hurd (now Lord Hurd) saying during his time as Home Secretary: 'I constantly saw on the poster of the *Evening Standard* . . . "Maggie Acts" on something. Often in those cases, she wasn't even aware of the situation. But the whole ethos of No. 10 was that it had to be "Maggie Acts".' Had Lord Hurd had a word with me, he would have discovered that I shared his concern. The media's obsession with Mrs Thatcher was, to say the least, demoralizing for ministers and therefore a source of potential tension. It did nobody any good – least of all Thatcher – for her to be seen to be doing everything and taking credit for everything.

When I could do anything about it, in the face of the media's determination to build up a legend, I did. For example, when South Georgia was recaptured Thatcher was elated by the snatching of this success from the jaws of Antarctic disaster and wanted to get the news out quickly. I was adamant she should not announce it and eventually we persuaded John Nott, as the Secretary of State for Defence, to do so with Thatcher supportively at his side. For the same reason I later forcefully voiced my concerns about Charles Powell's monopolization of her, especially abroad. I was above all a team player who all too often wished my team would play with me.

Let former Chancellor Nigel Lawson (now Lord Lawson) present the next charge: tabloidization. He claims that, although a former *Yorkshire Post* and *Guardian* man, I 'was only really at home with the tabloids – above all the *Sun*'. He even claims I had rebuked his press officer 'for lunching a senior *Financial Times* writer instead of the journalists that counted'. In his *The View from No. 11*, he adds even more absurdly:

> Margaret decided that she had no time to read the newspapers during the week. Instead, Ingham would get into No. 10 very early each morning, go through the papers himself, and prepare her a crisply written press summary. This had a selection and slant that was very much his own. It would usually start with the *Sun*, the paper he was closest to and which he had taught Margaret represented the true views of the man on the street. It was also the paper whose contents he could most readily influence. This led to a remarkable circularity. Margaret would sound off about something, Ingham would then translate the line into *Sun*-ese and feed it to that newspaper, which would normally use it. This would then take pride of place in the news summary he provided for Margaret, who marvelled at the unique rapport she evidently enjoyed with the British people.

So, while Heseltine has me inspiring leaders in *The Times*, Lawson has me damn near editing the *Sun*.

First, I would be amazed if the Chancellor's press secretary were not lunching with the *Financial Times*. But I often thought it would have helped if the Chancellor and his press secretary had paid closer attention to the more populist tabloids. It was not that I felt at home with them, especially the *Sun*; it was that I believed we had to talk regularly in their own language to all sections of journalism if we were to get over the Government's policies. And it wasn't that Thatcher decided she had no time to read the newspapers; she simply had no inclination. I had to devise a means by which we kept her in touch with what was going on. My press digest, compiled between 7 and 9 a.m., was the answer. I still store a decade of these digests in date order in boxes. I have looked at random at six days in each box. Not one single digest started with the *Sun*. Moreover, where I found it necessary to itemize newspaper coverage of a particular issue, I invariably started with the *Daily Star* and worked my way rapidly up through the tabloids to leave myself with time for a good read of the broadsheets.

Thatcher had in fact discovered and established a relationship with Larry Lamb, then the editor of the *Sun*, long before I went to No. 10. I seldom talked to editors: I worked through their political editors at Westminster and thereby reinforced their standing. I said what I had to say to them in plain English and, to that extent, it was probably more readily used than complex Treasury guff, if it served the correspondents' purposes. So the Ingham myth, which may have encouraged Blair and his team into its obsession with spin-doctoring, seems to have originated with some of Thatcher's colleagues. They have much to answer for – and so say most members of her party, if my travels across England in the last eleven years are anything to go by.

Their testimony – and the attempts by Labour MPs to excuse Alastair Campbell's every excess by reference to the Ingham myth – contrasts sharply, however, with that of the chairman of the Lobby in 1990. Writing to *The Times* just after my retirement in 1990, he said that the 'vast majority' of the then 226 accredited Lobby correspondents would agree with the warm sentiments expressed in a recent article by one of their number, Robin Oakley.

Very few of us recognize the image of Mrs Thatcher's former Chief Press Secretary as the manipulative character portrayed by Robert Harris [the novelist and a friend of Mandelson] in his book *Good and Faithful Servant*. Sadly, there is a danger that this version will enter the record as the definitive account of Mr Ingham's eleven years as 'sources close to the Prime Minister'. I believe that it is important to understand that Mr Ingham's first duty was towards the Prime Minister and not the media. That was certainly the basis on which we treated his briefings. There were times when he could not in all conscience tell us the whole truth. But I believe I speak for my colleagues when I say that he was unfailingly straight, honest and fair.

In the cynical world of Westminster that testimony will, of course, be brushed aside – however accurately it represented the majority of political correspondents – because the chairman of the Lobby in 1990 happened to be Trevor Kavanagh, political editor of the *Sun*.

16

Born in the USA

THE FINAL stop on the road to the age of the spin doctor is New York. It was there in October 1984 – an appropriate year, perhaps – that it arrived. It is said that the first recorded use of the term was by Saul Bellow in his 1977 Jefferson lectures. But the *New York Times* gave it currency in an article about the aftermath of a televised debate between the US presidential candidates, Ronald Reagan and Walter Mondale:

> A dozen men in good suits and women in silk dresses will circulate smoothly among the reporters, spouting confident opinions. They won't just be press agents trying to impact a favourable spin to a routine release. They'll be the 'Spin Doctors', senior advisers to the candidates.

That sounds more like the average diplomatic reception to me. There is an enormous amount of spin-doctoring going on whenever two or three diplomats are gathered together. Indeed, diplomacy is one long doctoring of spin. They tried to employ me on it during my time in Government as they steadily shifted the nomenclature of Europe towards the federal goal of a United States of Europe. What was the Common Market became the European Economic Community and then the European Community and now, pending further adjustment, the European Union. So far as I was concerned, these titles were all misnomers.

According to the *Oxford Dictionary of New Words*, in the jargon of US politics a spin doctor is a senior political spokesman employed to promote a favourable interpretation of events to journalists. Confusingly it adds, 'a politician's flak'. This takes us into another related world – that of the 'flak-catcher'. The dictionary tells us this is 'a person employed by an individual or institution to deal with all adverse comment, questions etc. from the public, thereby shielding the employer' – or, perhaps they should have said, trying to shield the employer – 'from unfavourable publicity'. How do you shield an employer from unfavourable publicity if the facts in the public domain are fundamentally unfavourable? It isn't possible.

Flak derives from the German initials of a compound word for 'pilot defence gun' which the Second World War converted into a term for anti-aircraft fire. After the war it came to mean in Britain a barrage of criticism and abuse. But in the USA it was in regular use in the 1930s as a term for a press agent, after a well-known practitioner called Gene Flack, who subsequently had his name clipped. So, according to the *Oxford Dictionary of New Words*, a flak is a chap who tries to turn negative publicity to advantage, whereas a spin doctor tries to get the picture right from the start and avoid the need for damage limitation. It all sounds a bit mob-handed to me. I have never known a press officer who did not try to get it right first time but also never hesitated to try to turn flak to his advantage.

Defined thus, there is nothing objectionable in the spin doctor, whether operating in his positive role of expounding a line or his negative role of diverting flak. There is nothing exceptionable in any human being putting the best possible gloss on his words, actions or intentions – or in his getting others to do so for him – and I do not see why politicians should be denied the opportunity in this egalitarian age of universal rights. The issue is how they do it and the extent to which they stretch the truth and credibility in doing so.

The anonymous *New York Times* wordsmith was not an innocent abroad. He knew exactly what he was doing. He was trying to nobble the jury, complementing the word 'spin' (as in 'to spin a yarn' or perhaps as in spin bowling in cricket), with the word 'doctor' (meaning to titivate, tamper with and even falsify) in order to brand with the mark of Cain all those in the business of liaising with and guiding journalists. This is out of the top drawer of relations between journalist and press officer. There has never been any love lost between them, even though – or perhaps because – they usually come from the same stable. The journalist thinks that the press officer is a journalist gone wrong, and the press officer knows the journalist is always liable to go wrong himself, except when by some stroke of luck, heroics of deduction, enterprise or leak he gets it spot on and thereby causes the press officer a great deal of trouble. The result: they are all spin doctors now. The term is so much more sinister and pregnant with skulduggery than mere 'press officer'.

Jeremy Paxman, the BBC *Newsnight* presenter, demonstrated the traditional loathing of journalists for press officers at an Imperial Cancer Campaign 'Turn the Tables' lunch over which I presided in the Savoy in 2000. By general consent, incidentally, Alastair Campbell wiped the floor with him as his interviewer. When Paxman was asked what he thought of spin doctors, he said he was reminded of Gwilym Lloyd George's monkeys: 'the higher they climb, the more revolting are the parts they expose'. In fact Lloyd George (the Prime Minister's younger son) was talking about politicians, but Paxman made his point. Yet it is a safe bet that, like all journalists, he has had his professional life saved from time to time by one of these revolting press officer monkeys. As they read this, the monkeys are no doubt silently telling Paxman where to stuff his nuts.

It is time to examine the monkey's tricks. Shorn of its *New York Times* or Paxman connotations, 'spin' – or presentation, as it used to be described – is as old as the hills. It amounts to nothing more than a line of argument with which to present a case. It is how the speaker sees the subject or situation he is dealing with. 'Lines to take' – the bones of an argument with which to present a policy, a decision or an action – are the weft not only of press officer briefs but also of ministerial and chief executive speeches. These 'lines' are almost by definition closer to the facts than, for example, the average newspaper's presentation of its circulation figures, which is among the most creative concepts of spin you will find in the public prints!

I first began to encounter the term 'spin doctor' in 1990. It had taken a good five years to cross the Atlantic. Then calls began to arrive in the No. 10 press office from journalists asking us for the 'spin' on this or that. We were rather tickled by these early displays of tradespeak, chortled rather mockingly down the line perhaps in the vain hope of making our clients feel a mite self-conscious about using the term, and proceeded to do what we and our predecessors had always done: we gave them our line on this or that.

And 'spin' would have come to mean no more and no less than presentation or briefing but for the now widely held conspiracy theory of government that the *New York Times* scribe so cleverly played upon in 1984. His spin doctor fitted the prejudices of the average journalist like a glove once the succession of scandals mentioned earlier had undermined the public's faith in the integrity of politicians.

But if spin adds up to nothing more sinister than plying a briefing line, how then does a Government press officer, operating under the appropriate rules and conventions, conceivably qualify for the dismissive title of 'spin doctor' in the course of his average week's work? And what actions are compatible with those rules and with generally acceptable professional conduct, in the face of journalists eager not just to report what is said and done but to make the news by licence, trivialization, simplification, selection, deduction, translation and exaggeration, and to cause the maximum trouble in doing so? Let us never assume that journalists are in the business of reporting mere rows; they aim at the very least for incandescent fury leading to irrevocable splits.

The propensity to exaggeration led me to give a mickey-taking briefing at the Milan European summit in 1985, when heads of state and government comprehensively fell out. For a while they were scarcely on speaking terms. I had to go down and tell the world's press in their tent about this curious eventuality, whereupon an *agent provocateur* from Fleet Street asked, 'And what does Mrs Thatcher think about this?' Since it was widely believed that she had only one emotion – fury – I resorted to understatement: 'She is not best pleased'.

I knew, of course, how this would be interpreted. 'Aha', I cried. 'I know what you lot will be writing tomorrow. Mrs Thatcher won't be furious. She won't be livid. She won't even be incandescent. She'll be positively erupting, Krakatoan on the Richter scale.' *The Times* the following day reported that 'sources close to the Prime Minister' had said that 'Mrs Thatcher was Krakatoan on the Richter scale'. Edward Heath inevitably went on radio and called for my instant dismissal, presumably for my insouciance. A seismologist even wrote to me and, in the severest possible terms, pointed out that volcanic eruptions do not register on the Richter scale.

It is obvious from this that Government press officers can, and do, tease their clients, but they are also in a serious business. Their first concern is to get inside the mind and under the skin of the minister, to know the minister's manifesto, programme – as outlined in the Queen's Speech – purpose, philosophy and nature, and how he or she reacts. They have to be able to interpret the minister's views and feelings unseen, and to get it right, or as right as does not matter. This means being able to produce an interpretation of those views and feelings that will stand the test of credibility, and credibility over time. I calculate that I was directly briefed by Thatcher on only about five per cent of the occasions on which I spoke for her. This underlines the risks that senior Civil Servants took with me by deliberately keeping me in the dark – had she been anything less than as readable as a book. They will say, in their cynical way, that it does not much matter if a press officer has to be denied, but a press officer cannot make a habit of being denied without also damaging the interests of the minister and Government. This is especially true if the press officer has a reputation, as I think I had, for trying to be helpful and getting it as right as possible.

The press officer's second concern is to know what is going on. The head of information has the privilege of regular, daily morning meetings with any minister who is concerned to keep on top of his job. In crises his or her presence will be much more frequent and as continuous as possible, consistent with keeping the media informed and keeping the minister informed of media thinking, rumours and tactics. Another invaluable but patchy source is meetings. Policy-making meetings give a 'feel' of the structure and fabric of a policy – why it has been constructed in a particular way – and the wherewithal better to explain it. Beyond that, the press officer can fall back on Cabinet and Cabinet committee minutes and policy papers, conversations with private secretaries and officials responsible for the formulation of policy. But this, of course, requires the ability to secure an uninterrupted flow of paper – as I manifestly did not always manage at No. 10 – and to persuade officials to loosen up.

The press officer's third concern is to anticipate events and trouble. Like the Boy Scouts, the press officer's motto is 'Be prepared'. This means keeping a diary. In departments this is primarily for the press officer's own departmental use but it is also part of the more elaborate 'grid', as it has come to be known in Blair times, bringing proposed events across Government together in one controlling document. The press officer reads the political scene like a meteorologist pores over his charts; he monitors newspapers, radio and television and he sniffs the air for topical issues that present an opportunity for effective message-bearing as well as those that create potential problems.

When he knows his minister is taking an initiative, the press officer assembles not only positive lines to take but also defensive points to deploy in anticipation of likely criticisms. When he is beset by a sudden storm, he cobbles together the best correct exposition he can summon up in the time available. He never says 'No comment'. If he does, journalists will assume he has something to hide, even if he is genuinely playing for time. He finds other ways of temporizing, such as 'When we have established the facts, we shall know what to say about them'. Unless, of course, his department's ignorance is the story.

His fourth concern, having got on top of his principal, his subject and the media, is to develop a presentational purpose or strategy. Perhaps the greatest benefit he can bestow on a government over time is the creation of a sense of presentational purpose, an impression of coherence. To this end the press officer develops a plan, in so far as this is possible amid the welter of events, for the positive exposition of what his Government is seeking to achieve and he uses events to underline those objectives. In the case of the 1979–83 Thatcher government, the Herculean objective was to stop the national rot by bringing public finances under control and controlling inflation; to put the trade unions within a framework of law to end decades of industrial warfare; to abolish regulations and to promote enterprise and the adoption of modern technology; and to encourage individual capitalism and responsibility. This involved breaking with the decayed post-war political consensus on the need to reconcile low inflation and a competitive economy with full employment. Impartial Government press officers did not put it like that. Instead, they played 'Spot the U-turn' with journalists, who widely expected Thatcher to return defeated to the old ways. Who could blame them when the penalty was unemployment in excess of 3 million? After all, Heath had turned in 1972 with unemployment approaching 1 million.

The press officer's fifth concern is to secure general recognition within the Government that its medium- and long-term reputation will suffer if the Government's presentation ceases to be credible. This will happen if its promise exceeds its performance, if its claims are risible, if it is perceived to be manipulating the facts, or if it acquires a dodgy reputation (even allowing for journalism's congenital suspicions of our governors). The press officer knows his sole stock in trade is credibility, the prime determinant of a government's longevity. As an employee of Government, he is there to sustain it in office by his spokesmanship, his wise counsel and his ability to co-ordinate the presentation of the Government's messages, to bring them together from the many disparate strands of a department – or, if he is in No 10, from across Government – into a coherent whole.

He has – or had – to do this within the constraints imposed by Civil Service rules and conventions: political impartiality, protecting public funds from being hi-jacked for party political purposes, giving honest advice, respecting Parliament's privilege to hold the Government to account and maintaining a low profile. If doing all of these things make someone a spin doctor, then I must plead guilty to having been one for nearly half my working life. But there is nothing sinister or Machiavellian in this definition. Is there then something in the way press officers perform their task in a modern democracy that could conceivably justify the pejorative description of them as spin doctors?

17

Line in the sand

A PRESS officer at work is like a nut being squeezed in a nut-cracker. He has to reconcile the interests of ministers with the secretiveness or caution of the official machine and the insatiable demands of journalists with the rules and conventions governing his status as a Civil Servant. His every utterance is a reconciliation, a calculation of how much or little he can credibly get away with, even when he acts on his own initiative to reveal matters that others would have preferred kept under wraps. His overriding duty is to his minister, acting in his official governmental capacity, subject to his also observing Civil Service rules and conventions for which he is answerable to his permanent secretary, the official head of his department. Added to this is a higher duty to the Government as a whole, a potential source of conflict that is fortu-nately generally resolved by ministerial restraint but which can create acute difficulties. For example, in the Matrix Churchill affair the late Alan Clark apparently ran his own private policy on arms sales, contrary to that of the Government. Perhaps predict-ably Lord Justice Scott, in his curious inquiry into the affair, passed over this conundrum in governmental relationships.

Whatever the theoretical circumstances, the practical reality – for myself, my predecessors and my successors up to 1997 – is that everything that passes in the course of a working day between press offices and media is the outcome of an internal tug-of-war between the forces of openness and the forces of secrecy. In this tug-of-war a good press officer will usually argue that a minimalist approach is unlikely to serve the interests of the Government unless it has no policy, or does not know precisely what it is. Sensible political correspondents know that a press officer cannot tell them everything. Their exchanges are thus partly conducted in a highly specialized code of sorts, which John Carvel, the *Guardian* journalist, confessed he found bewildering when he first joined the Lobby in the 1980s.

The essence of the code is understatement, circumlocution and steady doses of heavy implication woven into the inevitable Parliamentary jargon, however naturally forthright the briefer may be. Even if the system were more open, there would still be an addiction to understatement because the very existence of modern, commercial journalism raises the decibels, intensifies the drama and heightens the Technicolor, as with my intimation to reporters in Milan that Mrs Thatcher was 'not best pleased'. Press officers discount at source. It follows that when plain English is uttered it acquires a certain force, as did my 'bunkum and balderdash' to dismiss the more fanciful stories.

The press secretary's style is also part of the code. Harold Evans's outwardly relaxed and unhurried manner perfectly matched that of his Prime Minister, Harold Macmillan, who pinned a quotation in his own handwriting from *The Gondoliers* – 'quiet, calm deliberation disentangles every knot' – on to the then green baize door between the Cabinet Room and the old principal private secretary's office in No. 10. I never actually saw a handbag hanging from the door handle in my time but it would have set the tone for my more volatile nature, which Tony Benn has described as 'a simmering cauldron'. I once shattered my watch on the Lobby room table as I unintentionally banged my fist down on it for emphasis. Donald Maitland apparently anointed the Lobby with words in Edward Heath's time, just as I am told Gus O'Donnell marinated them in verbiage in John Major's early years. Evening newspapermen told me they often wondered whether they were going to get away from O'Donnell in time to file their stories before the noon deadline.

No one studies a press secretary for his mood music more closely than the Lobby journalists. If they could ruffle Harold

Evans, reduce Donald Maitland or Gus O'Donnell to monosyllables or induce a certain icy calm in me, they knew something was up. This is why some politicians would kill the Lobby stone dead, if they could. Lobby group therapy is not necessarily to the Government's advantage, and the attempt by a small group of editors in 1986 to close it down says everything for their sheer naïvety. By contrast, Chris Moncrieff, the former political editor of the Press Association, told me he had not the slightest intention of cutting himself off from any potential source of information.

A press secretary's approach to journalists is a crucial part of his armoury. His aim is to promote as sympathetic a view as possible of the Government's period in office, but journalists are red in tooth and claw. I knew therefore that they would be up to every trick in the book – and some not in it – to get a story that made life difficult for the Prime Minister or the Government. This was even true for her so-called supporters in the national press, who, at least in the 1980s, generally never lost sight of their commercial interest in producing a lively newspaper or programme. I therefore sought to pursue a tough but fair regime from the start. I did not expect them to stand any nonsense from me and I most certainly had not the slightest intention of standing any from them. I had seen where love-ins between government and media had got them in Harold Wilson's time. Later, John Major and Gus O'Donnell were taken to the cleaners, starting with a report that the Prime Minister tucked his shirt inside his underpants – a story that Alastair Campbell, in his time as a journalist, is credited with breaking, or at the very least circulating.

A press secretary also needs to understand before he starts how the world is changing around him. My experience had been not just of an increasing sharpness – not to say viciousness – in journalism, as evidenced daily by the gossip columns, where blood sport is brought to its ultimate refinement. It was also a time of declining party loyalty, not least in the Conservative Party, which had hitherto behaved like the Brigade of Guards. There was also a plummeting respect for rules and conventions, such as for embargoes on the publication of documents, which are primarily designed for the convenience of journalists so that they can prepare their reports from advance copies. To be fair, however, the journalists were only partly to blame for the increasing lack of respect for embargoes. One former colleague has told me of the despair in the Lobby in trying to get the Tory maverick Enoch Powell to observe his own deadlines on the reporting of his speeches. But the Lobby's own rules, which require journalists to refrain from reporting anything in the Members' Lobby, private rooms or corridors of the Palace of Westminster, or those parts to which they have access by virtue of their membership, were also increasingly ignored, primarily because Parliament permitted it.

I also saw decreasing reportage of Parliament and political speeches in favour of gossip and interpretation, with the result that the balance of journalists working in the Palace of Westminster between Lobby (the commentators and interpreters) and Gallery (the reporters) has been completely reversed over the last twenty years. The latest figures show commentators outnumbering reporters by 236 to 84, virtually three to one. And in an increasingly polarized world a disconcerting number of these commentators seemed to hint at, if not flaunt, their own political allegiance in a manner that raised doubts as to the objectivity of their output. I began to find myself alone in defending the BBC from charges of being anti-Tory, just as when I served Labour governments I had denied that Broadcasting House was a hotbed of Conservatism. It would be hard for me now to defend the BBC from charges of bias since Gavyn Davies, the Chancellor's well-heeled friend, has become chairman of its board of governors and Greg Dyke, a £50,000 Labour donor, its Director-General. This is not to mention the Government's wholesale recruitment of BBC journalists and other staff to special adviser and press officer posts, or of Lord Birt, Dyke's predecessor as Director-General, as Blair's ideas man. The concept of not merely having a BBC which is impartial but which is also seen to be impartial has flown comprehensively out of the window during Blair's media-centred tenure.

I also inhabited a world being shrunk by technology. The ability to flash moving pictures of events as they happened across the world into our living-rooms greatly increased the pace of politics. That put a premium on a government's speed of reaction and its sure-footedness in handling fast-moving events. I do not believe that governments should dance like puppets on a string to press, radio or television, but the nation does expect leadership in the face of earth-shattering events.

Another feature of the 1970s and 1980s was the rise of pressure groups, often described as Non-Governmental Organizations (NGOs). This was particularly true in the environmental area, as I discovered at the Department of Energy. These groups, in seeking to shape and direct Government policy, often developed an air of pseudo-scientific authority and ingratiated themselves with a media voracious for stories and itself riddled with campaigners masquerading under journalistic objectivity. All too often these groups were the first resort of journalists, who seemed to find them far more credible as informants than Government itself. In the same way that assertions by trades unions in the 1960s and 1970s attracted far less critical scrutiny than those by Government, so did NGO propaganda. Their news control methods had some similarities with those adopted by Campbell in his attempt to convert the GIS into a news factory.

Against that background Lord Deedes, who was Harold Macmillan's minister for press co-ordination in the early 1960s, is recorded in Nicholas Jones's *Soundbites and Spindoctors* as having come to the conclusion that modern Prime Ministers needed to have 'a real thug at their side to give them protection against the daily assault of the media'. Or, as Lord Deedes subsequently put it: 'In the circumstances in which Mrs Thatcher has had to work I think she needed a tough beside her and even Bernard Ingham's enemies among the press, and he has a quite a few, would admit that he is a tough.' The fact that the pressure and nastiness increased during the 1990s has been used as further evidence that I in some way provided an excuse for Campbell. But the important issue is not whether a press officer is tough or has the full array of qualities prescribed by Christopher Meyer, John Major's second chief press secretary: 'quick wits, sense of humour, histrionic skills, self-confidence and a thick skin'. What matters are the rules by which he plays the game.

There is one other factor that applied up to 1997: the Chief Press Secretary at No. 10 had no authority to order departments about in a Cabinet system of government of autonomous departmental ministers. Nor was he the boss of heads of departmental information divisions, such was the dispersal of power. He could try to persuade them to fall in with No. 10's view but he could not compel them, short of convincing the Prime Minister that she should make an issue of it with the minister concerned. And there was not much point in continually running to Thatcher on these detailed presentational matters.

My critics – and those who would excuse Campbell's accretion of power over the Government machine – say that this is disingen-uous, especially when in the last two years (1989–90), as I was approaching sixty and coming to the end of my career, I was also head of the GIS. I then acquired policy sway over recruitment, training and promotion in the GIS on top of an unrivalled knowl-edge of the talents and abilities of budding chief information offi-cers. It is also true that, where necessary, I could exceptionally ask people to move to a new post in an emergency. But I signed the reports of only my own seven No. 10 staff and not many more in the GIS management unit, and was asked to serve on only a few promotion boards set up by departments. My 'patronage' was, rightly, exceedingly limited.

It is not true, as Nicholas Jones claims of my time at No. 10, that 'as the years went by there were few within the information service who dared challenge him'. That is not my recollection of the GIS at the time, although it is true that I was often frustrated by the passiv-ity of the Monday evening meeting of departmental information heads. The reality of my position as chief press secretary in the 1980s also makes a mockery of the claim by Adam Raphael, then of *The Observer* and now of *The Economist*, that I touched off the Westland affair by telling Colette Bowe, 'You will . . . do as you are . . . well told'. Some journalists will believe any tittle tattle they are told and, as I advised Raphael at the time, will carefully avoid checking with a source if it might rob them of a story.

Against this background, there are a number of areas where the mainstream press officer's job can be distinguished from that of the spin doctor. The first is timing, which they say is of the essence in politics. For me timing was more of a problem than a weapon. It would have been much easier to be frank and open about the con-tents of interesting answers to Parliamentary questions or statements in alerting journalists at 11 a.m. to their imminence that day, but Parliamentary privilege got in the way. But if the minister who would have to answer for any breach of privilege in the Commons felt that the political benefit outweighed the risk, then he might use his political agents, whether MPs or advisers, carefully to leak the substance. That was his affair, but merely identifying forthcoming answers or statements which take issues further scarcely amounts to 'spin', let alone 'doctoring'.

Press secretaries are also often accused of trying to control the timing of the release of announcements or documents such as White Papers, or of keeping information close to their chests until it seems advantageous to release it. I plead guilty to spending most Monday evenings for eleven years in the company of departmental heads of information trying to ensure that important initiatives had a clear run on the chosen day, free from competition from other impending Government announcements. Imagine the reputation for incompetence that a government would soon acquire from the media if it brought out a week's crop of statements in one day. But the best-laid plans for a programme of announcements can be set at nought by an international disaster, terrorist incident or even a domestic sensation. The press secretary does not have much option but to withhold information, if he can reasonably do so, to allow his minister to complete consultations or inform the people directly affected by a policy announcement. If he is under instructions to keep information being sought under wraps for the time being (as distinct from suppressing it), then he would either have to take a flyer in releasing it and be judged after the event, in the belief that it was the only credible course open to him to protect his minister's interests, or somehow temporize to allow him to have it out with the minister. If he is ordered not to disclose certain information, he has no option but to obey until he has had an opportunity to challenge the minister's case and to warn him of the likely consequences.

Then there is the 'Jo Moore game': burying bad news under the weight of a hugely diverting story or letting it out late on the last day of a Parliamentary session or on a Friday afternoon, when most journalists (but not Sunday newspaper journalists or weekend duty broadcasters) are trying to get away for the weekend. This tactic may just work during a government's traditional 'honey-moon' after a general election, but not for long. It is one of the surer ways of dissipating goodwill and acquiring a slippery reputation. It just reinforces journalists' conspiracy theory of government and most of them are too wise and alert for this kind of trickery. Any self-respecting press officer would warn his department of the likely consequences: a worse story, which would have been better explained at the outset.

One of the functions of a press officer is to act as an intelligence agent. He is not there simply to convey information to the outside world; his job is also to gather information for his minister and department from his contacts with journalists. They are often revealing. Among many other things, they give early warning of the publication of attacks on Government policy. If it is spin-doctoring to arrange for pre-emptive strikes, whether by a ministerial press notice or broadcast, to set out the facts, then I must plead guilty to having practised the art. My job was to fertilize argument with fact. I have no time for reactive government; it should seek to command the public debate by factual argument. Whose fault is it but the Government's if the public get hold of the wrong end of the stick?

Similarly, while others may dismiss it as spin-doctoring, I see the canvassing of ideas as a feature of a healthy democracy. Ministers brief – or authorize briefings – in order to test out public reaction to concepts or initiatives that are festering in their souls. If they are elected to serve the national interest, it makes sense to see if the nation thinks their ideas will do so. Flying kites to see which way the wind blows is a political pastime. All too often the media can be relied on to canvass the least likely but most sensational option unless they are heavily warned off. The daily press is full of stories saying the Government 'may' do this or that, however unlikely it may actually be to do so.

Two variants of this that come closer to spin-doctoring are reducing the shock that might otherwise accompany harsh decisions and lowering the expectations of a policy for which there is popular support. The latter is a traditional Treasury ploy at Budget time. When I see figures bruited abroad in advance of the budget telling us how much people are going to benefit, I know they are going to get more on the day. Such briefing is designed to give them an even cosier glow on the evening after the Chancellor has spoken. Similarly, cuts in departmental allocations will inevitably prove to be less dramatic than forecast. It is a cynical game, but the Treasury is a cynical department. In my day it seemed remarkably willing to share its budget secrets with a certain class of journalist rather than with the Prime Minister's press secretary. No doubt these games were played 'to preserve the integrity of the GIS'!

More generally, I have always taken the view that it is madness on the part of a press secretary to encourage expectations. Is that spin-doctoring, or common sense? Perhaps Tony Blair now thinks it was madness to indulge in spin-doctoring since after promising the earth he has delivered little, apart from a reasonably prosperous economy, during his first five years. No Government has ratcheted up expectations more than his, with its declared ambitions and endless initiatives from May 1997.

In defensive mode the press officer may, as we have seen, confine himself to answering the narrow limits of the question rather than expanding into areas that might run him into an assortment of difficulties. Being 'economical with the truth', as it is described, is, I fear, an inevitable part of a press officer's armoury. A health scare – particularly relating to the Prime Minister – can have a variety of political and stock exchange implications, from confidence in the Government to manoeuvring for succession. A press officer, when asked, may have to be very economical with the truth in the first instance until he has had it out with the minister and convinced him of the desirability of setting the illness in its correct context.

Another vice often attributed to press officers and generally thought of as characteristic of the spin doctor – and a vice that I apparently shared with Christopher Meyer – is a vigorous approach to journalists. Nicholas Jones saw both Meyer and me as ever ready to divert attention from the subject in hand by 'playing the man instead of the ball', the reporter instead of the question. So far as I am concerned, this is a fair point. To maintain some control over briefings, I was on the look-out for journalists in the business of making trouble. When I thought they were up to no good, I made it clear in a robust way that I was not playing. The question often fell by the wayside. This was for me less a question of a deliberate determination to avoid an awkward question than an issue of relationships, which could be put to some severe tests in the course of the average working week. One of the problems that journalists present to all who have to deal with them is their over-sensitivity to ridicule. They are very good at dishing out criticism but incapable of taking it, as the distinguished journalist and historian Paul Johnson has readily acknowledged.

More positively, a press secretary will advise the minister on how best to get over his message, whether through Parliamentary means, broadcasts, speeches or briefings, or a combination of these. He will bargain for the best slot for his principal, almost certainly refuse a confrontational interview with an opponent – why give them a joint platform? – and generally try, by talking to the interviewer or producer, to elicit the line of questioning. In the case of a woman minister, he may have an added concern about the colour scheme of a TV set and make-up arrangements. He will prepare a brief for his minister, identifying lines to take and defensive points to make in anticipation of the rougher end of the interview, warn him of what came to be known as 'elephant traps' and suggest ways of putting over the message as graphically as possible.

This may involve devising sound bites. A press secretary does not disdain the sound bite, even though it is ludicrous to suppose that the ramifications of a complex policy can be encapsulated in a few words. He knows that press officers are there to help devise and convey the message.

To me such functions are legitimate. What is not legitimate is wilfully misleading journalists, leaking, favouritism, unprincipled opportunism, assorted intimidation and general skulduggery. When a press officer goes down that route to perdition, he becomes a spin doctor. In short, a press officer is an individual whose job is to manage relations with journalists within a code of ethics and with the long-term objective of maintaining and, if possible, enhancing the reputation of his employer and employing organization. To do that he must maintain his credibility. A spin doctor is an individual who, in providing a link with journalists, operates for the short-term advantage of his employer and employing organization, without ethical restraint. He soon becomes incredible.

The line in the sand marking the (possibly temporary) end of the age of the press secretary and the advent of the spin doctor can be precisely drawn: at 2 May 1997. That is when the press officer, governed by codes, rules and conventions, gave way to the spin doctor, operating regardless of those ethics and without the restraint of either the constitution or common sense.

18

Under new management

IT COULD not have been a more beautiful day when Labour took office on 2 May 1997, after eighteen years in opposition. I was briefly in Downing Street that morning for a BBC interview which ended up being done in an outside broadcast van at the Ambassadors' entrance to the FCO at the foot of the steps leading up to No. 10. A sense of relief to be rid of a tired and worn-out Conservative government was palpable. The people's joy was unconfined – or so it seemed from the crowd flooding into the street waving union flags. They turned out to have been imported rather like stage extras for the occasion from Labour Party HQ. When I read this later, I began to wonder what kind of government we had got.

Civil Service press officers I have talked to were at once elated and apprehensive. It is a familiar feeling, as I can testify as a veteran of changes of government and reshuffles which land you with a new minister overnight or, more often, over supper. My former colleagues looked forward to beginning again with a new, dynamic administration and to demonstrating that, as professionals, they could work effectively for any government the electorate bestowed on them. All new governments and ministers present a challenge, but they had no reason to suppose they were not up to it. They were naturally keyed up and apprehensive because press secretaries have only a matter of minutes to create a favourable impression in their initial meeting with their new minister. But this time there was an added tension: the reputation that Labour had won in opposition for running presentational rings round the Major government. These people were no slouches.

I had chronicled some of their ways in opposition in a column I then wrote for *PR Week*. On 21 March 1997 I reported that 'vibrators are in, courtesy of Madam Speaker Betty Boothroyd'. It was now permissible, I reported, to receive silent prompts in the Commons' chamber via a vibrating pager, but woe betide anybody if their electronic connections with the outside world made any noise. This ruling followed an incident when Labour's campaigns operator, Brian Wilson MP, felt impelled to intervene in the budget debate by his receipt of a paged message. The Shadow Chancellor, Gordon Brown, then put on a passable imitation of a puppet by repeating a section of his speech to polish up a sound bite after a TV reporter had told his aide (whose message was relayed via Mr Wilson's pager) that his first effort was no good for news purposes.

This, I wrote, is what happens when a party leader, having been forced to ditch his political baggage to make his party electable and having failed to put in place any alternative philosophy, has to resort to every PR wile to construct a new Labour image. 'The effort has produced a very bad case of spin-doctor fever', I concluded. 'It is what politics catches when it is felt that what parties look like matters more than what they stand for. That is why vibrators are now *de rigueur* in the Commons.'

A month later, on 18 April, I wrote:

Labour's bullying – about which journalists routinely complain – is another offence to be avenged in due course. But the real savagery will come if, in office, Labour continues to give preferential treatment, both in terms of leaks and briefing, to friendly journalists. I know because, as press secretary, I tried to institute a series of intimate Prime Ministerial briefings for senior political correspondents. Jealousy brought it down at the first fence. Prime Minister Harold Wilson's media relations fell apart because he showed favouritism to an élite. They called it the White Commonwealth. Mr Blair should learn from history.

On the very morning of Labour's victory I warned the GIS of the impending tensions because of the inexperience of Labour's likely ministers. It turned out that only six of the hundred or so had known the luxury of hearing a minion say 'Yes, Minister'. Even the Prime Minister and Chancellor were greenhorns, knowing nothing first hand of how the machine works and what makes it tick.

'Unless they are dramatically different', I wrote, 'they will have to be educated in precisely what the GIS can do within the rules which ban party politicking and polemics . . . one or two "hot" press notices may soon have to be aborted because they could only be properly sent out by Labour Party HQ. This can be a flash-point.' I added that, in the slightly longer term, there was the question of ministerial confidence in the machine: 'Labour may be suspicious of press secretaries who have served only Tory Ministers. But they will store up trouble for themselves if they by-pass the GIS by importing political apparatchiks. There are enough tensions with the arrival of a new government without creating them.'

That brought me to Alastair Campbell. 'Is he', I asked, 'going to be a GIS man or not?' And I continued:

> Does he want to work with the system or just look after his Prime Minister as Joe Haines did for Harold Wilson. On the face of it, given Labour's pre-election discipline, he will wish to keep a tight grip on both the Civil Service and political appara-tus. He can only do this if he makes the GIS feel wanted. But he should remember that departmental press secretaries owe their first loyalty to their Cabinet Minister, not to the Prime Minister. He can only proceed by persuasion.

Those extracts from three of my columns demonstrate why Civil Service press secretaries were more than usually exercised and apprehensive about the approach of the new government. They knew only too clearly Labour's urgent attention to the detail of presentation; their zealotry in pursuit of image, coverage and sound bite; their well-established favouritism and bullying of jour-nalists, which was not the GIS way any more than was subservi-ence to the media; their politicians' inexperience of office and the tensions that could cause; and the command and control tenden-cies of Mandelson and Campbell.

It is now clear that, even realizing this, they were unprepared for the shocks that awaited them as one by one they were toppled. Their first collective meeting with Mandelson and Campbell took place on Tuesday 6 May 6 1997, in the White Room on the first floor of No. 10, overlooking Horseguards Parade, as the Government began to shake down. Some who were there did not find it disturbing. At least one got the impression that Mandelson and Campbell were seeking the help of departmental heads of information in curbing the activities of their ministers and their special advisers. If so, it speaks volumes for their ignorance of the loyalty a departmental press secretary owes to his minister and for their perspicacity in identifying special advisers, as people who owe their position to individual ministers, as a potential problem. Others now recall the meeting as 'chilling' both for what was said and for its stage management.

There was a choice of drinks – wine or fruit juice – and at the end of a hard day the press secretaries tended to choose alcohol while the teetotal Campbell sipped fruit juice. Those present remember Campbell mixing but Mandelson making a late entrance and briefly addressing the assembly to the effect that the Government had inherited the GIS and those present. They would be given time – though their impression was not long – to prove themselves and they would have to be on their mettle.

Steve Reardon (Social Security) took responsibility for replying on behalf of his colleagues. I had asked Reardon in the late 1980s to move from the Department of Employment, where he had worked for me, to the Department of Social Security to look after the interests of John Moore (now Lord Moore). Reardon recalls telling Mandelson and Campbell that a number of those present had proved they were capable of working for governments of both political complexions and were at the Government's service, by implication within the usual rules. They were, as press officers, one of the few Civil Service groups who worked 'horizontally' across Government; that is, they moved on promotion through different departments, gaining wider experience of Government. And they knew each other personally and were used to working together.

Reardon, one of the earlier and more maltreated of GIS casualties, still harbours the worry with which he left the meeting – that his response may have signed 'a dozen death warrants' because Mandelson may have read into them some kind of threat from a vested interest group. His colleagues, both those who were axed and those who went of their own volition, are inclined to dismiss his worries. But they sensed they were in for a challenging ride. It turned out to be the roughest ever known, and the most unpleasant since Edward Heath's apparatchik the late Michael Wolfe made me an instant target in 1970.

Wolfe rang me up at home before even the Cabinet had been announced and gave me the impression that I was not long for the governmental world because of my political past. My sins in his eyes were probably multitudinous. I had been a (very unsuccessful) Labour candidate in the hopeless Moortown ward of Leeds City Council in 1965 and had written a vitriolic anti-Tory column for the Labourite *Leeds Weekly Citizen* in the mid-1960s. I had been a Labour reporter for *The Guardian* from 1965 to 1967 and one of a number of journalists recruited to the Government service, in my case via the National Board for Prices and Incomes, in the second (Labour) half of the 1960s. And then I had then been engaged, albeit unseen and unknown, by Barbara Castle as her speech-writer when in 1968 she went as First Secretary to the Ministry of Labour (restyled the Department of Employment and Productivity). I got the impression that all this was too much for Wolfe to swallow, even though I had been in the Government's service for three years and by then was an established Civil Servant.

I recorded in *Kill the Messenger* that I resolved to be as awkward as only a bloody-minded Yorkshireman could be. I wrote:

> Either I had been accepted as an established Civil Servant or I had not, but I was damned if I was going to be messed around by Michael Wolfe, whoever he may be. I do not know whether this communicated itself in the appropriate places, but when Paul Bryan, Minister of State, came to examine my credentials face to face I made it clear to him that I expected to be judged not by history but by performance. Performance was properly given its chance.

By coincidence Bryan, my vetting minister, had unsuccessfully fought Sowerby, where I then lived in West Yorkshire, in my earliest days as a junior reporter. He knew of me.

Wolfe demonstrated that there is no party monopoly in political vindictiveness. Mandelson and Campbell were at least prepared to say they were giving the GIS a chance, whether or not they meant it. They would not have been the first to have prejudged the accused. Unfortunately, the GIS has always stood charged with an array of crimes, from incompetence to laziness and from obtuseness to obstructiveness. Some of the mud sticks, partly because of the natural tension that exists between journalist and press officer. It is also the case that information officers are not there just to help the media, regardless of the context, and that they inevitably reflect the limits their political and official bosses often foolishly and counter-productively impose. But it was, is and probably always will be impossible to defend the GIS unreservedly. I never felt able to do that whether as a journalist or as a Government information officer over some forty years. I know its limitations as well as its potential power, which the system has – or had, until 1997 – sought to curb.

It is the sad truth that the public service provides a comfortable shelter for those of limited capacity and cossets those who want a quiet life. For that reason it puts a premium on the ability of a press secretary to motivate his team. But in a fast-moving department there is a limit as to how many passengers can be carried, and in No. 10 there is room for none. I would contend that, properly led, a good Whitehall press office is a match for the best. They are the sort of people you can go to war with. I know. I did.

None the less, as the Blair government began to eliminate the top echelon of the GIS I received a telephone call from a retired senior information officer urging me not, in retirement, to 'die in the ditch' for them as a former head of the GIS. He was trying to protect me; he thought I would damage my credibility if I tried to fight their corner too hard. I recognized that it was possible that, after eighteen years of working for the government of one party, the GIS had become set in its ways, slack and too comfortable. Inevitably its reputation suffered with that of the Major government, which towards the end cut a forlorn figure. I also acknowledged that, however reasonable I had found Campbell to work with as a *Daily Mirror* journalist in the 1980s, he might well have formed a poor view first hand of the GIS, especially as he had little time for the successive Conservative governments it had been their duty to serve. It seems unlikely that the GIS would have assiduously gone out of its way to help this anti-Government propagandist.

I very much hoped that those journalists who claimed that press officers never rang them back were grossly exaggerating, since during my eleven years in No. 10 I regarded the failure to return a call, as promised, as a hanging offence. Nothing could be more calculated to damage a press office's reputation, unless it be the immensely frustrating and provocative game by departments of passing journalists on from one to another on the narrowest of pretexts. It is unfortunately often necessary – especially in No. 10 – to refer callers to the expert department, but passing them from one to the other as an evasive tactic is quite simply bad public and press relations.

I acknowledged that the GIS might well not be up to Labour's campaigning speed, simply because it had never had either the status or the resources in terms of money, manpower and equipment. To my certain knowledge since 1968, it had had to manage an increasingly demanding 24-hour media as best it could, and never more so than in crises. As I have pointed out, permanent secretaries, the top officials in departments, have seldom been committed, still less compulsive, communicators. Their prime requirement of the head of information is to keep their minister happy and them out of the clutches of the Public Accounts Committee for permitting the waste of public money on unnecessary and invalid publicity. Career press officers also have to pace themselves. They are, as career communicators, in the front line of the daily battle with the media, and it makes eminently good sense for them to take advantage of quiet periods. In any case, quiet periods are a bonus, not a disaster, for ministers. They can devote their undivided attention to useful work.

Against all that, I knew what the adrenalin generated by a new government could do for press officers who felt they had something – their professional impartiality – to prove. I concluded that my former colleague was being unreasonably cautious in urging me to lie low rather than rise up in defence of the GIS from the mauling it was getting.

There could be one other reason for the carnage of top GIS officers: a government that had come to office with the declared overriding objective of securing a record (for Labour) second full term. As such, it was in permanent electioneering mode. Its very objective put it at odds with those whose entire professional upbringing required them to observe rules and conventions that insisted on political impartiality. In short, the two did not mix. The inevitable happened. Within a year twenty-five of those occupying the top forty-four posts in the GIS had moved on or out. Only one of the eighteen departmental press secretaries Labour inherited in 1997 survived to the 2001 general election, and he retired soon afterwards.

Of course, not all were fired. Some, such as Romola Christopherson (Health), retired. Others, such as Jean Caines (DTI), another who was once my deputy at No 10, went early of her own free will. Jonathan Haslam, the last of John Major's three chief press secretaries, took himself off to the private sector at the London Metal Exchange (not, he says, because he had a blistering row with Stephen Byers at the Department for Employment for blocking his attempt to use a departmental press notice for political propaganda). But no government accidentally presides over the removal within one Parliament of the entire top brass of its press and information effort, least of all a government besotted and obsessed with presentation and media. The inescapable conclusion is that it wanted them out of the way. And the dismal corollary of this is that it was allowed to get rid of them by a weak senior Civil Service, an ineffectual Civil Service Commission, a useless opposition and a poodle Parliament. At least the media took notice of the blood-letting.

19

Origins of the obsession

IN HIS widely praised biography of Tony Blair, John Rentoul perhaps puts his finger on the day New Labour's obsession with the media formally began. It was Sunday 15 May 1994, three days after the death of the Labour Party leader, John Smith, when Blair's leadership campaign met in a neighbour's house in Islington. Rentoul records that one participant remembers Blair saying, 'You have got to understand that the only thing that matters in this campaign is the media. The media, the media and the media.' 'Media, media, media' was, Rentoul says, the 'driving obsession of the campaign not just for the leadership but for the coming general election'. Hence the central roles for Campbell and, within days, Mandelson, although he was not at the meeting. The attempted seduction of the press barons and leading journalists, disillusioned with John Major, intensified and Rupert Murdoch succumbed, subject to one reservation on Europe. *The Sun* rose for Blair.

Not surprisingly, Blair's campaign team reflected his media obsession. Apart from Mandelson, who was initially under cover and code-named 'Bobby', and Campbell, then working on the *Today* newspaper, it included: Barry Cox, head of Current Affairs at London Weekend Television; Tim Allan, a researcher on Channel 4's *A Week in Politics*; Tom Restrick, former BBC TV producer eventually turned barrister; Chris Powell, an advertising executive and the brother of Jonathan Powell, who was to become

Blair's chief of staff, and of Lord Powell, for six years Thatcher's foreign affairs private secretary; and Philip Gould, the political consultant and focus group wonk who apparently fine-tuned Blair's presentation to the latest concern of his randomly selected voters.

It could be argued that this was not unduly media-laden, given Thatcher's supporting cast as leader of the Opposition and as party leader in government of Tim Bell (now Lord Bell), the Saatchi brothers, the late Gordon Reece and Harvey Thomas, the stage manager and later the party's director of communications. It cannot be denied that Blair sought to deal with substance with his dispatching of Clause 4, distancing himself from the unions and his commitments to pursue prudent economic policies and contain inflation. Nor can it be gainsaid that this conversion of Old Labour into New Labour needed selling to the public if Labour were to become re-electable. But whereas Thatcher brought a philosophy to the Conservatives from which flowed a programme that was sustained over a decade, Blair created a vacuum to be filled by the somewhat mystical 'Third Way', which remains undefined. Perhaps the best definition of the 'Third Way' is that it is whatever Blair decides it should be whenever he decides it. In these circumstances presentation becomes a way of government. To Mrs Thatcher, of course, there was only a right way and a wrong way.

According to Donald Macintyre, the *Independent* columnist, in his fascinating biography of Mandelson, 'Bobby' came to the Labour Party's publicity directorship in the autumn of 1985, 'nonplussed'. Macintyre reports Mandelson as saying many years later: 'I was 31, I'd just been appointed to a job about which I had absolutely no idea whatsoever and I had absolutely no ability or experience to do.' He had, however, had experience of working on LWT's *Weekend World* as a researcher and producer, which brought to journalism a curiously propagandist approach, in which they decided what line they wanted to pursue and then remorselessly interviewed their contributors until they got them to say what they wanted. It was perhaps good training for someone whose concept of political presentation I came to see as 'creating the truth' by way of laying down the line and repeating it as often and as smoothly as possible.

He also came to office on tales of what I got up to as Thatcher's press secretary. Indeed, Macintyre records Andy McSmith, then a Labour Party press officer and now with the *Independent on Sunday*, telling Mandelson that the job of communications director was really two jobs – publicity and handling the press – and that they needed a 'Harvey Thomas' and a 'Bernard Ingham'. McSmith thought it was more than one man could take on. Mandelson made it clear he had every intention of doing both. Macintyre records my specialities as 'hectoring journalists' (untrue, except when they were trying it on or had got their facts wrong), 'complaining to broadcasters' (untrue, except when they had got their facts wrong), and 'denouncing enemies in his leader's own ranks' (untrue, unless my attempts to explain the behaviour of Francis Pym and John Biffen justify the charge). I do not regard it as a mark of distinction that I was first canvassed as a role model for Mandelson and subsequently cited as the precedent for Labour excess.

Mandelson also quickly set out his approach to journalism in a quote for the advertising industry weekly *Campaign*. 'Of course we want to use the media, but the media will be our tools, our servants; we are no longer content to let them be our persecutors.' That quote no doubt reflects Labour's folk memory of the Attlee and Wilson governments' treatment by the media: searing experiences reinforced by the media's fierce approach to Neil Kinnock as leader of a Labour opposition.

Journalists also detected the early hand of Mandelson, the former TV producer, in ensuring the correct backdrop at a Labour Party conference. They reported that overnight those veteran left-wing MPs Dennis Skinner and Joan Maynard, who had glumly and ostentatiously sat on their hands during Neil Kinnock's conference denunciation of the Militant faction, had been replaced in the camera's eye by two solid trade union members of the party executive dutifully applauding in the right places. Mandelson is reported to have commented: 'Communications means throwing your net much wider than publicity. It means deciding what we say, how we say it, and which spokesmen and -women we choose to say it.'

The scene was set for control, control, control. Add to this Mandelson's workaholism, his modernizing and organizational ability, his Machiavellian tendencies and his pursuit of power through revisionism for a party to which he has a congenital loyalty, and the association between New Labour and spin-doctoring became inevitable.

Alastair Campbell came to politics, as political correspondent of the *Daily Mirror*, only months before Mandelson started to rescue the Labour Party from its disorganized anarchy. In what was then seen as increasingly unstable behaviour, he accepted an offer from the unlaunched newspaper *Today*, had a breakdown or some kind and was off work for about six months. Within a year he was back, teetotal, as political correspondent of the *Sunday Mirror* and, according to his biographer, Peter Oborne, 'renounced the trade of journalism – at any rate as it is commonly understood by those who practise it – and turned to something that he found very much more exhilarating: power politics'. In other words, he became Neil Kinnock's propagandist.

In fact, Oborne claims that as early as March 1987 Campbell, in a *New Stateman* article, described his Lobby journalist colleagues as 'cynical, cowardly and corrupt' for allegedly colluding with the White House to try to 'stitch up' Kinnock. This was the forerunner of many such collective and individual maulings of journalists by Campbell in defence of Kinnock over the next five years. He then moved between the *Sunday Mirror*, the *Daily Mirror* and *Today* before regularizing his position and becoming Tony Blair's press secretary in September 1994. He had proclaimed Blair as next leader of the Labour Party on the evening of John Smith's death. The former soft porn writer, bagpipe busker, croupier and journalist was only an election away from the centre of national political power.

I have several things in common with Campbell, apart from journalism. I was brought up just over the hill from his native Keighley. Like him, I support Burnley AFC, though I have long been absent from the Turf Moor terraces whereas he follows the team actively and assiduously. We are also both former BBC breakfast TV newspaper reviewers, and I must record that he, at least, brought to his office a certain charm and charisma. He has also demonstrated a strength of character by abandoning completely his heavy drinking. He undoubtedly has a genius for tabloid journalism, all Mandelson's obsessive ruthlessness, an outsider's rancorous lack of respect for individuals, institutions and traditions, and a generous dollop of menace. And as Kinnock's large helper, he was unencumbered by political baggage and roots, apart from a strong egalitarian streak.

He and Mandelson complemented each other. Whereas Campbell is a fierce, action-packed executive tactician, Mandelson brought a strategic sense that has by-passed Campbell. They also both learned their trade from scratch during what Oborne describes as the emergence of the new 'media class'. This, he says, has arrogated much power unto itself at the expense of the great institutions of the state and especially politicians. With some justification he claims that it prefers 'the short term to the long term, sentimentality to compassion, simplicity to complexity, the dramatic to the mundane, confrontation to sensible compromise'. I would add that in its competitive pursuit of commercial success it has also abandoned the concept of absolute standards for relative ones. This moral relativism is at the heart of the attempt by some journalists and broadcast presenters to use me to excuse Campbell's operational methods.

As Thatcher's press secretary, I sought to hold the line against the new class indentified by Oborne and perhaps previously known as the Fourth Estate. Mandelson and Campbell, with the aid of Blair, their consummate actor–leader, sought to dominate this class, in Mandelson's words to make it their 'servant' and to end its role as 'persecutor'. Superficially, they succeeded when roughly two-thirds of the press backed Labour at the 1997 election in a complete reversal of the position when Kinnock was defeated in 1992. They also held on to them, albeit a little less firmly, in 2001. One inevitable consequence is that no previous government has ever had such immediate, extensive and detailed biographical and analytical attention so early in its tenure. The tomes have spilled forth. They have produced much evidence of the Mandelson/Campbell methods as they measured themselves up for office.

First, and no doubt to Mandelson's greater credit than Campbell's, Labour's old penny-farthing machine had been converted into a Rolls-Royce, albeit of American design. If New Labour's style was not created in the USA, it was certainly honed there. The links with Clinton's team and his pollsters were close.

New Labour adopted some of Clinton's successful electoral messages. The concept of an open-plan war room was imported from Little Rock, Arkansas, to Millbank.

If, as Blair said at the outset, it was 'media, media and the media' that mattered, then the party had round-the-clock monitoring of press, radio and TV and Excalibur, their wonderful computer broadsword, all the better (and the swifter) to rebut the opposition and provide stilettos for the troops. Mobiles and pagers were everywhere, used to exercise a draconian discipline over those, high or low, who strayed off message. And to think that less than five years earlier I had ended my career as a Government press officer without ever having had the use and help or hindrance of a mobile, pager or computer!

With the aggression of a pit bull terrier Labour Party press officers, aided by Excalibur, harried the broadcasters, and especially the BBC, who strayed from Labour's perception of the truth. Challenging the news judgement of journalists and bullying them became routine. George Jones, the political editor of the *Daily Telegraph* and one of the most meticulous of reporters, came in for Mandelson's treatment in November 1996, when he reported that the Tories had costed eighty-nine separate Labour policy proposals at £30 billion, equivalent to £1,200 on the tax of the average family. When Labour called a rebuttal press conference, Mandelson greeted Jones with 'Applause, applause for George Jones. Straight from the *Newsnight* programme and Central Office.' Jones promptly walked out and Mandelson disappeared, apparently to avoid being filmed at this game.

In the context of the 1997 election Jones's brother Nick, of the BBC, the chronicler of governments' media relations, has told with some incredulity, even for one so assiduously targeted by Labour, how he endured similar treatment. In the final week of the election he had reported the threat of a fire service strike in Essex. He knew Labour would be anxious to play down the threat, but in his book *Campaign 1997* he writes:

Nothing had prepared me for the torrent of abuse which greeted me on checking in at the Millbank Tower media centre. Campbell was incandescent, verging on the incoherent, as he went on and on about my report for the 9 a.m. Radio 4 news on Prescott's remarks about the Essex dispute. 'So that's the story then, a trade union dispute . . . That was a nice, easy question you asked Heseltine, wasn't it? It was just a free hit . . . I just love the way you guys in the BBC decide what the issue is. John Major only has to fart to get on the news. If Blair does something positive you don't report it.' By now David Hill [Labour Party press officer] and Charlie Whelan [Gordon Brown's press officer] had joined in, jabbing their fingers, denouncing me as a prat and a wanker, as Campbell continued his tirade: 'What right has the BBC to set the agenda? The *Today* programme is just a radio version of the *Daily Mail*. You think it's the BBC's job to even things up for the Tories in the hope it'll make a difference.' Peter Mandelson, who on this occasion had remained aloof from the fray, gave me a supercilious look as he walked by and, with a majestic sweep of his hand, tried to be as dismissive as he could about my reporting: 'So, you've done it again, have you? You and the unions. The Third World War would break out and you'd ask a question about the unions.'

While he was in opposition, reporters claimed that Campbell was 'moderately even-handed'. The exception was the *Sun*. No one has yet satisfactorily explained the mechanism by which details of the Conservatives' 1996 budget were leaked. Sensationally, they were first given to the *Mirror*, which then handed back the documents to the Government after apparently taking the precaution of hinting at their contents to Labour. They then appeared in the *Sun* the following morning. According to Oborne, Mandelson was much more exclusive, singling out 'a tiny number of favourites . . . trusted souls' with whom he would share 'almost everything'.

Mandelson and Campbell also set out to control the agenda. Perhaps a classic demonstration of this technique was executed during the 1997 pre-election campaign by Charlie Whelan, who served Gordon Brown in opposition and at the Treasury until he became counter-productive. Whelan's job was to excite interest in the speech the Shadow Chancellor was to make the next day, announcing that a future Labour government would stick to the

Tories' spending plans and not raise the basic or top rates of tax in the next Parliament. He briefed one set of journalists on the spending commitment, which led the newspapers and major bulletins the following morning. They were also told he would not make any mention of his tax plans. But no sooner had he done that than Whelan rang other correspondents on duty early the following morning to alert them to Brown's intention to trail his promise on tax in an interview at 8.10 a.m. on the BBC's Radio 4 *Today* programme. It could so easily have gone wrong, had he got his correspondents mixed up or they had talked to each other. Luck was with him and the Chancellor took the day by storm, two stories tumbling out one after the other, leaving the Tories flat-footed.

A sane man would, of course, ask himself how much this trickery, not to mention deceit, really mattered in the great sweep of political history. It was rational to think 'Not much'. The Conservatives were in chronic, tired disarray, in spite of producing the best-performing economy in Western Europe, and Labour looked vital, energetic and on top of things. But serious Civil Servants, and not least serious Civil Service press officers, could only ask themselves whether these operational methods would be left behind when Labour achieved power. They soon found they were the continuing order of the day in government. And so we entered the age of the spin doctor.

20

Special advisers

THE AGE of the spin doctor would not have blossomed, if that is the right term, in government but for a sub-species of what are called special advisers to ministers of the Crown. These advisers come in many forms, and none more special than ministers' wives and families. If they cannot keep ministers' feet on the ground, who can? Then they have their candid friends to give them their frank assessment of their policies and performance out of the goodness of their hearts and without thought of reward. I suppose Harold Macmillan's John Wyndham was the unpaid, candid friend writ large and translated into No. 10.

Another variety of advisers are the genuine experts, often academics and usually of a minister's own political persuasion, who have made a study of a particular subject or have substantial professional or business experience and are willing to devote at least part of their time, generally in return for a reasonable consideration, to helping the minister to devise policy and commenting on policy proposals made by his officials. These are the special or policy advisers, whom I knew for the whole of my quarter of a century in the Government's service.

It is entirely reasonable for ministers to employ such experts at the public's expense. They have a contribution to make, even if it can sometimes be exaggerated, especially when they are purists without the flexibility of approach necessary to adapt to political practicality. But their very presence in the office can be stimulating and valuable, even as purists, and some of them probably benefit as much from their experience inside government as the minister does from having them working on the case, as it were. Academics repeatedly tell me that there is no substitute for hands-on experience.

Since Edward Heath's time there has been a variant of these experts, working in policy units in No. 10 or Cabinet Office. Heath created the Central Policy Review Staff (CPRS), in which outsiders and Civil Servants worked together in the service of the Government as a whole in the Cabinet Office. Wilson had about five, mostly outsiders, working in a policy unit in No. 10 from 1974 to 1976, and from the first in 1979 Thatcher formed a slightly larger unit in No. 10 under a succession of outsiders, including John Redwood, subsequently a Cabinet minister. I can testify to the value of such special advisers when I wanted to go into the background to an issue.

They were employed by the Prime Minister or Cabinet minister in his department on a personal basis for the duration of his ministerial tenure or, if he stayed the course, for the term of that Parliament. They were then subject to reappointment. None of them, whether in No. 10, Cabinet Office or departments, was supposed to have any authority over Civil Servants. Nor could Civil Servants boss them around. In practice, No. 10 has always tended to provide exceptions to the general rule. Joe Haines, in the Wilson government, certainly had authority over press officers in the No. 10 press office. John Redwood also had authority over Civil Servants in Thatcher's policy unit. They coped with their anomalous position with restraint and good sense. But like all other special advisers, they were temporary Civil Servants appointed under Article 3 of the Civil Service Order in Council (a regulation governing the conduct of the Civil Service) and were required to conduct themselves according to the Civil Service code. Their only difference from the real thing – and this is what Article 3 provides for – was their exemption from appointment on merit in competitive circumstances and the requirement to behave with political impartiality and objectivity, so that they might retain the confidence of future governments of a different complexion. They were only there for at the most one term, though they could be reappointed.

If that were where special or policy advisers began and ended, probably not a single eyebrow would have been raised by even the most strait-laced or hysterical members of the body politic. The institution of special or policy adviser was, and remains, an eminently common-sense arrangement where it brings in people with a depth of experience, even with a political sympathy. As the Code of Conduct for Special Advisers says, their employment 'on the one hand adds a political dimension to the advice available to ministers and on the other provides ministers with the direct advice of distinguished experts in their professional field while reinforcing the political neutrality of the permanent civil service by distinguishing the source of political advice and support'.

But man – and especially ambitious, thrusting political man – is unfortunately given to exploiting the potential of any situation. Thatcher recognized this on arriving in Downing Street. She had been elected on a pledge to bring order to public finances. Profligacy was out, and economy was in. I arrived to find the No. 10 press office had been shorn of a post and for the next eleven years I had to find a way of coping with my 'establishment'–eight souls who would have to settle for a life of unrelenting, if exciting, toil. And she wasn't going to let her Cabinet ministers blow a hole in her savings by importing a tribe of special advisers.

Yes, she said, they could have their special advisers, if they really must. After all, she could not really deny them, given that she had a policy unit and a political secretary. But she let it be known that she did not see why Cabinet ministers with several junior ministers – ministers of state or parliamentary under-secretaries – needed special advisers to keep them in touch with political thinking. What is more, Cabinet ministers had their parliamentary private secretaries, and if they were not in touch with political thinking, they ought to be. Their job was to liaise with their fellow Parliamentarians. In other words, the emphasis in the Thatcher years was on special advisers with professional expertise to help drive through the reforms and stop the rot.

The very idea that ministers might need special advisers to link with the press when they had press secretaries and press offices and junior ministers and parliamentary private secretaries and Tory Central Office would have provoked a dismissive sniff. But in my direct political experience the role of special adviser was also a means to bring on young political prospects. Eric Varley had thrust upon him in the Department of Energy in 1974 a young, long-haired ginger scouser called Steve Bundred, who went on to become a force in London local government. Tony Benn brought with him to the same department Francis Cripps and also Frances Morrell, who, having gone through the hippy stage, would, in my view, have made a good MP. I found her blessed with common sense, which occasionally made her an ally of mine in persuading Benn to follow, or perhaps more often not to follow, particular courses.

In my more ungenerous moments I used to rail against the abuse of the special adviser as a finishing school at public expense for ambitious young political activists. In truth, it was probably worth it in the form it then took. Michael Portillo, for example, appeared as a special adviser in the Department of Energy in 1979. But I still felt, in my careful, non-conformist way, that the public should be told and allowed actively to approve how its money was actually being used.

After the sustained asceticism of the Thatcher years John Major's more relaxed regime allowed the special adviser tally to rise a little to the unprecedented height of thirty-eight, but their activities were not a public issue. I have not the slightest doubt that many of them talked to journalists, and I know of at least one case in the Thatcher years when a head of information's position with the media was undermined by a special adviser: not merely by his accessibility to the media but his use of it for his minister's ends. But as John McGregor (now Lord McGregor), a Cabinet minister in five departments under Thatcher and Major, put it to me when discussing the activities of Blair's crop:

> I do not recall our Conservative governments ever getting into any difficulties with special advisers, especially of the sort we have seen so regularly with Jo Moore and other 'spin special advisers' under Labour. We kept them under better control. They knew their roles and did not engage in the kind of activities we have seen from these Labour special advisers. As far as I know, all their relationships with Civil Servants in their depart-

ments were good and they did not step over the boundary marks.

The fact remains that the institution of special adviser was ripe for exploitation by the ruthless. The Code of Conduct for Special Advisers that the Blair government inherited defined what they could do, at the request of the minister, as: reviewing papers going to the minister and giving him political advice, 'devilling', speech-writing, generating long-term thinking through policy papers, contributing to policy planning, liaising with the party and outside interest groups, helping to brief party MPs, attending (but not speaking at) party functions, taking part in party policy reviews to represent the Government's thinking, and providing expert advice as a specialist. It made no mention of relations with the media, even though some had tried their hand at it before then. Given the natural tendency for people to stretch codes rather than just observe them, it is not surprising that New Labour promptly wrought havoc.

A new edition of the code in 2001 caught up with reality. Paragraph 3 in the list of special adviser roles permitted (point 9) 'representing the views of their minister to the media, including a party viewpoint, where they have been authorized by the minister to do so'. This cautious sanction was in line with the recommendations of a 1998 review of the GIS by Sir Robin Mountfield, permanent secretary at the Office of Public Service, designed to bring special advisers under better control. None the less, the spin doctor had formally arrived in Whitehall, even if he was called a 'special adviser'.

He would have had a hard time establishing himself under any Government before 1997 because of other strictures in the Code of Practice. Paragraph 6 says

They [special advisers] are employed to serve the objectives of the Government and the Department in which they work. It is this which justifies their being paid from public funds and being able to use public resources, and explains why their participation in party politics is carefully limited. They should act in a way which upholds the political impartiality of civil servants and does not conflict with the Civil Service Code. They should avoid anything which might reasonably lead to criticism that people paid from public funds are being used for party political purposes.

The new 2001 code tried to rein them in as they went about their media work. A new Paragraph 9, dealing specifically with contacts with the media, reads: 'Departmental heads of information are responsible for managing press and publicity operations in their department and should be kept informed of special advisers' contacts with the news media not only to ensure consistency of briefing but also to ensure that contacts are recorded.' In other words, while special advisers may brief the press, they should do so in active partnership with the responsible Civil Servant – the departmental head of information – and, in doing so, should conduct themselves with integrity and honesty, observe discretion and behave with moderation. Those words – integrity, honesty, discretion and moderation – are all used in the code. It is not a licentious document. On the contrary, there is enough in it to asphyxiate a spin doctor at birth.

So what went wrong? The popular but superficial answer is Campbell's terms of employment. They presented Cabinet Office with a problem in 1997. The Order in Council had been tightened up in the later 1980s to restrict special advisers to purely advisory roles. If it had been left like that, it would not have permitted Campbell or Jonathan Powell, Blair's incoming chief of staff, to perform the executive jobs – including giving orders to Civil Servants – that the Civil Service knew had been allotted to them. So the order was amended to allow up to three special advisers in No. 10 to fulfil executive roles. Only two have so far been appointed: Powell and Campbell. This gave Campbell no greater privilege than had been enjoyed by such previous political appointees as Joe Haines, who behaved carefully. Nor did Campbell's contract go beyond exempting him from political impartiality and objectivity, subject to the requirements of the Civil Service code. The intention was not to let Campbell off the leash. In fact, the whole arrangement was intended to keep him on it.

So from 2 May 1997, when Blair entered Downing Street, there was a well-established system in operation for controlling the operations of special or political advisers which had more or less worked under previous administrations. There was no excuse for any abuse, which could have been immediately snuffed out by ministers once it had been brought to their attention.

The inescapable conclusion is that ministers either did not understand the limits under which their special advisers should operate or could not have cared less about them. There is evidence to support both conclusions; indeed, there is evidence that one flows from the other. It is also fair to say that those who might have cared about codes, contracts and conventions had no incentive whatsoever to crack down on their abuse since the entire culture of the Government was to campaign, vigorously through the media, for a full second term.

Ignorance of the law, or of codes and rules, is of course no excuse, least of all in ministers, who generally are not allowed to move without legal advice. But this was no ordinary incoming government. It was an administration with next to no experience of it. This is what comes of our governance being in the hands of one party for eighteen years.

Blair revealed his utter ignorance of the terms and conditions of employment of his chief press secretary as late as the spring of 1998, when he had been in office for nearly a year. A fortnight earlier Blair had been on the telephone to Romano Prodi, then the Italian Prime Minister, and sought his reaction to Rupert Murdoch's £4 billion bid for the media empire Mediaset, owned by a former (and future) Prime Minister, Silvio Berlusconi. Prodi preferred it to remain in Italian hands and Blair relayed this to Murdoch. The bid was rejected. The exchange would probably have been regarded as innocuous, had Blair not so assiduously and successfully courted Murdoch before coming to power. When it surfaced in the Italian press, Blair was mocked for running Murdoch's errands. Campbell dismissed the idea that his boss had lobbied for Murdoch's business interests as 'crap'. The British press thought he had misled them and ructions followed.

This was the cue for Gerald Kaufman to urge the Prime Minister to respond to Tory attacks. Blair obliged. He said: 'There is one reason why the Opposition attack the press spokesman: he does an effective job of attacking the Conservative Party.' This was an extraordinary thing for a Prime Minister to say of a press secretary paid for out of public funds. It revealed an amazing ignorance of long-standing conventions as well as of what his press secretary was, and was not, supposed to be doing within his contract and codes. Is it any surprise, in view of that answer, that the activities of his government's massively increased number of special advisers became an issue? They would have become the subject of public scrutiny on grounds of numbers, even if there had not been a single spin doctor among them. It is estimated that, in practice, as many as half of the eighty-one special advisers eventually acquired by the Blair government – more than twice the number in Major's time – were dabbling with the media. And if this is what the Prime Minister, in a Government preoccupied with central control and media manipulation, thought their proper function, who would expect greenhorn ministers to rein in their so-called policy advisers?

Campbell had a clearer idea than his boss about the limits within which he operated. In June 1998 he told Andrew Tyrie, a Conservative member of the Commons select committee on public administration: 'What would be wrong is if I were using that position to promote and further the interests of the Labour Party by abusing that position constantly by attacking your party.' That answer was not entirely in line with the code of conduct for special advisers. It says: 'They should avoid anything which might reasonably lead to the criticism that people paid from public funds are being used for party political purposes.' That does not permit the occasional – let alone the constant – attack.

But it became evident that a certain amount of fudging had gone on when Sir Richard Wilson, the secretary to the Cabinet, heroically tried to rescue Blair before the same select committee. First he claimed that the point Blair was making was that Campbell had been very effective in attacking the Conservatives when Labour was in opposition. If so, Mr Blair had made the point very badly. Sir Richard then added, 'I do not think [Campbell's] job is to go over the top and attack the Opposition with bricks and bottles.' This begs the question as to what weaponry might be appropriate.

In practice, Campbell has been remarkably restrained in his public attacks on the Opposition, given the atmosphere since

2 May 1997 and his boss's naïvety. Moreover, while the argument against the Government's spin doctors is that they should not be paid by the taxpayer for performing the party political role of winning the next election through the media, there have been few instances of their being accused of hurling 'bricks and bottles' at the Opposition. Instead, the criticism is of the ruthlessness and cynicism with which the game with the media and public has been played in pursuit of a party political objective: the perpetuation of Labour in power.

21

The bloodletting

THE BLAIR concept of government in continuous campaigning mode collided immediately with the GIS. Those information officers who thought they would not have long to prove themselves were right. The purge began within three months of Labour coming to office. There is no evidence to suggest that it was planned or centrally controlled. Indeed, the evidence, such as it is, suggests that the first moves in the elimination of the top echelon of the GIS were among the few events that occurred in Whitehall in the late summer of 1997 beyond the ken of the control freaks. There is, however, a suspicion among former GIS staff that, once one of them had been turfed out, it became almost the fashion to get rid of them by a variety of means.

It all began on the morning of Friday 25 July 1997, when Peter Mandelson paid his first visit as Minister without Portfolio in the Cabinet Office to Northern Ireland. He was due to speak to members of the Northern Ireland Information Service (NIIS), a body separate from but related to the British GIS. Before he did so, Andy Wood, the service's director and press secretary to a succession of Northern Ireland ministers for ten violent and traumatic years, thought he had better take him on to one side to warn him what none of his press officers then knew: that he (Wood) had been sacked by Mo Mowlam because of 'a lack of chemistry.' Wood is convinced that Mandelson was genuinely surprised, and shocked, when he learned of this. It certainly taxed the minister's diplomatic qualities when he eventually spoke to the NIIS. A couple of months earlier Campbell had personally penned Wood a note of appreciation after Blair's first visit to the province: 'Many thanks for all your help. Please pass on to your colleagues my thanks for a great team effort. I hope the "new Labour, new Stalinism" was not too much of a burden.'

Wood learned of his enforced departure not from Mowlam but from his permanent secretary, Sir John Chilcot. He was told, 'Mo wants a change. It's a matter of personal chemistry and style.' There was apparently no criticism of his abilities, performance or track record. Indeed, Chilcot told him that Sir Robin (now Lord) Butler, then Cabinet Secretary, saw him as 'a big hitter'. He was, in fact, such a big hitter that he had been in the frame a year earlier for the post of head of the British GIS, which I had held from 1989 to 1990. At one point he was led to believe he would become 'head of profession', as the head of the GIS is described, undertaking it in tandem with his Northern Ireland duties, reportedly much to Chilcot's delight.

It would have been surprising had there been criticism of his performance. I can testify, as one who inherited him as a press officer in No. 10 from the Callaghan government, that Wood is a tough, enthusiastic, no-nonsense professional, with a background in local newspapers and BBC national radio and TV news. He is a committed communicator who bore the heat and burden of the day with distinction in Northern Ireland, to which he bravely went to live with his young family in 1987. He was particularly hot on maintaining Civil Service impartiality and had been known to argue the details with Cabinet Secretaries. He may not have been everybody's cup of tea. I myself have found that not all abrasive Yorkshiremen are. Judging from what Wood himself says, he had certainly not endeared himself to Richard Needham, the Old Etonian former Tory Northern Ireland Minister who was famously revealed as having described Thatcher as 'that cow' on his mobile phone just before she paid a visit to the province. Wood claims he has evidence from journalists that Needham put in a bad word about him to Mowlam.

I regard personal chemistry as one of the more disgraceful ministerial excuses for dumping a press secretary because it is subjective, emotional and not susceptible to rational examination. Nor is it in the spirit of impartiality with which a Civil Servant inherits the politician the system lands him with, and is in turn inherited by the politician. In fact, in my time, moving from one department to another with a minister with whom your chemistry was wonderful was severely frowned upon and every effort was made to prevent it. Chemistry potentially opens up the system to political preference. It is not a ground for divorce that should be readily accepted. It is one of only last, desperate resort. Nor was it accepted by Chilcot, for whom Wood has considerable respect and appreciation. Chilcot could not prevail, but Wood says he later told him that he took some pleasure that autumn in appearing at a meeting with Mowlam with a copy of *PR Week* under his arm, recording its top PR award of the year: to Wood. I should advise the reader that I was chairman of the judges' panel.

Nevertheless chemistry is important. It is better that a press secretary, like a minister's principal private secretary, should get on with his minister. But they should be given time to grow on each other. While first impressions are important, instant rapport is not necessarily a prerequisite for an effective working partnership. I had never known a single one of my seven Cabinet ministers from Barbara Castle to Margaret Thatcher before I was taken on by them, apart from Maurice Macmillan, who had been MP for Halifax while I was a *Yorkshire Post* reporter there. I had little idea what they initially thought of me. But I learned to respect every one of them and I have reason to believe that that respect was reciprocated. What matters, and ought to matter, much more than chemistry is whether the press secretary is competent, energetic and positive in outlook, and whether he gives straightforward, candid advice.

Wood had long since passed all four tests with a variety of Cabinet ministers but found his reputation being undermined well before he was fired. Mowlam arrived in Northern Ireland with two special advisers: one political and the other responsible for the media. No one knows the mechanism by which Wood soon came under fire, along with Sir David Fell, head of the Northern Ireland Civil Service and No. 2 in the NIO, in an unsigned article in the monthly Northern Ireland political magazine *Fortnight*. As a family man, it was Wood's custom to take some annual leave during the school holidays in July, the dreaded marching season in Northern Ireland, while keeping in touch with the situation so that, if necessary, he could return to the office. That July he informed Mowlam's private office that he had booked open tickets so that he could fly back quickly from Athens if circumstances required. He noted it was the first July that he was being publicly criticized in the press for his absence. After he had been sacked, it was also floated as a reason, beyond chemistry, for his services being dispensed with.

He did not go quietly. He saw no reason why he should when Mowlam's regime continued to undermine his reputation after he had left the Northern Ireland Office (NIO). The *New Statesman* in October recorded her view that he was 'not up to the job' and he was described as 'anally retentive' on RTE, the Irish broadcasting network, in the spring of 1998. After the abuse in the *New Statesman* Wood telephoned Mowlam's private office to complain but failed to prevent further attacks on him. Against that background he agreed in 1998 to write for the *Sunday Times* about his years at Stormont, including an unflattering account of Mowlam's early lavatorial court. Wood probably did himself no good with that article, but no one can say he was not provoked. As the first press secretary to be culled, he was treated appallingly. If Blair's government had set out to cow the GIS by the manner of his removal, they could not have handled it better – or worse.

Wood maintains that he was not offered any real alternative job. The initial idea was for him to 'go and review the Scottish Office Information Service'. When he pointed out that that would take all of two months and he asked what would follow, he was told 'Well, we'll have to see. Robin (Butler) doesn't want the public service to lose you.' Another idea was to work on the handling of major terrorist incidents in the Home Office. After a few days the Scottish offer was upgraded to 'do the review and then take over as director'. Another press secretary's job was evidently on the skids.

Wood discovered Elizabeth (Liz) Drummond was on her way out when, in the interests of finding alternative employment, he was asked to go to Dover House, the Scottish Office's headquarters in

London, for an interview. He had questioned the wisdom of his appearing there and, on second thoughts, those who had asked him to do so reached the same conclusion. He was diverted by mobile phone from Dover House at the last minute, either because the next victim of the purge was there or because the atmosphere was so febrile that people might have put two and two together. He was later interviewed and turned down the Scottish job because he would have been worse off. Drummond was the first press officer I recruited to Thatcher's No. 10 press office through the training scheme that my first deputy there, Neville Gaffin, devised to overcome the earlier sacrifice of a post in Thatcher's drive to encourage wider economy in Whitehall. We offered six-week experience secondments to the No. 10 press office and these proved invaluable in discovering GIS talent. Drummond had experience of the Price Commission and DTI before No. 10 and afterwards in the NIO, the Home Office and Westminster City Council before becoming Director of Information in the Scottish Office in 1992, where she served Ian Lang and Michael Forsyth before Donald Dewar. She was popular with journalists.

She had a torrid time with Forsyth, who provided a foretaste of the Labour obsessions to come. He was hyperactive as a junior minister in the late 1980s, when I was wheeled in by the Scottish Office to frustrate his plans for an expensive presentational revamp of the department. As Secretary of State, he came in like a tornado which never blew itself out. In his book *Open Scotland* Professor Philip Schlesinger, of Stirling University, quotes a senior member of the Scottish Office Information Directorate as saying: 'It was a story a day. That was his policy. He was an opportunist. He was the despair of many civil servants. One resigned saying he was "completely unreasonable".' He demanded everything of press officers and his own private office, neither of which had sufficient staff to cope.

Worse still, according to Schlesinger, Drummond saw Forsyth as anticipating the 'blame culture' that the GIS experienced under Labour. He quotes her as saying:

All we ever got from him was: 'You're not doing this. Why aren't you doing that?' He used to think up gimmicks and we used to have to think up gimmicks to promote him. It all came from him. You know, the things he did Ian Lang wouldn't have been seen dead doing . . . cosying up to Mel Gibson and walking up the High Street in a kilt.

Forsyth left the Scottish Office with low press office morale and a significant turnover of staff. And then came Labour. After the initial enthusiasm Drummond found herself trapped between No. 10's demand for Forsythian frenzy and Donald Dewar's relaxed approach to publicity as he concentrated on devolution. On the one hand Dewar was locked in perpetual discussion over a fresh constitutional start for Scotland, while on the other his special advisers Wendy Alexander and Murray Elder demanded publicity – almost any publicity.

Drummond is quoted as saying:

Basically, the two special advisers seemed to have no idea what the press office was for and what their role was. We were getting instructions to organize a press conference tomorrow about such-and-such, without us being asked whether we thought the story was big enough . . . There's been a number of instances of press conferences recently where remarks are coming in the papers as to why did they have that press conference? I suppose it comes from years of opposition. It was go out and sell this one, go out and sell that one. They were wanting to have a press conference on everything, which to my mind was debasing the currency.

Journalists also found it difficult to make the transition from Labour in opposition to Labour in government. They objected to speaking to press officers when for years they had been speaking directly to politicians who were now ministers. One wonders what good it would have done them ringing up Alexander, who is described in *Open Scotland* as talking 'very loud and very fast. She talks so fast it is hard for your ears to keep up with what you're hearing, let alone with your brain keeping up with what she's thinking. Some of her ideas are off the wall. And she doesn't listen. She never listens.'

Bedlam seems an accurate description of the Scottish Office in the late summer of 1997. By then Drummond was hearing on the grapevine that 'they' were not happy with her. She was certainly not happy with them. The Scottish media were also moaning that the new Government was highly active 'down South', whereas nothing much seemed to be happening in Scotland. She had a private breakfast with Dewar to try to clear the air, only to discover that, whatever No. 10 and Dewar's special advisers might require, he was 'not interested in quick headlines'. He wanted to get the devolution policy right. Drummond had had a serious operation in Forsyth's time and her idea then of retiring early had been turned down because she was 'much too valuable'. After talking to Dewar she rang her permanent secretary, Sir Russell Hillhouse, to resurrect the idea. Soon afterwards she had a meeting with Hillhouse and his head of personnel, who confirmed 'they' wanted her out. She was both shocked and relieved, and left at the age of fifty for voluntary work and journalism in Edinburgh. For a time Gordon Brown's brother John, PRO to Glasgow City Council and with a background in TV, was the favourite to succeed her. Perhaps wisely, he pulled out on the day of the selection board.

The cull of top information officers continued relentlessly with Jill Rutter at the Treasury and Gill Samuel at the Ministry of Defence. The Treasury, like the Foreign Office, using diplomats, had made it their practice to have their press office led by an administrator. In effect, they used their press offices as finishing schools for their high-flyers. It gave them a taste of the real world. Understandably, Rutter found life with Charlie Whelan, Gordon Brown's media relations import, impossible. She also found she had little to do. When she complained to her permanent secretary, Sir Terry Burns (who had also been sidelined by Gordon Brown), that three-quarters of her job had gone, he told her 'Well, just do the quarter that's left'. She preferred to depart presentation – or what Whelan's freewheeling left of it – for another life.

Gill Samuel, an experienced professional information officer, had enjoyed excellent relations with secretaries of state at the DTI, Transport and the Ministry of Defence. Yet a few months after the 1997 election she found her job as press secretary and chief of information at Defence eliminated by downgrading. It was described as 'structural change'. For years she and her predecessors had exercised overall control over MoD, Army, Navy and Air Force public relations. Under the restructuring, responsibility was divided between the directors of public relations for the three branches of the armed services and a new 'Director of Information Strategy and News'. Within two years of her departure the MoD rediscovered the need for top-level direction and co-ordination of media relations, and Samuel's post was effectively reinstated. Her permanent secretary there was the celebrated Sir Richard Mottram, who subsequently made a habit of losing official spokesmen in the Environment/Transport complex in the persons of Simon Dugdale and Martin Sixsmith, not to mention lesser press officers, and, of course, Jo Moore. Samuel relished her years as a Government spokesman but she has now built a successful career in the private sector and has not looked back.

Steve Reardon, the man I asked urgently to move from Employment to Social Security to look after John Moore's media interests, was arguably the worst treated of the lot. The terminal cause was Harriet Harman's salary. She returned to the Social Security Department from a Cabinet committee at which ministers had discussed their pay, 'cock-a-hoop' over their decision to take their entitlements, even though Gordon Brown objected. Like other press officers, Reardon came under pressure from journalists to reveal his minister's attitude to her salary entitlement. He checked with Harman's private office, who saw no reason why her intention to take her full entitlement should not be disclosed. He reposed too much trust in his officials. The following day the Chancellor bounced his colleagues into giving up £16,000 a year, restricting themselves to £87,000 of their entitlement. Harman had egg on her face, whereupon one of Harman's policy advisers informed the press that Reardon was 'dead meat' two days before he got the ominous call from his permanent secretary, Ann Bowtell, easing him out of his job.

The ministerial salary issue came after sustained 'daily fire' from Harman, conveyed by Bowtell (never the minister) about the alleged shortcomings of his press office. Reardon resisted pressure to ditch some of his staff because he saw no justification for doing so. He has his suspicions that the problems over Harman's salary were seized on to get rid of him and to remove an obstacle to press office changes.

To explain his going Reardon devised, at the behest of his department, the phrase 'the need for a change of style', which makes a change from 'lack of chemistry'. He was given no option of alternative employment in the Civil Service, even though he says he had received top marks in his annual 1997–8 appraisal, accompanied by glowing reviews from his permanent secretary. He told the Commons' Select Committee on Public Administration that this suggested that, for whatever reason, he had become *persona non grata* with the Government as a whole and with the Civil Service in particular.

He ended up for a time in the same room as Andy Wood at the Home Office as they considered, both aged over fifty, what to do to repair their shattered careers. Wood put his thoughts on handling major terrorist incidents down on paper, while Reardon wrote a report on improving coverage for crime statistics and securing a better press for the judiciary. Both recall with rich irony that the room to which they were dispatched out of sight and out of mind was Room 101 in that part of the Home Office designated as the 'Grey Area'. It was while suspended in this Orwellian grey area between careers that Wood decided to go freelance and Reardon to become the Institute of Directors' director of communications.

Sheila Thompson had served the Conservative Lord Chancellor, Lord Mackay, for seven years when she was landed with what many would regard as a fate worse than death: Lord Irvine of Lairg, New Labour's Lord Chancellor. In his first year in office the press had a field day scrutinizing Irvine's every move for fresh evidence of what the *Sunday Times* described as his 'accelerating self-destruction, political naïveté and pompous self-importance', not to mention his lifestyle. He became known as Lord Irvine of the Wallpaper because of the cost of the wall-covering in the refurbishment of his official residence in the House of Lords. Thompson found that Irvine was initially suspicious of the Civil Service after eighteen years under the Tories and that increasingly her advice was unwelcome, when it was sought. She was certainly not asked her view on a political speech he made at the Reform

Club in which he likened himself to Cardinal Wolsey in terms of his constitutional importance. Had she been consulted, she would have advised against the comparison – as she later told him. She also told him, when her situation was coming to a head, that it was he who had given the speech to the press, even though it had been delivered under Chatham House rules – that is, not for reporting.

By the end of 1997 Irvine was seen as a loose cannon on the Government's decks. He then summoned Thompson to a meeting in the company of her permanent secretary, Sir Thomas Legg, the Lord Chancellor's Department's policy director and a private secretary. Two things became clear. First, Irvine did not understand the role of a Civil Service information officer and the constraints under which they operated. Legg felt obliged to try to describe the boundary between political and departmental work. Second, Irvine wished to have his displeasure with the way he had been looked after recorded. Hence the presence of a private secretary to make a note. Irvine concluded the meeting by saying it had been 'good to clear the air' and asking Thompson to prepare a media plan for forthcoming departmental initiatives. A week later she learned that even before the meeting Irvine had instructed Legg to appoint a director of communications two grades above her rank. She was given to understand she could apply but she would not be appointed, however well she performed. She left in May 1998, with the sympathy of the press, for private sector PR after declining an offer to stay on as deputy to the newly appointed director.

Andrew Marre (Culture, Media and Sport), and Philip Aylett (International Development) were surgically removed by being forced to compete for their own jobs. Graham Blakeway (Agriculture) was neatly ousted by a restructuring device that also eventually killed off Drummond's No. 2 at the Scottish Office. Marre went off to the private sector and Aylett became head of the press operation at the Committee on Standards in Public Life. It must have come as a comfort to Aylett, who had also worked for me at No. 10, to discover that some standards were still presumed to exist.

As the toll of press secretaries mounted, one man still hanging in there was Simon Dugdale in John Prescott's vast empire embracing the environment, regions and transport. I discovered Dugdale when he was nominated by the Newcastle upon Tyne office of the COI for a six-week secondment to No. 10. He is a quiet, straight, immensely competent press officer with an excellent presence and an iron will. No one quite understands how he managed to last just over a year with Prescott, with whom 'survival was better than par', according to Sir Andrew Turnbull, Dugdale's first permanent secretary before he went off to head the Treasury. I worked with Turnbull, who has become Secretary to the Cabinet, when he was Thatcher's last principal private secretary before her resignation. He is a philosophical man.

Dugdale found the huge department challenging before it acquired transport under Prescott. It seems to have become a nightmare welding transport into it amid the chaos that is Prescott, although Dugdale refuses to discuss his time with the Deputy Prime Minister. He says he is not in the business of 'tittle tattle, anecdote and gossip'. But it has been possible to piece together through other contacts Prescott's bad-tempered tantrums and bullying, his instinctive rather than intellectual, ordered way of working, the failures of Prescott's private office to include Dugdale in important meetings and the operations of the minister's tribe of frenetic political advisers. There are stories of press officers working into the early hours on trivial matters and of one being castigated at 4 a.m. for being unable to say whether they had achieved a 'correction' in a national newspaper. Eventually staff was haemorrhaging at 30% a year and morale in a department that had been attractive to staff with the advent of a new government had slumped alarmingly as the 'blame culture' took hold.

Dugdale has restricted himself to saying that he had travelled the world with Prescott trying, and failing, to get him to settle down during the long hours of flight to discuss his information division and presentational issues. In the end he found it impossible, like others in the department, to do anything right. By July 1998 a special adviser told him Prescott would prefer someone else to accompany him on a visit. This warning sign was quickly followed by the discovery that a review was being imposed on his division by No. 10.

He told his permanent secretary, by then Sir Richard Mottram: 'I have torn this place inside out and upside down to give them a fresh start. If they want to impose someone from No. 10 without having the decency to tell me, I have got my pride. I am off.' And off he went on six months' gardening leave. During that time he says he never heard another word from Mottram, even though a secondment had been discussed. He resigned, to become a free-lance consultant, on the day the department received its Investors in People status, which he had helped to secure since his division had been chosen as a sample for examination in the qualifying process. No one, says Dugdale, seemed to detect the slightest irony.

Only one information chief inherited by Labour in May 1997, Pat Wilson, remained in post at the 2001 election and he retired soon afterwards from the Welsh Office, which had been rendered effectively redundant following devolution. There is a great deal of bitterness among those who disappeared about the elimination of the top echelon of an impartial and independent GIS, especially in the light of the 'abject' performance of Labour's special adviser–spin doctors. They and they alone, former GIS members say, are responsible for wrecking the Government's reputation within the life of a single Parliament. They have a point.

I have discussed with many of those who were forced out, as well as with those who left of their own accord, their impressions of what happened, including Labour's self-serving claim that they were no good. They acknowledge that they were not working in shifts to accommodate Campbell's 24-hour media, but they main-tain there was ultimate cover. The concept of 24-hour media was nothing new, but the idea that the manpower and resources would be available to provide continuous cover was novel. They certainly recognize that the GIS lacked the staff and the units and the tech-nology as compared with the Labour Party. This was not because they would not have welcomed them but because the Civil Service was committed neither in spirit nor in budget to serving the media age. It may be argued that that was the GIS's own fault. But it also knew instinctively what it could get away with in a machine driven by economy rather than need.

They ruefully and pointedly note that in my eleven years the No. 10 press office managed to provide some sort of presentational co-ordination, monitoring and intelligence service with eight people. The 2001 COI directory of information and press officers lists seventeen staff in No. 10 press office alone. It is a fat booklet compared with pre-1997. And not only have numbers soared; grades, and with them pay, have also jumped. Moreover, a No. 10 press office with an unprecedented staff of seventeen is only half the story. It ignores Campbell's units for strategic communications and research and information. What, they ask, eyes rolling, do they all do since there are now mercifully many fewer ministerial articles in newspapers?

My former colleagues generally reject the argument that they were not up to it, given the resources. But they readily accept that they could never be up to the demands of an incoming government bent on starting the next election campaign from its very first day in office, especially when they must keep out of party politics, maintain impartiality and prevent the public purse from being used for party political purposes. From the very beginning in 1945 it had been recognized that the GIS should never play that role. From 1997 not only was it expected to do so; when it stood true to its principles – as it must – it was purged.

On reflection, my former colleagues recognize that any attempt to play the media relations game by the Civil Service book was not regarded as upholding the proprieties but as negativism and obstructionism. It was perhaps virtually impossible to survive at any level of seniority as a proper Civil Servant in a press office after 1997. I had found it difficult enough in other times with other *mores*. The system looked with suspicion on activist, inventive press officers with a flair for communication. They were inclined to become what is called 'over-committed' and to 'take too much upon themselves'. If you were what I would regard as useless and incompetent, you conformed to the received wisdom as to why you were in information. The GIS suffered for decades from class snobbery. It was very definitely second-class behind the administrative Civil Service. It had to be kept in its place.

Against that background my former colleagues are not in the least surprised that those recruited to follow them were administrative Civil Servants or journalists with attitude – in other words, Government sympathizers. It was only natural, they felt, that the administrative Civil Service would wish to see part of the action now that Labour had made communications so much more important. The administrators given the job might be media inno-cents abroad – perhaps not a bad thing for a government seeking to bend the Civil Service to its will – but they could easily be found a new job, unlike specialist information officers, if they somehow failed.

Not to put too fine a point on it, my former colleagues feel they have been let down by the senior Civil Service. I am sure they are right. I say this with sadness, as one who paradoxically would never accuse the late Sir Denis Barnes (Employment), the late Sir Jack Rampton (Energy), Lord Armstrong of Ilminster or Lord Butler of Brockwell (former Cabinet Secretaries) of failing me. It is only fair to their successors to say they never had to put up with five years of a Blair government.

22

Alarms and inquiries

A s New Labour progressively eliminated grandmother from the scene, they just as assiduously tried to teach her to suck eggs. Alastair Campbell began at the meeting in No. 10 with departmental heads of information six days into the Blair government. He told the assembled throng that he wanted the GIS to be more interventionist and proactive. They should be able to tell him what tomorrow's 'story' was – in other words, to control the news agenda – give a 24-hour service, correct a 'wrong' first edition story immediately and reiterate again and again Government messages. 'When you and I are heartily sick of repetition,' he is reported as saying, 'that is when we are getting through to the outside world.' Or not, as the case may be: the public gets bored too.

Campbell's assurances that there would be no great purge of GIS members and that he would not use the GIS for party political advantage looked threadbare by the time of his next pronouncement, on 26 September 1997. As the culling proceeded, he called on the GIS, in a letter to 'colleagues', to 'raise its game'. The text of his unclassified summary of a discussion with heads of information reads as follows:

There are four key messages which underpin this Government's agenda and should be built into all areas of our activity:

1) This is a modernizing Government. It is modernizing this country's constitution, its institutions, its economy, schools, NHS etc.
2) This Government is delivering on its promises.
3) Its policies are in the mainstream. It is a Government for all the people.
4) The Government is providing a new direction for Britain.

Everything we do should be speaking to these key themes.

As I said at our first meeting in May, given the power of the media, communication of policy is integral to any Government's activities. It is not an optional extra. We have a duty to explain. This provides a real opportunity for the Government Information Service to raise its game and be right at the heart of Government.

The change of Government has involved a huge transition for the Civil Service. There has been some negative publicity about the GIS, but as I said on Monday the Government is perceived as doing very well and you must take your share of the credit for this. Equally I am well aware of the huge amount you do which is not high-profile, but important and valuable none the less.

That said, I do believe our collective communications across Government could be improved. There are several areas which need to be addressed:

1) Media handling needs to be built into the decision-making process at the earliest stage. As a policy is devised, how it will be explained and communicated should be an integral part of the process. My sense is that in many Departments policy is discussed and developed on a completely separate track and the media plan is then added on at a much later stage. We need to be in there at the start.
2) More emphasis needs to be put on media strategy. I often get the impression that events happen and the mentality surrounding them is one of damage limitation. This is perhaps an understandable legacy of the last administration. But big positive announcements are not getting as good a show as they should. The Government must lay down big messages around every event.

There are three parts to any story – the build-up, the event and the follow through. My sense is that it is the middle of these three that gets all the attention. There is insufficient attention to advance publicity – the briefing of editors, feature writers and others both before and after. That is why we have been encouraging Departments to give us ideas for the Sundays with varying degrees of success. Formulas have developed which you should challenge. Do you always need a press conference after a Commons statement, for example? We should all be constantly looking for new ways to communicate.

3) Everything should be seen as part of a wider whole. Announcements should not be made in isolation but with regard to the bigger picture.

4) We should always be ahead of the game. We should always know how big stories will be playing in next day's papers. This requires a combination of judgement and telephone legwork, but it is a vital early warning system. Decide your headlines. Sell your story and if you disagree with what is being written, argue your case. If you need support from here, let me know.

5) We must respond faster. If a story is going wrong, or if a policy must be defended, we must respond quickly, confidently, robustly.

Thank you for the points which you raised with me. Some I have already begun to address. Others I will feed into the Mountfield Review.

In conclusion I believe there is a very bright future for the GIS, and a tremendous opportunity to re-establish yourselves at the very heart of Government.

There must have been hollow laughter around Whitehall at Campbell's belief in 'a very bright future' for the GIS and its taking its share of the credit for the perception of the Government when its leaders were being axed. That laughter would have become hollower at the idea of the GIS 're-establishing' itself at the very heart of Government. His own complaint about the need for media handling to be built into formulation of policy confirms my continuing experience of the system's 'optional extra' approach over decades to the issue of presentation. It had never been at the 'very heart of Government'.

Unless Campbell was being stupid, only one conclusion can be drawn from his letter. It is, quite simply, that whatever he may have disarmingly said about politicization and purges, he was absolutely determined to bend Government information officers to his will to secure the return of a Labour government in 2001–2. That will was entirely party political and his methods reflected that fact in mounting a continuous and unrelenting re-election campaign. To this end he sought to convert the GIS into a proactive and interventionist news factory aiming to control the news agenda and impose its view of a story on the media. That is the only possible interpretation of his fifth point of the areas needing to be addressed – requiring the GIS immediately to correct 'wrong' stories. Judging by his own pursuit of journalists, it covered 'wrong' angles as well as 'wrong' facts, indeed the entire presentation of a story. He was also determined to bend the media, via the GIS, to the Government's every will.

In its previous fifty years the GIS had always tried to give major Government announcements as clear a run as possible from competing Government initiatives and known external events so that publicity for them could be maximized. There is nothing new in Labour's celebrated events 'grids', or diaries, apart from their talking about them, their elaborate nature and the manpower required to produce them. The GIS had sought to influence the treatment of announcements by the media through a press notice and their minister's exposition of the policy development on the day. It had briefed editors, leader writers and correspondents both immediately before and after announcements as a matter of routine. It had tried to get the media to correct mistakes of fact as soon as it spotted them, notorious though the media are for seldom, if ever, publishing corrections. But it had not been in the habit of challenging the media's news judgements either in advance of or following publication, unless they were based on a mangled concept of the facts. To do so would have been incompatible with a free society, in which individuals are entitled to their own interpretation of events. It was becoming rapidly clear that in Campbell the GIS had acquired a propagandist of the first water, and to hell with a free press.

This was amply confirmed by his 'four key messages'. Each one is fundamentally party political. The furthest that a GIS member could go in conveying this Campbell flavour would be to report the Government as saying that it was seeking to modernize and provide a new direction for Britain and to that end to deliver on its promises. He would also be able to confirm, if it were the case, that a specific minister had described its policies as 'mainstream'. But there could be no question of his asserting the four key messages off his own bat. That would have compromised his impartiality and rendered him partisan. Whether or not he understood what he was doing, Campbell was clearly setting out to politicize at least a branch of the Civil Service.

The notion that Campbell is, or was, naïve, that in spite of his good intentions he stumbled into politicization, does not wash. Nobody with even a rudimentary concept of Civil Service impartiality could possibly have penned those four 'key messages' for use by Civil Servants. The inescapable conclusion of his first few months' operations is that he sought to push the GIS into becoming not only more 'professional' (which was perfectly legitimate, depending on the definition of the word) but also partisan (which was not). It is perhaps a tribute to the practised impartiality of the GIS that so little blatant party propaganda got through the system to see the light of published day, especially in view of Steve Reardon's account of the activities of special advisers in the DSS. In his memorandum to the Select Committee on Public Administration, which subsequently conducted its own 'inquiry' into what was going on, Reardon wrote:

> The drafting of departmental press releases was closely scrutinized to the point of obsession by the special advisers who frequently issued instructions about drafting and redrafting directly to junior press office staff without my knowledge [regardless of the prohibition in their contracts]. There were frequent arguments about the proper language to be employed in a departmental draft and special advisers sought to reproduce the tone of

the Labour manifesto and repeat its election commitments as emerging news.

There will, of course, be those who point out that the GIS, throughout my time and before, operated under guidance on publicity, which reads:

Government publicity should always be directed at informing the public even where it also has the objective of influencing the behaviour of individuals or particular groups. It is possible that in serving the public in this way a well-founded publicity campaign can redound to the political credit of the party in government. This is by definition a natural consequence of political office and has been accepted as such by successive governments. But it has equally been accepted that it must not be, or be believed to be, either the primary purpose or a principal incidental purpose of a campaign.

Others may raise specific campaigns that were thought to have stretched that guidance to its limits and even beyond. One was Lord Young's DTI 'Enterprise' campaign of upwardly thrusting arrows in the 1980s, which caused an immense amount of teeth-sucking in Whitehall. But the fact remains that the Campbell doctrine does not simply aim at well-founded campaigns or technically excellent public information work that may have an incidental political benefit; the overriding objective, the primary purpose of his key messages, is to set the work in a party political context and extol the entire performance of the Government responsible, with the aim of securing its re-election.

However successful the GIS may have been in upholding the impartiality of departmental output, the Queen has been less well served by the custodians of public service impartiality. Her speeches at the state openings of new sessions of Parliament have attracted withering comment. Simon Hoggart, the Parliamentary sketchwriter of *The Guardian*, noted in November 1999 that the Queen's Speech used to be 'couched in dry, flat, dull language and contained brief descriptions of the coming year's legislation' but that after 1997 it began to be 'padded out with New Labour jargon'. He cited 'a dynamic, knowledge-based economy', 'trans-parency', 'providing people with the opportunities to liberate their potential' and 'meeting the challenges of the new millennium' in the one delivered on 17 November 1999. This was, he said, just some of the 'cringe-making, jaw-sticking, tooth-furring drivel which the poor woman had to read from the throne'. No wonder, he said, she seemed to be infected with a greater ennui than ever. 'It was without doubt the worst Queen's speech I have ever heard', he concluded. 'In fact, it wasn't really a royal speech at all, but a party political broadcast.' It would have clearly benefited from GIS editing. Unfortunately, there were not many GIS senior staff left with a knowledge of the proprieties.

Long before then – in fact, within a few months of taking office – concern had been mounting about the Government's approach to presentation and the sacking of departmental press secretaries. The Cabinet Secretary, Sir Robin Butler, was moved in September 1997 to appoint an inquiry 'to consider proposals to respond to concerns about how far it [the GIS] is equipped in all areas to meet the demands of the fast-changing media world; to build on the skills and resources of the career GIS; and to maintain the estab-lished, and recently re-confirmed, propriety guidelines'.

The job of chairing the inquiry was given to Robin Mountfield, the now knighted and retired permanent secretary in the Office of Public Service, who had spent much of his career in DTI national-izing and then privatizing industries. His fellow members, along with Campbell, were: Andrew Silverman, Peter Mandelson's private secretary as Minister without Portfolio; Conor Ryan, a special adviser from Education and Employment; Mike Granatt, head of the GIS; Michael (now Sir Michael) Scholar, Permanent Secretary at the DTI, with whom I had worked when he was Mrs Thatcher's economic affairs private secretary; David Wilkinson, director, Machinery of Government and Standards, in Mountfield's department; and Margaret O'Mara, the Treasury's principal estab-lishment (personnel) officer.

The group was not chosen to sell the pass and generally did not do so. Instead, it produced a report that I would have been only too delighted to implement, subject to a few reservations. In fact, I said publicly at the time that I wished I could have had such a report behind me, filling my sails when I was chief press secretary. For me and my generation of information squeezers of the bureaucratic stone Mountfield's greatest achievement was his strictures on the approach taken by his fellow mandarins to communication. We heard sweet music as we read:

> We agree with the view that within many departments insufficient emphasis is placed by Civil Servants involved in policy development on the communication strategy that every important initiative or decision will require. Some observers have noted something approaching disdain for media and communications matters. This weakness must be addressed, so that policy staff naturally think about communications aspects and involve professional communicators early enough to contribute substantially.

This recommendation did not have pride of place in the report. Yet what was wrong with the system – a weakness, as Mountfield describes it, that had kept presentation starved of men, resources and the wherewithal of fact – was its attitude to communication. It, and the GIS, came at the end of the queue. It was all too often an afterthought, the sort of issue dealt with in a few seconds at the end of the meeting. An entirely different attitude – a positive approach to communication – might not have pre-empted the presentational paranoia of New Labour, but it would have made it much more difficult for it to behave as ruthlessly as it did.

As things turned out, Mountfield could have saved his breath because, once it became clear that the Government put a premium on good communication, the mandarinate rapidly began to put their own people in the top information jobs. At the same time they wrecked the career prospects of members of the GIS – who had, of course, always been dispensable – thereby entirely defeating Mountfield's objective. But Mountfield should take credit for trying. He hit the nail on the head, even if he was forced to fall back on the old remedy that some of us had long tried, with very limited success: promoting interchange between GIS staff and administrators so that each got experience of the other's work and needs. Mountfield also proposed a step change in training to promote awareness of the importance of communication among policy makers. The test of his achievement will be what happens to the bureaucrats' interest in communication when Blair is no longer Prime Minister, after the ridicule that his government's approach to media management has begun to attract.

For the rest, Mountfield sought to protect the propriety of GIS members, to bring special advisers under better control through improved co-ordination, to make the No. 10 spokesman routinely quotable, to modernize and equip press offices for the supposedly new but in reality rather long-in-the-tooth 24-hour media age, and to raise GIS performance through training and extensive check-lists, which are mostly common sense. In a last mad moment of absurd gimmickry he also changed the name of the GIS to the Government Information and Communication Service (GICS) to signal a shift of direction from 'reactive answering of questions' to 'proactive exposition and justification of policy'. So that was how I got my reputation: from the 'reactive answering of questions'!

Mountfield was perceptively tough on special advisers, who have ultimately, in the unfair form of Jo Moore, revealed their utter cynicism and the extent to which they can spin out of control. He was preoccupied with making the relationship between minister, press officer and special adviser work. To do that, he said, each of them needed to recognize the others' proper role and the constraints on them. They also needed to keep in very close personal contact, because for one side to be kept in ignorance of statements, guidance or briefings is a situation fraught with danger. And Cabinet ministers and permanent secretaries needed to spend time ensuring that press officer and special adviser work together. We have since seen that in some cases Mountfield might just as well not have bothered.

He was widely acclaimed, and unaccountably still is, for reforming the system by which No. 10 briefs journalists. From 1945 to 1997, as I have explained, in order to help preserve the constitutional convention whereby ministers are the front men and officials the backroom boys, No. 10 press secretaries briefed unattributably. They were not identified as the source, though

John Major made a small concession in 1990 by allowing No. 10 to be identified as the origin of a briefing. Mountfield cut through this and put Campbell and all other Government spokesmen on the record in the vain hope of trying to cut out media gossip and lend identified authority to authentic Government statements. But there was to be no personal identification of the briefer other than 'the Prime Minister's official spokesman' and the broadcasters' cameras and microphones were not to be admitted in order to preserve the myth, under Campbell, of ministerial superiority and visibility.

It did not, of course, end unattributable briefing, which follows the on-the-record bit wherever a journalist seeks clarification or a private chat. (The White House press secretary in the USA similarly goes on briefing unattributably once he has done his bit for radio and TV.) Nor did it prevent someone very close to the Prime Minister (still not positively identified despite the on-the-record rule) from describing Gordon Brown as 'psychologically flawed'. For all the on-the-record reform, this is still a hole-in-the-corner government populated, in Clare Short's words, by 'people who live in the dark'. Nobody has ever discovered who canvassed the demise of Frank Dobson, Chris Smith, David Clark, Gavin Strang and Clare Short almost before they had got their feet under the Cabinet table in 1997.

Still, Mountfield represented a considerable advance, provided his report could be made to stick. But buried away in an annexe designed to promote good press office practice was an apparently innocuous piece of advice that could have become a question of Parliamentary privilege if MPs still took any pride in their institution. Mountfield, I am sure, did not write it. Nor, I am equally sure, did those who compose it mean ill. But they played right into the hands of Campbell's manifest contempt for anything, including Parliament, which gets in the way of his political mission. Page 2 of 'Press Office Best Practice', annexed to the Mountfield report, includes these words: 'Trailing helps set the context and the news agenda, but it must not offend Parliamentary protocol'.

Right from the start the Speaker, Betty Boothroyd, was repeatedly upset by the Government's practice, now routine, of 'trailing' – that is, leaking on its terms to pliable journalists – every announcement immediately in advance of its publication before Parliament was informed. Yet there in black and white, in the GIS's own practical guidance, lies the sanction for it, however contradictory it may be, since trailing and Parliamentary protocol – the right of MPs to hear and question policy developments first – are almost by definition incompatible. It is no good MPs saying they did not know. One can only conclude that they put their political advantage in having their Government's policies leaked by dictation to tame journalists before the authority of the Commons. Alternatively, they may think that in this media age their Parliamentary privilege is 'old hat' and impractical. If so, they should redefine their privileges.

On one other point, the sacking of heads of information, Mountfield is felt by those who were sacked to have run away. That is entirely fair. In rehearsing the concern that led to his inquiry, he merely refers to 'the departure from their posts (for a variety of reasons) of a number of Heads of Information'. He could, if he chose, argue that an inquiry into their sacking was not within his terms of reference. I also wonder how far he would have got if he had tried to investigate their departures with Campbell as a member of his inquiry team, though there are those who were forced out who speak of Campbell's concern to retain them. Yet to accuse Mountfield of running away is harsh. He devotes part of his report to trying to prevent ministers from using 'lack of chemistry' as a reason for ditching a press secretary in the way that Andy Wood, for example, was dumped in Northern Ireland. It is worth quoting Mountfield's acidic Paragraph 70:

> Sir Michael Bett, the First Civil Service Commissioner [an independent appointment under the Civil Service Order in Council] has indicated he would not be inclined to favour changing the rules to allow a minister to choose between qualified candidates on grounds of personal chemistry. He thought personal chemistry should not be overstated as a requirement. Professional ability and normal inter-personal skills should generally be sufficient. A lack of personal chemistry could, of course, develop and might in exceptional cases need to be dealt with: but to elevate chemistry to a key criterion risked its exten-

sion into political stance. Moreover, heads of information appointed from an open competition would be appointed for a substantial period – typically as a career move, initially for 3–5 years. To allow a chemistry criterion for the appointing minister might quickly be made nugatory if the minister were shuffled. Appointments could not sensibly be vulnerable to successive chemical reactions.

The Civil Service Commission may now, in the light of experience, turn to examine 'the need for a change of style' and information division 'restructuring' as reasons to dispense with press secretaries.

Inquiries are, of course, only as good as the intentions of the Government to implement their recommendations. No one knows whether the Government's abuse of the GICS would have been worse but for Mountfield. But one thing is clear: it did not take much notice of it, except in beefing up resources, starting with a recommendation to introduce a Strategic Communications Unit (which sacked heads of information had been advocating), of some six people to improve co-ordination across Government. The fact remains it is an intrinsically valuable report, which for once took communications seriously.

This is more than can be said for inquiries by the Select Committee on Public Administration and by Lord Neill's Committee on Standards in Public Life, to both of which I gave evidence. The former was pathetic and the latter ineffectual – so ineffectual on special advisers that Neill's successor began another examination of the species in 2002. Neill recommended that there should be a statutory limit on their numbers (whereupon they increased) and completely ignored in his recommendations the issue of their employment in media roles. Obviously, I impressed him and his committee less than I do more worldly people about the risk of politicization when I asked them to put themselves in the position of a humble press officer. Imagine, I said, one who had seen the head of his information division fired, knew the Prime Minister was obsessed with publicity, had a No. 10 press secretary in Campbell who had told the GICS to 'raise its game', had a minister absolutely dedicated to do No. 10's media bidding and at least one of the minister's special advisers breathing down his neck in drafting press statements. 'What would you do in those circumstances?' I asked the committee. 'Why, keep your noses clean.'

As for the Select Committee, under Rhodri Morgan, it published its report early in August 1998, just after the Commons had risen for the summer recess. I had not expected much from it since the Labour majority of MPs on it had spent their time examining me on my every alleged indiscretion as No. 10 press secretary in order to justify Campbell's behaviour. It never bothered to interview a single sacked information head, though it invited them to send in written memoranda. It found no clear evidence that Campbell provided some journalists with special treatment after he himself had denied doing so and three Lobby and Press Gallery representatives had disingenuously or cravenly finessed the issue. Yet within a year Peter Oborne, in his book on Campbell, was taking the lid off the Blair government's rank favouritism.

As I wrote at the time:

> Like Swiss bankers during World War II, they [the Select Committee] went about their business with their eyes and ears shut. They decided it was not within their remit to go into the 'unusual turnover' in departmental heads of information since the election – not even when more than half of the heads or deputy heads of information in the main ministerial departments have moved on or out, often propelled by a ministerial boot. And not even when, as their report says, some press officers believed their departure 'was caused by the desire of ministers for information officers to be less neutral than they thought was compatible with their regular civil service terms of employment'. Instead, they took Stalin's way out: if there is a problem, liquidate it. They called on the Government to explain why a GICS is necessary and why it shouldn't be integrated into the mainstream civil service on the spurious grounds of improving career opportunities.

For the rest, the Labour majority contented itself with prescribing codes, reviews and vigilance. It also squashed the Tories, who had given the Cabinet Secretary, Sir Richard Wilson, a hard time on policing Campbell's activities, in their attempts to put some backbone into the report. The Tories wanted special advisers undertaking significant amounts of party political activity to be paid by the party and not by the taxpayer, and to have the Speaker's concerns about the sharp growth in Government announcements by pre-briefing journalists before informing Parliament investigated by another Commons committee. Labour also sat on a Tory plan to make Campbell, in the interests of transparency, keep tapes of his Lobby briefings for twelve months – a move triggered by his revelation that the recording of his controversial briefing on Blair's contacts with Romano Prodi over Rupert Murdoch's interests had been wiped clean by reuse.

Not one of the checks on an over-mighty Government utterly besotted with spin-doctoring was in working order: not the Cabinet, not Parliament, not the watchdogs nor, in the absence of all these, the senior Civil Service, and certainly not British journalism. No wonder things went from bad to worse.

23

Dissipation

EVER SINCE Tony Blair came to office I have pondered on the rationale for his government's remarkable approach to media relations, founded, as it is, on the short-term finessing of events, issues and situations. Only one explanation makes sense of its spin-doctoring: an arrogant contempt for Parliament, party, press and people, probably partly born of fear of its historically fractious party and the press. Parliament and the Labour Party have been treated like dirt, the press, radio and television used and abused and the people dismissed as dimwits, apparently thought to be incapable of forming judgements over time about the manner of their governance. The utter lack of a strategic sense and the stupidity behind this take my breath away.

Within two and a half years of taking power – by the dawn of the new millennium – it was obvious that the Blair government was politically the most profligate in our post-war history in all bar one crucial particular: its election pledge to provide stable economic growth with low inflation and to promote dynamic and competitive business and industry. It has not yet – or so far as the people notice – dissipated the Tories' golden economic legacy.

It came to office with, on Blair's own admission in his manifesto, 'a limited set of important promises'. Of course, all parties generalize in their manifestos, but a look at eight of Blair's manifesto ambitions shows how careful he was in opposition to avoid offering hostages to fortune.

Making education his 'number one priority', he merely promised to increase the share of national income spent on education. He left himself massive room to increase revenue by simply ruling out any increase in the basic or top rates of income tax. With an exceptional flourish of numbers, he promised to get 250,000 young unemployed off benefit and into work. He promised to rebuild the NHS, reducing spending on administration and increasing it on patient care. No more than that. He would be 'tough on crime and on the causes of crime' and halve the time it took persistent juvenile offenders to appear in court. That's all. He would build 'strong families and strong communities' and lay the foundations for a modern welfare state in pensions and community care. More generality. He also promised to safeguard the environment and develop an integrated transport policy to fight congestion and pollution and to 'give Britain the leadership in Europe which Britain and Europe need'. And that, apart from a ninth promise, which I shall come to presently, was his 'contract with the people', deliverable in five years.

It was nice work if you could get it, given that the economy was pretty well proof from all bar an international recession and that the unions had been tamed. Uniquely in fifty-two years of our post-war political history, Blair came to office not on a sea of troubles but on the flat calm of a golden dawn. The barometer had never been set fairer for a modern incoming British government.

If the circumstances of New Labour's accession to power demanded anything, it was a display of cool, calm competence, of a clear determination to set about fulfilling the spirit of the Prime Minister's pledges in opposition. Given his huge majority and the political atmosphere, he could reasonably expect the indulgence of time would be granted by the people. The situation also demanded a certain resolve on the new government's part to conduct itself with due propriety. After all, it had floated to office on what it had magnified into oceans of Tory 'sleaze'. The people were expecting something better. In fact, Blair's ninth pledge was to 'clean up politics' and put the funding of political parties on a proper and accountable basis.

The last things required were frenzy and gimmickry. And yet even before Blair had entered No. 10, flag-waving party workers had been summoned from Labour Party headquarters at Millbank to make his public reception memorably enthusiastic for the cameras. He was spin-doctored into Downing Street. Looking back on it, nothing became the manner of his arrival more than its deceitful pretence. It turned out to be merely a token of the hyperactive manipulation that was to follow. And while it proceeded, ministers steadily rid themselves of the experienced Civil Service press secretaries who, if they had been accorded a hearing and given the opportunity, would have reduced the frenzy and decibels and promoted a reputation-preserving longer-term approach to the serious business of government.

What is clear is that the GIS had no responsibility for the worst of the Government's presentational failures in its first year, which in turn laid the foundations for the arrogant, contriving, back-biting and ultimately squalid reputation it acquired from such episodes as Lord Irvine's expensive wallpaper, the Millennium Dome project, the chaos over the euro, the Ecclestone affair, Geoffrey Robinson's £12 million Guernsey Trust, the evasion over Blair's intercession with the Italian Prime Minister on behalf of Rupert Murdoch, and the confused approach to the Sierra Leone arms affair. As usual, the Blair government sacked the wrong people.

It is, of course, only fair to make allowances for the manic energy with which Blair's government set about its task after eighteen years in opposition. It was itching to do things. It wanted to demonstrate its vigour in contrast to the Major government's grey fatigue. But governments are not elected solely for their vigour. They are sent to Westminster to give the nation the benefit of their judgement. Yet if there is one quality the Blair government consistently lacked in its first five years, it is judgement in the presentation of its works. The result is that, leaving aside ominous stirrings of dissent within itself over policy, it has long been seen as 'all spin and no substance', even by its own Parliamentary supporters.

Characteristic of the presentational obsession of the Labour government's early years was the frenetic performance of Blair himself and Cabinet ministers as newspaper columnists. No wonder the Downing Street press machine was bloated by Thatcher standards. It regularly annexed space in which professional journalists might otherwise have informed, entertained or outraged us by churning out mind-numbingly boring accounts of the Government's rescue of this 'great people', as Blair described the British in his manifesto. John Rentoul, in *Tony Blair Prime Minister*, reckons Blair averaged one and a half articles per week in the national press in his first year. Twenty of them appeared in the *Sun*.

The lack of judgement in both ministers and editors was as stupendous as the outpouring. No doubt, as a new Prime Minister on an exciting voyage of discovery, Blair felt he had something to say. No doubt the press was as anxious to provide the new, available incumbent of Downing Street with platforms to get on good terms with him. But the last thing No. 10 should do is to hold up the Prime Minister to bemused ridicule, as the prolific nature of his virtual pen succeeded in doing, and thereby cheapen the product. Nor should it be seduced by the press's fawning accessibility. Blair allowed himself to sign much inconsequential rubbish and editors freely consented to be stuffed with it for an astonishingly long time, a poor reflection on the judgements of both.

Another aspect of this rush into print is the light it casts on Blair's 'media, media, media' mentality. It would have been impossible to enlist Thatcher in such a campaign, even if I had wanted to. She was generally incapable of approving drafts on the nod, as Blair must have done. For her style, substance and the framing of thoughts counted and were not to be skimped, whatever the reason. I once penned for her a *News of the World* column she had been invited to contribute. She said she liked it, but that did not stop her reordering, editing, polishing and honing it right up to the last minute, even as we flew across the Atlantic. Her speech-writing marathons were legendary. The conclusion must be either that journalism was Blair's early way of governing or, more likely, that what mattered to him was not quality but activity for activity's sake in his quest for a second term. It seemed that he would sign almost anything rather than be away from public view. The public's impression of his dynamism mattered more to him than his substance. For this he was soon *en route* to a reputation for superficiality.

Mercifully, the longer the Government was in office the less we had Government journalism inflicted upon us. It was a different tale with initiatives. They continue to pour from the Government. Oliver Letwin, the Shadow Home Affairs spokesman, told the

Tory Party spring conference in Harrogate in 2002 that David Blunkett had produced twenty-nine 'police initiatives' in the ten months since he became Home Secretary, not to mention 'forty-one crime fighting units . . . 376 crime and disorder reduction partnerships, a crime targets task force and an active community unit'.

After three years, as Alastair Campbell retreated from daily briefing of the Lobby into a more 'strategic' role, *The Times* was moved to criticize several other features of the Government's dynamism. It said:

> The constant repackaging of previously proclaimed proposals, double counting of numbers to produce the most favourable interpretation of spending plans and fiscal tricks such as the different manner in which inflation rates for pensions and petrol prices are produced have become a source of irritation. If the last Conservative administration was perceived as 'sleazy', the present Cabinet is courting the impression that it is too 'sharp' for comfort.

The Times, like the rest of the media, had only itself to blame. The press had allowed the Government to get away with it for three years, in sharp contrast to their vigilance while I was in No. 10. The first question asked of me about any initiative was, 'Is it new money?' Journalists quite reasonably wanted to know whether the finance set aside for any particular initiative came under previously announced public spending plans or was in addition to them. Presumably Blair and his ministers overwhelmed them by their flood of purposive press notices. They certainly accepted at the time – though months later they finally woke up to it – the treble, not just double, counting in Gordon Brown's budget arithmetic. After his boost for spending following the Government's initial restraint, I managed with the help of an MP through the Commons' Library, to square the circle of the prudent Chancellor's largesse on, for example, education. He proposed boosts in successive years of £3 billion, £3 billion and £4 billion. To those of us educated in simple arithmetic, that adds up to £10 billion over three years, subject to adjustment for inflation. Treasury maths converted this effortlessly into £19 billion by the simple process of

£3 billion in the first year, £6 billion in the second (the first year's £3 billion plus the second's £3 billion), and £10 billion in the third year (£3 billion plus £3 billion, plus £4 billion); 3 + 6 + 10 = 19. It was not until after I had solved the riddle of the Chancellor's prudent largesse that I found Peter Riddell, of *The Times*, referring in his column, without much explanation, to his double and treble counting. Playing games with figures is classic spin-doctoring: communication without ethics.

As ministerial articles followed one after another and initiatives were endlessly recycled, so the Government machine-gunned public services with targets. After three years the Liberal Democrats announced a remarkable discovery. They had counted 8,636 new goals set by Blair's government since coming to power. Their MP Malcolm Bruce painted a picture of public sector workers 'drowning in a tide of Government goals'. *The Mirror*, the Government's fairly reliable friend, listed the totals department by department: Education and Employment 4,585; Culture, Media and Sport 1,117; Home Office 614; Treasury 460; Environment, Transport and the Regions 429; Agriculture, Fisheries and Food 285; Defence 277; Cabinet Office 227; Trade and Industry 190; Lord Chancellor 124; Health 99; Social Security 95; International Development 48; Foreign and Commonwealth Office 41; and others 45.

The newspaper had immense fun with the detail. It said that the Culture department's targets outnumbered its staff 4:1. A community health trust boss said he found his targets out by accident. The Ministry of Agriculture, Fisheries and Food (MAFF) had to maintain the percentage of people saying they 'eat as much meat as ever'. Environment required the Countryside Commission to 'influence 17% of "activity" on public rights of way'. And the DTI set the Atomic Energy Authority to 'increase favourable media coverage by 43.9 to 50%'. Of course, these targets were not announced, but they were always liable to surface because of their ridiculous nature. When they did, they gave a new twist to the Government's reputation for frenzied activity and freakish desire to control. And since this was a Government to whom presentation was everything, they contributed substantially to the impression that there was precious little common sense at the centre.

The judgement deficiency was further highlighted by Blair's chronic inability to underplay anything. He is not only the first media Prime Minister – though Harold Wilson was perhaps a prototype – but also the first Prime Minister chronically and dangerously addicted to continuous hype. John Rentoul, in his biography of Blair, summarizes Blair's early extravagant language:

> Rhetorically, the scale of his ambition was unlimited: to remoralize British society; to refound the welfare state; to create a coalition of political forces which would dominate the whole of the 21st century; to secure peace in Northern Ireland; to provide leadership for the whole of the European Union; to make Britain 'a beacon to the world', and even to eliminate world poverty.

Blair went on to pledge an end to child poverty in twenty years, felt the hand of history upon him in Northern Ireland, and in 1998 proclaimed the Millennium Dome to be 'Britain's opportunity to greet the world with a celebration that is so bold, so beautiful, so inspiring that it embodies at once the spirit of confidence and adventure in Britain and the spirit of future in the world'.

It is one thing to talk up a nation; it is entirely another to promise it the earth in the most extravagant terms. The people began to get the impression that Mr Blair would say anything if it served the purpose of the moment. Paradoxically, the great control freak found it difficult to control himself or perhaps to be controlled by his own spin doctors, who cannot, if they pretend to any judgement, have failed to warn him of the inevitable consequences of unbridled euphoria. After all, Campbell said on polling day, 7 June 2001: 'Campaigns are won throughout the Parliament, not just the final weeks of the election campaign.'

After four years of him the people – or those who bothered to vote – gave Blair another chance because there was no alternative but, as he recognized, they expected him to start delivering. On the morning of his return to office, *The Mirror* featured pictures of Blair, Gordon Brown, Prescott and Cook, saying, 'What the hell are you lot looking so smug about? Get back to work'. Instead, the Government carried on promising and failing to deliver. Within a month Blair was pledging to match EU spending on the NHS within four years, though he withdrew the promise six months later, just before a Treasury official said they hadn't a clue what the EU level was. Stephen Timms, junior Education Minister, confidently saw a shortage of 8,000 teachers being met within a month, only to have to admit failure.

By the autumn of 2001 various ministers were admitting that things were worse in at least parts of the NHS and on the railways than when Labour took office. And a *Guardian* poll found the proportion of people trusting politicians had sunk to an all-time low of 16%. That is where frenzied, hyperactive, obsessive spin-doctoring, lacking the measured judgement Civil Service press secretaries were brought up to provide, gets you.

24

The new thuggishness

NOTHING REPRESENTS greater misjudgement in the Blair government's presentational policy than its approach to journalists. It is easy to see why in opposition Mandelson and Campbell adopted what might be described as their terrorist regime. They analysed journalists' paranoias and played upon them. It is less easy to understand why they persevered with that regime into government, when common sense (and harsh experience) teaches that the media worm always eventually turns on a government and consumes even the hand that feeds it. What, they should have asked themselves, will it do if we routinely abuse it? After five years they are beginning to find out.

Journalists lead a wretchedly frenetic existence. They often spend long hours of waiting and boredom punctuated by periods of manic activity to catch editions. The periods of super-activity, synthesizing ingenuity, flair, imagination and formulaic writing, are driven by taskmasters called news editors who are in fierce competition to produce the most commercial product. They demand stories and more stories, stories that no one else has got so that they can claim to have beaten the opposition and thereby theoretically increase their commercial attraction, though 'exclusive' has become an extremely elastic term. Journalism is thus a craft or trade that runs on nervous tension of a very high octane.

Mandelson and Campbell did not have to work this out. It is obvious to all who inhabit the ephemeral world of the media. To some extent both, but more especially Campbell, had lived it. They were, no doubt, shrewd judges of individual organs and the susceptibilities of journalists working for them. As their pursuit of Rupert Murdoch to the ends of the earth – or, at least, Australia – showed, they knew who they wanted on their side. And they had a pretty good idea how to keep them there, at least for a time: by showering journalistic favours – stories – upon them, to the disadvantage of their competitors. The result has been the most distorted period of news dissemination by Government this country has known.

Of course, favouritism is not new any more than Treasury leaks of supposedly the most sensitive issue of the year – the Chancellor's budget – are novel. Ministers and even officials had their manifest favourites throughout my time as a press secretary, and the results were often plain to behold in a particular day's press. I marvelled at the accuracy of the budget prognostications of some Treasury favourites the weekend before or on the morning of its delivery while, of course, the Treasury tried to keep me in the dark, saying it was all far too market-sensitive. As a general rule, however, Government press secretaries did not indulge in favouritism – a fact that emphasizes the Mandelson/Campbell regime's lack of use for them.

Favouritism can take several forms. The most familiar is now seen virtually every day in our newspapers: the selective 'trailing' in a particular newspaper or group of newspapers of a policy development or initiative immediately before its formal announcement. This has been practised from the very beginning of the Blair government. It plays on the journalist's desperate need for an exclusive story and, given that the account dished out is reasonably accurate, is calculated to keep that journalist and his newspaper coming back for more. It may, of course, differ subtly from the eventual substantive announcement and, as such, is a cynical abuse of power which reduces journalism to a client fourth estate.

Nicholas Jones, in *Soundbites and Spindoctors*, stops some way short of suggesting that I practised this. But he does claim that 'those reporters who were employed by newspapers sympathetic to the government had no wish to sour relations by challenging him [that is, me] needlessly. They knew they had every chance of speaking to him by phone after the organized briefing, when they might find it easier to obtain the information they wanted.' It comes as news to me that the late Gordon Greig, of the *Daily Mail*, for example, ever bothered his witty head about relationships in his baiting of the press secretary at afternoon lobbies. But then he knew that I was not going to hand an exclusive to the *Express* by way of reprisal. It is also a fact that I spoke personally whenever I was free to political editors and senior correspondents who rang me, whether or not their newspapers were sympathetic. I also sought to make sure that junior press officers knew the line I would take, though I acknowledge that the journalist prefers to get it from the press secretary rather than his subordinates.

Understandably, journalists are not keen to advertise their relations with No. 10 or any other informant. Peter Oborne, of *The Spectator*, in his biography of Blair's press secretary, is so far much the most forthright chronicler of Campbell's favouritism. He contrasts the fortunes, once Blair arrived in Downing Street, of George Jones, the political editor of the *Daily Telegraph*, and Philip Webster, his counterpart on Murdoch's *The Times*. Jones, he says, 'had been the favoured recipient of whispered confidences from [Tory] Cabinet ministers' for a decade. These then dried up and he found himself in the wilderness, 'starved of the oxygen of information', while Webster turned the political news pages of *The Times* into 'Fleet Street's closest equivalent to a notice board for the Government'. Stories started to fall into his lap. He even scooped the world with a leak of the new Poet Laureate, which rather annoyed Buckingham Palace. Close observers of major public appointments and the honours lists have noted that leaks of even these are employed in the Blair favouritism game. Witness the confident leaking of knighthoods for Mick Jagger and Bobby Robson well before publication of the Queen's Jubilee birthday honours list.

Why should No. 10 bother about the sensitivities of the Palace when it takes not a blind bit of notice of those of Parliament? Even Betty Boothroyd's successor as speaker, Michael Martin, widely regarded as a Government placeman, has continued complaining. Nothing changes. Nothing is allowed to get in the way of what is felt to be the Government's advantage.

Oborne also shows that favouritism was employed as part of the armoury for winning power, as well as for trying to hold on to it. He records Alan Rusbridger, editor of *The Guardian*, as saying that Campbell in opposition 'used to ring up to cajole, plead, shout and horse-trade. Stories would be offered on condition that they went on the front page. I would be told that if I didn't agree they would go to *The Independent*. They would withdraw favours, grant favours, exclude us from stories going elsewhere.' To Rusbridger's credit, *The Guardian* has remained a potential irritant of the Blair government, regardless of its disposition towards it.

Another variant of favouritism is the withholding of a government's favours from a newspaper or a broadcast programme. It is claimed that programmes that irked Thatcher suddenly found that no senior minister would go on them to be interviewed. It comes as a surprise to discover that No. 10 in the 1980s was able to exercise such iron control. It is true that I had the devil of a job to persuade Thatcher to give interviews to some journalists, such as Hugo Young, of *The Guardian*, though I did once manage it. What is more, Young rose to the occasion magnificently with such a powerful account in 1986 of her opposition both to sanctions against apartheid and to apartheid itself that editors of more supportive national dailies rang me up wishing they had been able to run his article. In other words, Thatcherite pogroms and discipline have grown with the years and the legend.

One ban did, however, operate. Late in the 1980s, near the end of the Thatcher era, the late Brian Redhead, my former *Guardian* colleague and one of the presenters of BBC Radio 4's *Today* programme, called me a 'conspiracy'. He refused to apologize, so he was given to understand that he would never get another interview with Thatcher. And he didn't. I would, however, have been happy to consign Thatcher to John Humphrys's tender, loving care, if I could have been sure that the programme would not have slipped in Redhead as interviewer. Humphrys is tough, persistent and probably interrupts too much, but he is fair and straight. He has been up in arms about Blair's sustained determination to give his interrogations a miss.

Oborne claims that any programme that questioned the glowing public image of Blair and his Shadow Cabinet found itself ostracized long before they won the 1997 election. This is presumably why he says my 'influence over the young Campbell can hardly be overstated'. I suggest it might be more accurate to say that what can hardly be overstated is the influence of Campbell's (and Labour's) grossly exaggerated – and self-servingly exaggerated – impression of my operations. They have never hesitated to employ it in their defence.

Part of that legend is my abrasive relations with journalists. Yet when I retired I told the BBC – and I have since reminded Lord Birt of this – that I forecast that the Thatcher years would go down as among the most halcyon in the history of Government and broadcasters. And if they were halcyon for broadcasters, they can be taken to have been idyllic for print journalists, since most of the political pressure on Thatcher to complain was exerted by MPs, usually with a somewhat coloured view of the script, over broadcast bulletins or programmes rather than newspaper articles. Nicholas Jones, in his chronicles of 'spin', would not entirely agree but fails to identify the reasons why I blasted journalists when I did. There were two: when journalists had got their facts wrong or had built a theory on the mangling of those facts; or when they had not played fair or in the spirit of agreed arrangements. Not so Campbell, if Oborne is to believed. If even the running order – that is, where a story appears in the bulletin, never mind its content – is not to his satisfaction, he will take action in a Kremlinesque way. 'Some BBC producer will receive a sharply worded call of protest from a Downing Street or Labour Party aide. Normally, that is sufficient to correct the direction of the bulletins. If it is not, and the matter is important, Campbell will take it up at a much higher level.' So much for our free, independent media.

James Margach, in his book *The Abuse of Power*, recounts how Prime Ministers from Lloyd George to Jim Callaghan (with whom his chronicle ended) have sought to 'crush' critical reporters and even newspapers. Thatcher impulsively and momentarily banned some newspapers from her household until I suggested that I at least had better read them to find out what they were up to. But I can recall only one occasion when it was felt I had not played fair with a Lobby correspondent. That was when I revealed in open

Lobby that I thought George Jones, Nicholas's brother, had asked 'a silly question'. The Lobby elders got very stroppy about that. What a different world of old-fashioned courtesy the 1980s were! On the other hand, I remember several occasions when I rejected attempts by editors to get me to tell them frankly what I thought about their political staffs. I was not playing that game.

Oborne gives the impression that, under Blair, journalist-bashing is rather routine, albeit not by the Prime Minister himself. He claims that New Labour spin doctors have 'never hesitated to destabilize journalists by going behind their backs to bosses'. Not so Mandelson and Gordon Brown. Such is their sensitivity that they seem to have been very catholic in their destabilization *en route* to government. Mandelson once wrote to Rupert Murdoch to try to get him to sack Trevor Kavanagh, political editor of the *Sun*, once described by the former Tory Chancellor Kenneth Clarke as 'the most influential man in British politics'. It is also claimed that both Kavanagh and his deputy, George Pascoe-Watson, survived a Brownite camp move against them. When Kavanagh told me of Mandelson's effort, he claimed that on this sector of the media subversion front Campbell 'plays it straight, so far as I can see'. Oborne, however, says that just before Labour came to office, Campbell rang David Montgomery, at that time boss of *The Independent*, to try to oust Andrew Marr, at that time the newspaper's editor and a valued ally of Labour and now the BBC's political editor, for daring to criticize Labour's European policy. Campbell is also reported to have told Ewen MacAskill, a *Guardian* political correspondent, in 1998 that 'if you carry on in this vein, we are going to tell our people not to buy you'.

The evidence from this and from private discussions I have had with journalists is that between them Mandelson and Campbell brought a new thuggishness to relations with journalists. Technology only facilitated this development. When journalists wrote their stories on paper, they composed in private. It is true that they then had to telephone them to their offices and might be overheard doing so unless they took precautions. The advent of computer screens opened up the process, and Lobby journalists have told me that Campbell and others have had no compunction in reading, commenting on and effectively marking their handiwork. In fact, Chris Moncrieff, of the Press Association, said he rewrote on principle if his story passed muster with them.

The new thuggishness, or extremism, even stretches in the interests of political advantage, or perceived advantage, to favouring helpful journalists to an individual reporter's exclusive. One of the cardinal principles of the GIS in which I worked was that a journalist's exclusive must remain secure with you as a Government press officer. If the journalist came to you to check facts about his exclusive story, then, no matter how sensational, that exclusive must remain his property. You would be grateful for the tip-off and beaver away at preparing a briefing against its publication. But on no account would you wreck that individual's exclusive by making it available to journalists who you might think would deal with it more sympathetically. That meant you were very careful about who you let into news that you had gathered of an impending scoop, and about when to tell them.

Joe Murphy, then political editor of the *Mail on Sunday*, is on record as confirming this. 'It used to be the case', he says 'that when a journalist found something out it belonged to him or her. Now the party machines feel that any information about themselves is their own property and they can give it to friendly papers or do what they like with it.'

Two examples culled from the Blair regime illustrate how things have changed and why journalists might now be very reluctant to check information with Government press officers if, by doing so, they think it will be handed over to their competitors. Not surprisingly, one of them concerns Joe Murphy. He discovered in 1996 that Harriet Harman, like the Blairs later, had decided to send a son to a grammar school. By dint of some smart telephoning, he identified the school, in Orpington, which alerted the Labour Party. Campbell is credited with handing this scoop to the *Daily Mirror* and *The Independent*. Their efforts, such as they were, to reduce Labour Party outrage over this espousing of selective schools failed completely.

The Harman episode is eclipsed in its cynicism by Campbell's treatment in government of the *Daily Mirror* in the early summer of 1998. The paper's then political editor, Kevin Maguire, hit on the bright idea of President Clinton using its pages, while he was in London for the G8 summit of the world's leading economies, to address an appeal to the Northern Ireland electorate to vote in the impending poll for the Good Friday Agreement. Campbell backed the idea with the US embassy and Maguire was set to work to produce a draft, only to suffer the mortification of finding his handiwork, which he thought was being edited, being splashed by the *Sun*. When Maguire and his editor, Piers Morgan, went to war, Campbell's explanation was 'I did this for peace'. Morgan is reported to have replied, 'Sure, peace with Murdoch'.

As George Jones told me in 2001: 'Things are not the same as they were in your day.'

25

Results speak for themselves

IF ANYTHING marks the style of Tony Blair, it is his smiling, 'Call me Tony' informality. This is curious in a man who has done so much to model himself on Margaret Thatcher, who was and remains the epitome of serious formality. She had very little time for the supposed sartorial informality of G7 (now G8) summits of the world's leading economies or at the US President's mountain retreat at Camp David. She was open all hours for business and dressed for it.

Blair is the most casual Prime Minister we have had. It comes over as a studied casualness but it is remarkably sustained, even for the consummate actor that Blair has become in the hands of his Svengali, Campbell. It is the same programmed performance that initially caused him to hide away from trade union leaders when cameramen were about, and to strive for such common touches as practiced strap-hanging on the London Underground.

He also has a remarkable ability to rise to the occasion and reflect the nation's mood, as for example after the September 11 terrorist assault on the USA, in his tribute on the death of the Queen Mother and his response, I am sorry to say (since I did not recognize the Britain that then emerged), when Diana, Princess of Wales, was killed. He will never pull off a greater presentational coup than when, having scarcely found his way around No. 10, he and Gordon Brown put our inflationary destiny in the hands of an independent Bank of England. And he can be bold, almost to the point of recklessness, in foreign affairs: with his plunge, for example, into Kosovo and his immensely forthright backing for President Bush over the war against terrorism and initially over Iraq.

Yet his administration's handling over the last five years of the great issues and crises that buffet governments reveals nothing so much as its incompetence in matters of presentation. What has become plain to see is the Blair government's determination never to make a clean breast of things; only to manoeuvre, duck, weave, manipulate, mislead and spin partial tales until the whole issue is covered in cobwebs. Revealed in all their tawdry detail are the sheer cynicism of its approach to its great responsibilities, the squalid nature of its machinations – and a chronic lack of judgement. It cannot blame the GIS for all this because these crises were handled not by Government press officers but by its very own spin doctors. They have certainly been no better than the GIS at coping with the secretive tendencies of the bureaucracy, whether of party or Government.

Within six months of its coming to office the Government's reputation was seriously damaged by the Ecclestone affair. The bones of the story are that Blair and his family were entertained in July 1996 to a day out at Silverstone by the tycoon Bernie Ecclestone, who had made the sport big business. Blair seems to have impressed Ecclestone, a former donor to the Conservative Party, since he handed over £1 million to Labour after Gordon Brown had pledged in January 1997 not to raise income tax rates. If Labour held to its promise, Ecclestone, reputed to be earning some £50 million a year, would still be quids in. More than five years after the event, it was claimed that Blair's chief of staff, Jonathan Powell, actually solicited the donation.

In the May 1997 election Labour also pledged itself unequivocally to ban tobacco advertising and the Health Secretary, Frank Dobson, soon promised a draft bill to do that and to outlaw sponsorship by tobacco firms, though sports heavily dependent on sponsorship would be given time to wean themselves off it. The EU followed this up with its own proposals to legislate on the issue, and Ecclestone's team argued that Formula I would be forced to stage more races outside Europe, to Europe's loss. Having got nowhere with their representations to Dobson, his junior minister,

Tessa Jowell and the sports minister, Tony Banks, they sought a meeting with Blair in October. Blair, having been a recipient of Ecclestone's hospitality and knowing that he had given £1 million to his party and that his party were seeking a further donation from him, not only received Ecclestone and his team in No. 10 but afterwards asked Dobson to look at ways of protecting sport in general, and Formula I in particular. Within a month the story blew. Blair was left trying to defend himself against the allegation that Ecclestone's donation had secured a change of Government policy. His plight has to be seen against his pledge to clean up British politics.

The basic facts of the case suggested that Blair and his advisers were either very stupid or utterly arrogant in their recklessness. At that stage in their government, the most likely explanation is reckless arrogance. This tends to be confirmed by Campbell, who claims he wanted to come (relatively) clean at the outset. He failed to persuade Blair and his advisers, including the Lord Chancellor, Lord Irvine, to lay some of the unpleasant facts on the table. Instead, they embarked on a cover-up. After the party had told Ecclestone it could not accept his further donation, No. 10 stalled in the face of journalistic clamour while it sought the confidential advice of Sir Patrick (now Lord) Neill, then chairman of the Committee on Standards in Public Life. Their purpose was to ask whether they should accept his further donation, having just piously refused it, rather than whether they should return Ecclestone's original £1 million. At the same time they sought to imply that all this was done in an orderly fashion after their policy U-turn and before they came under public pressure. Neill understandably advised them to hand back the £1 million as well, to avoid the appearance of undue influence on policy.

He did not put it quite like that because he did not know what the donation was worth. Nor did the public. No. 10, the Chancellor and the Labour Party all tried to keep the amount under wraps until eventually after five days Ecclestone himself named the figure. Blair still managed, in a statement to the House, to withhold his party's interest in securing a second donation from Ecclestone until Neill's letter leaked out. After all this subterfuge, machination, dissembling and evasion, which prolonged the agony and underlined the impression of a government up to no good, Blair eventually had to fall back on what was billed in advance as an apology via an interview with John Humphrys on BBC's *On the Record* programme. It was an anaemic affair since he seemed to apologize not for what had been done but for how it had been handled. He told that bit of the nation which watches TV at Sunday lunchtime: 'I hope that people know me well enough and realize the type of person I am to realize that I would never do anything to harm the country or anything improper. I never have. I think most people who have dealt with me think I am a pretty straight sort of guy.'

Peter Mandelson's gloss on the entire affair becomes hilarious in the light of subsequent events. He said: 'The Government acted out of character. We acted against our principles – that honesty is the first principle of good communications; that quick communications are essential to good government; and that the purpose of communicating is not to stall or hide but to put into context and explain.'

Nearly five years later it began to seem the Blair government's inept handling of these events might be attributable more to stupidity than insouciant arrogance (though arrogant they certainly are). They had clearly learned nothing from the Ecclestone affair in their handling of the Mittal mess, otherwise known as 'Steelgate' and dismissed by Blair as 'Garbagegate'. In this case an Indian steel billionaire, Lakshmi Mittal, with a home in London, gave £125,000 to the Labour Party just before the 2001 election. Two months later Blair sent a favourable letter about Mittal's company to the president of Romania, where Mittal was trying to buy a huge steelworks, even though his company was registered in a Caribbean tax haven and employed only ninety people in the UK. It later seeped out, as things tend to do in these situations, that the Department of International Development, under Clare Short, had backed a cheap loan of £70 million from the European Bank of Reconstruction and Development to support the Romanian steelworks privatization. That again appeared to help Mittal's purchase.

Once again, Mr Blair was forced to defend his probity. In doing so, however, he seemed to forget that journalists are ferocious in their pursuit of a 'scandal' and intelligent enough not only to ask extremely awkward questions but also to ferret out the answers. After a week of turmoil the *Sunday Times* was left saying that the 'Government's spin machine was looking like a conman caught *in flagrante delicto*'. The Government had, after all, changed its story on Mittal several times: it had claimed that Mittal's donation came after the election, that the Romanian deal had been completed when Blair signed his letter, that Mittal's company was British, and that the letter Blair signed had not been changed to remove a reference to Mittal being his 'friend'.

The result in February 2001 was headlines such as 'Lies, damned lies and Labour spin' (*Sunday Times*) and 'When spin turns to lies – does Number 10 know the difference?' above a leader in *The Observer*. Andrew Rawnsley, author of 'the inside story of New Labour' was moved to write in *The Observer*:

> Does this latest imbroglio with a tycoon tell us that the Prime Minister is a pretty bent sort of guy? . . . Does Jonathan Powell, chief of staff, keep a tariff of charges in his bottom drawer? You know how it would go. One hundred and twenty five thousand buys a snow job for an Asian millionaire in the form of a helpful letter to a foreign government to win him a steel deal . . . For a million, Bernie Ecclestone receives a full-on change of policy which directly favours his business. When you look for the unvarnished truth, is that how it works?

Blair would deny it all. He is, after all, 'a pretty straight sort of guy'. But incidents such as the Ecclestone and Mittal affairs, or the story of Paul Drayson (chief executive of PowderJect Pharmaceuticals, who gave £50,000 to the Labour Party and won a £32 million Health Department order for smallpox vaccine), left Bill Morris, general secretary of the Transport and General Workers' Union, voicing his concern in April 2002. 'It seems to a lot of people', he said, 'that the party is more or less abandoning its roots and the party is almost up for sale to the highest bidder.' And two months earlier a *Sunday Times*–YouGov poll of 3,113 people had reported that Labour was regarded for the first time as significantly more sleazy than the Tories.

I cannot with confidence and honesty say that I would have handled these situations better, given the chronic secretiveness of the bureaucracy and the endlessly naïve or desperate hope that springs eternal in most politicians' breasts that the less the press are told the less will come out. As I have indicated, it is a fight within Government at the best of times – let alone *in extremis* during a scandal – to strangle a damaging story with all the facts at the outset. Yet it seems obvious that, the less that is explained and the more that is left hanging unanswered in the air to fuel media suspicions, the longer the scandal will run and the more damage will be done to the Government's reputation. In other words, spinning – which is what the Blair government does instinctively when it lands in a scrape – is counter-productive.

There is some evidence that Campbell may sense this, while none the less being obsessed with manipulation. His reaction to the discovery of Robin Cook's extra-marital affair and his initial handling of former Welsh Secretary Ron Davies's resignation suggest a desire for clean breaks. Indeed, his handling of the Davies business was almost textbook, aided by an unusually continent Metropolitan Police force. He was able to break the story on the Government's own terms, though trouble followed as journalists pursued the many questions about Davies's behaviour that were left untidily inviting investigation.

Campbell's strategic nous is another matter. A press secretary concerned to maintain the reputation of a Prime Minister whose Government won office by playing on Tory 'sleaze' and committing himself to 'clean up politics' has only one viable presentational policy. It is to present an open, candid face to Britain, to stamp on anything that compromises its integrity and to play it straight. But the results of New Labour's first five years speak for themselves: the people now wonder whether they can believe a word their government tells them. They think it is 'all spin'. Far from being geniuses, Labour's spin doctors have proved to be a disaster. Far from sustaining the Government in office, they have undermined it by their approach.

26

Spin doctors: the toll

IF ONE test of a government in this media-sodden age is the ability of its spin doctors to hold on to their jobs, Blair's is a mess. The arch-spinner Mandelson was forced to resign not once but twice from the Cabinet within a single Parliament, a record that is unlikely to be easily surpassed. Mandelson, above all, should have known how to handle his public relations and to control his amazingly young apprentice spinner, one Benjamin Wegg-Prosser. Charlie Whelan, Gordon Brown's incredible import from the trade union world, was drummed out of the Treasury because he was a loud-mouthed menace to collective responsibility. Campbell had to be kicked upstairs after three years because he, rather than Government policy, had become the story. He was grossly overexposed but remained director of communications over a widening field, eventually taking in the Central Office of Information, the in-house communications consultancy and campaigns management centre. I never had control of the COI. And Jo Moore eventually paid the price in the Department of Transport for exhibiting, even by the Blair government's amazing standards, an exceptionally crude and unfeeling cynicism in her approach to presentation. The Government becomes an even bigger disaster area when the details of their spin doctors' departures are examined, revealing the extent of the menace inherent in the special adviser phenomenon and the Government's debilitating deficiency of judgement.

Mandelson's failure is the most extraordinary of all. He had the intelligence to recognize that Old Labour was unelectable and the political acumen to guide its conversion into a potential government. He had the sense to see that its conversion would not be enough without a determined effort to 'sell' its transformation to the public. He then exhibited the energy and will to convert what Harold Wilson described as Labour's 'penny farthing' apparatus into what the Conservatives recognized as a Rolls-Royce of a campaign machine. He was undoubtedly one of the major architects of Labour's return to power in 1997. And yet by the next election he was languishing on the back benches and reduced to making a defiant and embittered 'I'm not a quitter' speech on his re-election as MP for the Hartlepools. He scarcely had time to demonstrate his ministerial potential, but I suspect he can be ranked as one of the great wastes of political talent that litter the post-war years if not, for want of proof in office and Parliament, of the stature of, for example, Enoch Powell, Tony Benn and Michael Heseltine.

The reason for Mandelson's failure to blossom can lie only in his personality. Having discounted luck, it is not usually necessary to look much further for a clue to a political career. Personality counts for much in politics, whatever Tony Benn may have told me when I was his press secretary. 'It's issues which count', he drummed into me, pronouncing issues as 'ishoos'. Well, policies – as I would have put it – certainly matter a very great deal. Gritty, worked-out policies, as distinct from mere promises and rhetoric, are crucial, if not to a government's success – that depends on their results – but to its credibility. But without the ministerial personality to drive those policies through, and to keep his or her feet on the ground while doing so, little is likely to be achieved. As an apparatchik, Mandelson seemed to be heavily endowed with the right combination of intelligence, charisma with purpose, determination, energy and a will to succeed. But his biographers testify to his instability as an individual. He is highly sensitive and petulant. His tiffs with Blair remind me of what Harold Wilson had to put up with from Marcia Williams (now Lady Falkender). He is clearly devious, horribly self-centred (as many politicians are) and does not inspire trust. Too many journalists have come to discover his capacity for nastiness and slaver for the chance of getting their own back. He is – or was – a socialite who lives too much of his life on the edge, and who chanced too much in his relations with the rich and in his quest for a good address. So when he fell from grace people revelled in putting the boot into him.

With Mandelson as the chief designer of Labour's new approach to presentation, it comes as no surprise that the spin-doctoring machine he devised reflects the reputation of the man. While it can have its brilliant moments, it is obsessive, hyperactive, manipulative, sharp, more concerned with creating impressions than with exuding integrity, aggressive and unreliable. It is the very antithesis of the GIS approach, which is to preserve long-term integrity, if necessary at the expense of short-term advantage. No wonder the GIS and Mandelson's machine didn't mix.

His two downfalls show worrying evidence of the spirit that all too often seems to have driven wider Government presentation – namely, an utter brass neck. His first resignation is a classic example. It was over a £373,000 loan some six months before the 1997 election from Geoffrey Robinson to help Mandelson buy a £475,000 house in Notting Hill, west London. Mandelson had kept his loan secret from Blair and from the Department of Trade and Industry, where he became Secretary of State in July 1998.

He had done so in spite of at least five factors that should have counselled frankness. First, he had been ruthless at Labour Party headquarters in eliminating would-be Parliamentary candidates whose political, business or personal life might damage the party. He should have practised what he preached. Second, Labour had ruthlessly exploited 'Tory sleaze' in opposition. Those who aspire to live in glass houses should not throw stones. Third, the Ministerial Code, previously called Questions of Procedure for Ministers, says 'no minister or public servant should accept gifts, hospitality or services from anyone which would, or might appear to, place him or her under an obligation'. It also enunciates the general principle that 'Ministers must ensure that no conflict arises, or appears to arise, between their public duties and their private interests, financial or otherwise.' In other words, they must not only be clean but also be seen to be so. Fourth, Mandelson's department was conducting an inquiry into Robinson's business interests and his past links with the former proprietor of the

Mirror Group of newspapers, the late Robert Maxwell. And finally, there is the simple matter of common sense, which teaches that when the vultures are massing in the hope of picking your bones, you should not give them an opening.

The opening was a relatively long time coming. Gossip columns had been commenting for some time on Mandelson, the man of property, on a £43,000 Parliamentary salary. Mandelson had not exactly discouraged media interest in himself as an elegant man about town with a good address. The magazine *Punch* had concluded in February 1998 that 'a pal who did not like to see him slumming it' had been generous to him, since his mortgage was only £150,000. The dam eventually broke just before Christmas 1998 amid a welter of competitive journalism. Reporters had expected the political commentator Paul Routledge, a close friend of Charlie Whelan, who had had a long-standing feud with Mandelson, to throw some light on the source of his wealth in his biography of Mandelson, publication of which was imminent. But it became known on 21 December that *The Guardian*, apparently independently, was about to publish the results of an investigation and the story immediately had lift-off.

The Government machine was able immediately to show that Mandelson had ensured that both he and his ministerial colleagues at the DTI were isolated from the Robinson inquiry. Against that background Mandelson toured the studios as the story poured out, trying to make what he described as 'a clean breast of it' and to persuade the world there had been no conflict of interest or infringement of the ministerial code. He is not without courage or determination in defending difficult cases. His line was a mixture of contrition and cheek, which has become the trademark of Labour operations. Yes, with hindsight, he said, it would have been better if all the facts had been out. But no, there was no infringement of the ministerial code and no conflict of interest and therefore the question of resignation did not arise.

But as the media pursued the loose ends, Mandelson seemed remarkably vague about whether he had declared Robinson's loan in his application for a £150,000 mortgage to Britannia Building Society – applicants were supposed to say whether they intended to borrow any more money to buy a property – or declared the loan in the register of MPs' interests. He eventually released a letter showing he had sought the advice of the Parliamentary Commissioner for Standards, saying he did not think it needed to be registered because it was not a gift or gained through his being an MP. It was all to no avail. He resigned within two days, saying on the one hand he did not believe 'I have done anything wrong or improper' but on the other that he should not have entered into the arrangement and that, having done so, he should have told Blair and other colleagues. He failed the acid test of a communicator: the test of credibility. The *Daily Telegraph* commented: 'It is a measure of the mix of ambition, greed, talent, flamboyance, charm, vanity, social climbing, insecurity, shallowness risk-taking, corner-cutting and sheer comic lack of self-awareness that make up Peter Mandelson that only he could take seriously the version of events he described.' That mix helps to explain the shallowness of Labour's spin doctors.

It does not say much for Blair's depth that he brought Mandelson back into Cabinet as Northern Ireland Secretary after little more than six months and was ditching him again after another two years, with Mandelson again protesting his innocence of any wrongdoing. It says even less for Mandelson's presentational abilities that he is reported to have claimed that he fell again because there was no 'line to take' – in other words, no briefing line to stick to. Yet there is evidence from the astonishing amount that has already been written about the Blair government that he was very twitchy about the second issue which drummed him out of government, possibly for good. Why on earth, if he felt so threatened, was he not more careful with the line he took?

This second resignation turned on the activities of the three rich Hindujah brothers from India. They were well known to many Labour politicians, including Blair, underwrote the Faith Zone in the beleaguered Millennium Dome project and found the Blair government far more accommodating about awarding them passports than John Major's had been. Essentially, when the press forced the issue about representations on the Hindujahs' passport applications, Mandelson sought to soothe. In a statement that he offered to Campbell, he said that, to the limited extent that he was involved, he had always been very sensitive to the proprieties, that the matter had been dealt with by his private secretary and that he did not support or endorse this application for citizenship. But the Home Office 'line to take' said he had made verbal inquiries of Mike O'Brien, the responsible Home Office minister. Had he done so or not? It seems in the end that Mandelson went, claiming he was a victim of the media, essentially because No. 10 had had enough of his unreliability in the run-up to the 2001 election. Blair was desperate to win. Mandelson was a risk they could carry no more.

Mandelson's first resignation was very quickly followed by two others – those of Geoffrey Robinson, the Postmaster-General, and of Charlie Whelan. Whelan's resignation is more than a footnote in the annals of the age of the spin doctor. He is, in fact, the phenomenon writ large, noisily, uninhibitedly and disastrously across it. This is not to say that Whelan is not articulate, cunning, profane, aggressive, and cheeky with it. I can only imagine – and shudder at the thought of – what he did to the cloistered calm of the Treasury fifty years after Sir Stafford Cripps shook it up with his drive to explain. Few would also suspect that he is the son of a Civil Servant, the product of a minor public school and a former Communist. He learned his spin-doctoring with the Amalgamated Engineering and Electrical Union and had been with Gordon Brown for five years when the parting came early in 1999.

If Christmas had been miserable for Mandelson, the New Year was menacing for Whelan. He was widely credited with having been the source of the information about Mandelson's loan, although he and Routledge denied it. But Whelan had done enough in his short Treasury career to have earned a reputation for causing trouble. He brought all of New Labour's crude determination to browbeat into capitulation journalists who do not do as they say. He is even recorded as unplugging a BBC camera and standing before it to prevent the media asking awkward questions of Gordon Brown. He saw his job as controlling the news agenda and output on behalf of his boss, from whom he and Ed Balls, the Chancellor's special adviser, were almost inseparable. In fact, some journalists came to see the Brown/Balls/Whelan team as economic management by other means: spin. But more importantly, he represented the most dangerous feature of Labour's spin doctors – their commitment to the one minister to whom they owe their jobs, to the exclusion of concern for the welfare of their Government. These Praetorian guards, with their narrow fixation on the interests of their minister, have undoubtedly been a menace since 1997. And while Mandelson and Campbell recognized their dangers and tried to enlist departmental press secretaries' help in curbing their activities, the GIS were not going to play that game on behalf of No. 10. Departmental press secretaries, to repeat, owe their first loyalty to their minister.

All Governments are an explosive mixture of personal ministerial rivalries, and few smouldering relationships have been as extensively documented as that between Blair and Brown. Whelan not only stoked the embers; he applied the bellows. As a commentator in *PR Week*, in the run-up to the 2002 budget, he wrote:

> No. 10 always try to sabotage the day, either by forcing the Chancellor to change his plans or by leaking details to undermine the Treasury. Gordon Brown is far too canny to be blown off course by Tony Blair and his henchmen. Brown simply refuses to give details of the budget to anyone next door and the conversations he has with Blair are usually private . . . It [the budget] gives him the chance to spell out the policies he believes in and also the chance to differentiate himself from the blandness of Blair.

And so, he said, 'The Chancellor and his team will spend the next few weeks moulding people's expectations with nods, winks and even a few leaks – some true and some not. This is probably the most important task the Treasury spinners have.' Whelan is remarkably frank about how he went about his job in the Treasury and makes it absolutely clear he was not a governmental team player; he played for Brown.

But Whelan also played for himself and counter-productively became a TV star. He foolishly backed an ITV fly-on-the-wall two-part series on Brown's transfer from opposition to government. In the first part, after being seen threatening a reporter and being accused of telling journalists half-truths, he said: 'You just have to be economical with the truth . . . you should never lie, but it's very difficult.' The second part not only demonstrated the tensions between the Brown team and the Treasury but also Brown's obsession with media. Within five months of arriving in the Treasury Whelan was the story. His name was up in lights only ten days after the broadcast of the second TV programme. The *Financial Times* in September 1997 authoritatively forecast that Britain would join the single European currency soon after the 1999 start date and well before the next general election. Then on Friday 16 October 1997 Brown gave an exclusive interview to the helpful *Times* (about which the *Sun*, another Murdoch newspaper, was briefed), saying 'it is highly unlikely that Britain can join in the first wave'. He did not actually rule it out, but both newspapers carried the Brown message: he was ruling out joining the single currency for that Parliament.

To make matters worse, Whelan then excelled his extrovert self outside the Red Lion pub in Whitehall. In tipping off selected journalists about the *Times* exclusive he briefed them on his mobile phone in the crowded precincts of the pub, shouting, according to someone standing next to him at one stage: 'Yes, Gordon is ruling out British membership of the single currency for the whole of this Parliament. No, it doesn't say that in the interview but Gordon is effectively ruling out joining in this parliament.' The person next to him, overhearing his phone conversation, was – not surprisingly given the location at the heart of political Westminster – a young Liberal Democrat press officer. He and a colleague promptly made political hay by getting their Treasury spokesman, Malcolm Bruce, on BBC's *Newsnight* programme even before the story had appeared in print.

The Government had been caught spinning red-handed. And, as so often before and since, it kept on spinning. No. 10 tried to claim credit when Blair zapped Brown's attempt to rule out entry. There followed a frenzied period of bewilderment as to what the Government's policy was, media recrimination over having been used and misled, and political demands for Parliament to be recalled since this was an issue vital to Britain's future. Worse still, the story had implications for the stock market. As luck would have it, Brown had to switch on a new electronic trading system in the City the following Monday. And as he did so, the massive screen behind him went red, showing billions of pounds being wiped off share values. Two days later Blair was booed, jeered and catcalled when he visited the London International Financial Futures and Options Exchange, although Campbell claimed he had a 'warm and friendly' reception. Such are the wages of spin.

Apologists for the Brown regime will say that all this is reminiscent of the effect I had on sterling with my remark that the Government 'would not throw good money after bad defending the pound'. But my remark was made openly in a formal Lobby briefing and turned out to be dead accurate. The Treasury subsequently raised interest rates decisively to head off the slide. It turns out that Whelan was dead accurate, too: the Government still blows hot and cold over joining the euro.

But the issue was not his accuracy. His performance was seen as evidence of the indiscreet cross the Government would have to bear if he continued in office. It bore that cross for just over eighteen months, in spite of attempts by No. 10 to persuade Brown to drop him. For once, Whelan was as silent as the grave when the media eventually turned their attentions to him after the demise of Mandelson and Robinson. At the end of 1998 he retired for the Christmas festivities to the Scottish Highlands and then, on his return on 4 January 1999, he told Campbell that he intended to resign 'as soon as an appropriate opportunity becomes available'. In a statement, repeating his denial that he had leaked information about Mandelson's loan, he said: 'I do, however, take the view that the job of press secretary becomes extremely difficult if the spokesman, not the department he serves, becomes the story and the subject of excessive attention.' It had taken a long time for this penny to drop. But he was not the only slow learner.

27

11 September: the nadir

WITH MANDELSON and Whelan gone – or, perhaps more accurately, out of office – Alastair Campbell has for several years been the sole survivor of New Labour's leading extremist communicators. As Blair's director of communications (as he eventually became), he was monarch of almost all he surveyed, presiding over all aspects of the Government's communications, the various units established in No. 10 for planning, propagating and monitoring the Government's messages and rebutting those of opponents, and unprecedentedly the Central Office of Information. He also shunted the Chief Whip out of that lovely house No. 12 Downing Street to claim it as his own. As I remarked at the time, this proved my first theory of politics: that the worse you do your job the bigger the office you acquire.

Mandelson may properly be credited, if that is the right word, with inventing the new 'terrorist' approach to media relations, but Campbell is its operator. He is a sort of Stalin to Mandelson's Lenin. He is not, however, professional head of the GICS, as it was renamed under him. That post is held by a Civil Servant sitting in Cabinet Office: Mike Granatt, a very experienced departmental head of information who also presides over the Government's Civil Contingencies Unit for coping with emergencies. Nor is Campbell any more, if he ever was, the Chief Press Secretary in No. 10. He was replaced after little more than three years, ironically by not one but two Civil Servants: Godric Smith, a protégé of Romola Christopherson at the Department of Health, and Tom Kelly, one of the shoal of former BBC staff recruited by Blair, in his case in Northern Ireland.

Of course, nobody imagines for one moment that Campbell, having withdrawn from regularly briefing the press and more accurately described as Blair's political commissar than chief press secretary, is not still pulling the strings. The twice-daily jousts between No. 10 and the Parliamentary Lobby journalists may be more civilized for his absence, but nothing fundamentally has changed, even though No. 10 tried to kid the nation soon after the 2001 election that spin was a thing of the past. The Government is still all smoke and mirrors, and will probably continue to be so until it is ignominiously dumped by an ungrateful electorate for its manifold pretensions and is released from its media dementia.

If the elusive 'Third Way' is anything, it is government by media manipulation. As such, it is unsustainable. The Blair government may bribe the media (by favouritism over exclusives and access), second-guess them, bully them, cajole them, trade with them and give them the cold shoulder, but it does not ultimately own or control them.

And yet the Blair strategy of government by media proceeds as if propelled by some extraterrestrial force, incapable of taking in the consequences of its earthly actions and of adjusting its performance in the light of experience. If the Bourbons have never before run Britain, they do now. As the boss, Blair is ultimately responsible for this almost unbelievable shallowness, but all too often Campbell seems the ventriloquist to Blair's dummy.

In his short life as the Prime Minister's chief press secretary, Campbell presided over an unprecedented cull of senior Civil Service information specialists. He created a hyperactive news machine, placing stories where they would be treated most sympathetically and challenging the media's judgement whenever it did not serve the Government's purpose, even down to the story's angle and running order. Initiatives became two a penny and were recycled endlessly; every expectation was encouraged; none left undoused. Campbell regularly appeared arguing the toss in newspaper correspondence columns. He was too often for his own good accused of misleading journalists, though some seemed to be lost in admiration at his ability 'to stitch them up'. Others confessed their concern to keep on the right side of the man arguably closest to Blair. Not surprisingly, his abrasive methods were followed by the more ebullient of his fellow special advisers in departments. Command, control and threaten were their watchwords, as journalists testify to their performance at photocalls and on election battle buses.

Campbell arrived in No. 10 with a determination to tear up the old GIS rule book and rewrite it without regard to longer-term consequences. The wonder at his performance was exceeded only by that at the media's, which, with notable exceptions after the normal honeymoon period, indulged Blair's government in a way that amazed all who had handled press, radio and television in previous Labour and Conservative governments. As one BBC veteran put it to me, surveying the open-plan office floor of 4 Millbank, the centre for radio and TV coverage of politics close to the Palace of Westminster: 'This lot have either forgotten or never understood that their job is to make life difficult for Governments.'

Labour politicians even seem to be largely immune – give or take Robin Cook and Stephen Byers (after he had resigned) – to the kiss-and-tell stories that beset John Major's period in office, when the media systematically hunted to the wrong bed the most obscure Tory back-bencher. Just as Campbell was not even-handed, neither were the media. It was as if some editors and journalists wanted to be spun. Some clearly still do, though there are fewer of them since the 2001 election.

Things began to go sour on the eve of the new millennium, before the day dawned on the year in which the Labour Party was to celebrate its centenary. With almost classic Tsarist disdain for the plebs and public relations, ministers took the short route from Westminster via the Jubilee Line to the grossly expensive Millennium Dome while the rest, including, God save us, editors, were made to queue endlessly and chillingly at Stratford in east London. The Queen went by boat. The formal opening, for those of us who watched it on television, was a sickening experience, representing all that was and remains brittle, contrived, politically correct and insubstantial about New Labour. Accordingly, the Government entered the twenty-first century in the doghouse. It remained there as the Dome's dismal patronage and the scandal over its thirst for National Lottery cash and its mismanagement developed.

The Dome's insatiable appetite for public money coincided with a flu epidemic that focused public attention on overcrowded hospitals, cancelled operations and the movement of patients across the country in search of a bed and treatment. Even corpses were stored in refrigerated lorries. As medical luminaries piled in with their criticisms of the NHS, Blair took to Sir David Frost's Sunday morning sofa and pledged to match EU average health funding – a promise that became a mere aspiration within twenty-four hours after Gordon Brown had paraded his stern girlfriend Prudence before him. In April 2000, when he was under pressure on law and order, he wrote a 'Touchstone Issues' note to aides, later leaked, calling, among other things, for 'an initiative, e.g. locking up street muggers. Something tough, with immediate bite that sends a message through the system . . . I should personally be associated with as much of this as possible.' This surfaced when he slipped into a speech to nonplussed German academics the idea of on-the-spot fines for drunken louts, which chief constables promptly dismissed as 'unworkable'. Two years later we had almost a repeat performance. Put on the rack in the Commons over soaring street crime and violence, he promised it would be brought 'under control' within five months. Twenty-four hours on, his officials back-pedalled furiously, refusing to specify the meaning of the term or a target figure by which his pledge might be judged.

It seems that Blair, no doubt advised by Campbell, will say anything to get out of a tight corner and then have his words massaged and finessed into meaninglessness. He displays the spin doctor's preoccupation with the moment and an utter contempt for the public.

As Blair's *annus horribilis* – AD 2000 – proceeded, he had the mortification of seeing Ken Livingstone become Mayor of London. He was barracked by the massed ranks of the Women's Institute in conference. He spent Bank Holiday penning a riposte to the claims in the *Sun* that he was beginning to lose the next election, a hyper-sensitivity that rightly earned him the headline 'Rattled'. And Campbell withdrew from front-line relations with the Lobby. A reflective Blair announced, 'We don't need to fight over every headline' – as superb an example of spinning as could be imagined from the addict.

Superficially, this might have suggested that Blair and Campbell were waking up to reality. The *Times* had noted that in 1998 Campbell had been mentioned by name in 2,241 stories – a higher figure than that achieved by nine members of the Cabinet. Yet no sooner had he entered his retreat two years later than he was the star of Michael Cockerell's fly-on-the-wall spin-doctor programme on BBC 2. While preparing for the programme, Cockerell telephoned me. I said I was astounded Campbell was lending himself to a film about his job, let alone a fly-on-the wall film, to which Cockerell retorted that I had done the same thing myself. That, I said, was disingenuous. He knew very well that all I had agreed to, in consultation with the Lobby's officers, was a brief glimpse of my briefing the Lobby in my room in No. 10 for atmospherics.

As with all such programmes, we got no more from the artificiality that sets in immediately a camera intrudes than a hint of the frustrations, calculation, cynicism, manipulation and interdependence inherent in Government–media relations. But we did get an unflattering view of Blair in a supportive, walk-on role in Campbell's manipulative shadow and another reminder that Campbell learns nothing from experience. Once again the focus was not on the Government's message but on Campbell himself and the games he plays.

Blair recovered from the setbacks of 2000 to win the 2001 election with only a slightly reduced majority. He had achieved his objective on coming to office of winning a second full term. His government's extremist approach to communication seemed to have served its purpose. But what was novel in the Mandelson/Campbell lexicon of spin-doctoring during its first Parliamentary term became routine, in spite of No. 10's pronouncement of the death of spin. Blair even refused to disclose whether his youngest son, Leo, had had the controversial MMR inoculation against measles, mumps and rubella, as parents worried over the jab's effects on their children, on the pretext of protecting his family from media intrusion. Yet, as journalists pointed out, he had used his children for political purposes when he judged it to be to his advantage. Only New Labour fanatics were left to take the Government at face value; the rest scarcely believed a word it said. They had come to expect to be conned, to the serious detriment of politics and those who practise it.

Then came 11 September 2001 and Jo Moore's e-mail. Stephen Byers took Moore to the Department of Transport, Local Government and the Regions (DTLR) when he was made Secretary of State after the 2001 general election. She has been described as 'a doctrinal dominatrix'. According to Whelan, she is 'one of the unsung heroes of Labour's long battle to become electable' and 'one of the most effective, hard-working and loyal press officers I've ever met'. But within an hour of the hi-jacked airliners crashing into the twin towers of the World Trade Center in New York she had e-mailed colleagues in the DTLR, where she was a special adviser, saying: 'It's now a very good day to get out anything we want to bury. Councillors' expenses?' There is, of course, nothing new in the concept of slipping out unpopular or embarrassing news in the knowledge that it will be swamped by major events. Nor is there anything new in the appreciation of the risk run by those who fall for the temptation of being found out and pilloried. But what was new in Moore's e-mail was its tunnel-visioned callousness, its narrow-minded preoccupation with Government advantage. It is not the sort of advice I thought I was paid for as a Government press officer. We were supposed to protect the integrity of our ministers and departments by having close regard to the overall circumstances and the potential consequences of our actions.

Given the tensions later revealed in the department over Moore's aggressive approach to media management, it took an unconscionable time – a month – for her crassness to seep out. The new press secretary of three months' standing, Martin Sixsmith, had succeeded a man who had been moved after resisting Moore's attempts to recruit a junior press officer into a smear campaign against Bob Kiley, the London transport commissioner. When the news broke, complete with photocopies of her infamous e-mail, Blair and Moore's minister, Stephen Byers, came under pressure to sack her. Inconceivably, they did not do so, in spite of the clamour in the

Labour Party. Instead, they felt her 'error of judgement', for which she apologized, after a fashion, did not warrant her dismissal, even though Blair had shown no compunction in presiding over the destruction of the careers of the top echelon of the GIS for behaving properly. Even Whelan called for her dismissal in his *PR Week* column. He wrote:

> If we thought my continuing presence in the Treasury would damage Brown, that is nothing to the damage that Moore has caused to the Government. The longer she stays the worse it gets, yet for some reason . . . Blair has failed to sack her. Instead, we've had No. 10 inventing a row with the BBC and poor old Kate Adie [about the publication of Blair's travel plans] to try to divert attention from the story. Now we've had the biggest insult to our intelligence ever. Number 10 actually had the nerve to brief hacks that Blair has instructed all special advisers to stop spinning. He should tell his spin doctor to stop spinning and sack Jo Moore. That would at least undo a little of the damage her actions have caused.

Blair did not take Whelan's advice. Inevitably, Byers, her protector, became even more damaged and Moore a marked woman. Inevitably the Tories demanded, but never got, an investigation into all Government announcements since 11 September. Equally inevitably, the media went on the alert for the slightest whiff of 'burying bad news' and concluded, for example, that Byers had conveniently announced the decision to put Railtrack into administration on the day military strikes began against Afghanistan. But Moore seemed to have got away with an act of amazing stupidity for such an experienced operator. A month later, however, it was reported that she had ceased to be a spin doctor and reverted to being a special policy adviser.

And then on 14 February 2002 the *Daily Express* and the *Mirror* led with 'exclusive' reports that Moore had been at it again. This time she was accused of wanting to release figures about rail safety and punctuality on the day of Princess Margaret's funeral. Subsequent accounts suggested that this was indeed true. Sixsmith was reported to have slapped her down with an e-mail that read:

'There is no way I will allow this department to make any substantive announcements next Friday. Princess Margaret is being buried on that day. I will absolutely not allow anything else to be.'

In fact, Sixsmith sent an e-mail to Byers, copied to Moore, among others, and published by the *Sunday Times*, which read: 'You spoke about possibly making this announcement [about rail performance indicators] on Friday. We should *not* do it on Friday, as that is the day on which Princess Margaret is being buried. There are too many connotations to the word "buried" for us to do anything that day.'

No sooner had he set foot in the department than Sixsmith, a former BBC correspondent in Washington and Moscow and a Labour sympathizer, though committed to Civil Service impartiality, had found Moore trying to 'bury bad news' about Railtrack under the Chancellor's pre-budget statement. He had also apparently incurred the wrath of Byers and Moore for eventually securing, after a stand-off, the services of a Civil Servant as his deputy, appointed by an independent board, rather than a former woman colleague of Moore's at a public affairs consultancy. The leak of the spat over the proposed publication of recycled rail punctuality figures on the day of Princess Margaret's funeral immediately cast serious doubt over whether Moore could last another moment.

This time Byers agreed to Moore's resignation on condition that Sixsmith went, too. Although Sixsmith had done no wrong, Byers announced that he had accepted his resignation, which Sixsmith had not offered. This caused the permanent secretary at the department, Sir Richard Mottram, to fire off five short explosive and expletive-filled sentences when he realized just what a hole he and his department had been dumped into by New Labour's addiction to cynical spin. There was much more of it to come, as Sixsmith stood out for a statement clearing his name – which he did not get – and was warned by Mottram that if he continued being awkward the No. 10 machine would make his life very unpleasant. Mottram even made a personal statement in an attempt to try to put the lid on the crisis, an unprecedented event in the memory of Lord Armstrong of Ilminster, former secretary to the Cabinet. After a week Sixsmith was reported as saying he had done his best to help the Government resolve the issue, but had been left 'stupefied by their attempts to exculpate themselves and put the blame on others'.

Sixsmith's plight shows what can happen under a Blair government if you inconveniently make a stand for sanity. It demonstrates how members of the GICS can be vulnerable if they get in the way of a minister and his special adviser or spin doctor. It is a chilling insight into how politicization of the Civil Service can occur. It may be dismissed by the likes of such apologists as Peter Riddell in *The Times* as exceptional. But what cannot be dismissed is the nasty nature of the Blair government in its preoccupation with perception at the expense of truth.

28

The domino theory

NEW LABOUR'S fifth anniversary was a disaster caused entirely by its addiction to spin. Stephen Byers resigned as Minister of Transport, admitting that, 'with hindsight', he might not have become such a media target if he had persuaded Jo Moore to resign after her notorious e-mail. That, he said, was the decision (to which Blair was party) that led the media to scrutinize his conduct in detail. They had much to scrutinize as well as his transport policy, which a Commons select committee described as vague, confused, ill balanced and poor value for money. There was his running battle with Martin Sixsmith over his departure as his director of information, along with Jo Moore. Byers's controversial effective renationalization of Railtrack turned into a furious row over the alleged attempt, by another of his special advisers, to seek information, again by e-mail, to discredit a Paddington rail crash survivor, a woman who provided evidence suggesting Byers had lied to Parliament over Railtrack. On 7 June 2002 – the anniversary of the very day that Blair won his second term – the *Daily Mail* led with 'How Blair's ruthless spin machine set out to destroy this brave woman'. The *Sun* commented: 'The behaviour of New Labour spin doctors is beneath contempt.'

A week earlier, as Byers departed ministerial life, newspapers, if not the *Daily Express*, were screaming about Blair inviting into No. 10 for tea Richard Desmond, the owner of the *Express* and of other titles described as pornographic. Eight days after Byers approved his takeover of the *Express* the Labour Party banked Desmond's donation of £100,000. Labour's spin doctors defended it on the astonishing grounds that the party does not make moral judgements about the people who support it.

Then in mid-June Downing Street rather ignominiously withdrew a complaint against *The Spectator*, the *Mail on Sunday* and the *Evening Standard* for claiming that Blair had sought a larger role in the Queen Mother's lying-in-state. No. 10's addiction to spinning instead of just letting the matter drop, having withdrawn its complaint, led it to produce a 29-page dossier which gave its row with Black Rod, the Queen's representative in Parliament, a new lease of life. The *Daily Mail* led with 'The smearing of Black Rod', claiming 'New Labour turns its venom on official who humiliated Blair'. This came only a few days after Downing Street had yet again tried to persuade the public that it had abandoned spin – an assertion that began to look farcical when a speech by Blair they had trailed failed to produce the promised blitz on shirkers.

The Government's lead steadily shrank to a mere three per cent, according to one poll. Robin Cook, leader of the Commons, became the most senior serving minister to inveigh against spin, in terms that contrasted Blair's 'packaging' with the late John Smith's 'blunt honesty'. Peter Hain acknowledged Labour had a 'trust problem' and that the damage caused to its reputation by rows over spin and sleaze could wreck its hopes of holding a referendum on the euro next year, only then to be himself accused of 'fibbing' over the outcome of a European summit in Spain. Lord Hattersley said that Alastair Campbell should go because he had become a liability. As the newspapers speculated rather tentatively about Campbell's demise, Charles Clarke, chairman of the party, went into a fearful rage about the media for criticizing a government that was 'whiter than white'. Its criticisms were 'pious and hypocritical, sometimes entirely manufactured', he said. He got little sympathy. No. 10 tried to spin him out of the ridicule into which he had plunged himself. 'What Charles is saying and what we agree with', they asserted, 'is that it's important judgements are made on the basis of fact. No one says the media can't criticize. But despite the brouhaha about so-called sleaze, nothing improper has been shown to have happened.' The *Mirror* despaired: 'New Labour is spinning to its grave.'

After five years spin doctors had reduced Labour to an appalling mess. Even David Blunkett, the Home Secretary, succumbed to the pressure – or went 'bonkers', as the *Mirror* put it – by claiming that the press were 'almost on the edge of insanity'. In the words of Peter Mandelson, Labour had lost public trust by its 'clumsy, crude over-use of spin'. 'Too much of what the Government is doing fails to make an impact because its words are dismissed as spin', he confessed.

The toll on the reputation of the most popular Prime Minister in British political history was revealed by the *Daily Telegraph* in a YouGov poll, when compared with one by Gallup in 1998, a year into his administration. Blair continued to score very high marks for confidence and energy – 85% compared with 93% in 1998 – and for being statesmanlike (60%–71%). He was also well ahead of Gordon Brown, who had just delivered a remarkably well-received tax-raising budget, as the public's choice of Prime Minister. Less helpfully, he had also maintained the impression that he wanted to please everybody (77%–79%).

But the real damage had occurred in the public's view of his strength as a Prime Minister and his honesty and trustworthiness. Both had plummeted, from 81% to 48% and from 77% to 31% respectively. He had reinforced the view that he lacked strong principles and relied too heavily on PR men and spin doctors – up respectively from 28% to 44% and from 52% to 71%. These findings were confirmed by an ICM poll for the *Daily Mirror*/GMTV, which showed the disillusionment in the body politic. Some 64% said Blair was too interested in image.

On this evidence it can scarcely be said that Blair's obsession with 'media, media, media' has served him well, For all his studied attention to his image, it was seriously on the slide. He seemed to be a man of easy principles with a dubious attachment to rich cronies who seemed to be doing rather well out of his government. Of course, it is impossible to know what impression the people would have had of him if his government had not been ruled by spin doctors. It is conceivable that it could have been worse, because we must at least recognize the possibility that their fiercely energetic efforts to project him in the most favourable light had some success in delaying the formation of unwelcome perceptions.

My view is that his reputation in office has been sustained only by the strong performance of the economy – and his government's welcome failure overtly to damage it – and the lack of a political alternative. It is at least possible that, had the old-fashioned and, by Campbell's standards, disengaged GIS been responsible for handling his presentation, he would have looked better for longer through its more measured, less frenetic approach.

The picture YouGov leaves is of an energetic politician energetically exposing his essential shallowness to the nation as the result of the endless machinations of his media minders dancing to his choreography. This proof of the inability of public relations specialists to turn water into wine, which I have always regarded as axiomatic, should come as a comfort to those who fear that spin-doctoring is a virus threatening the health of our democracy. The central, unresolved question is whether a bad government can, by presentational means, be prolonged in office through a general election into a further undeserved term. As yet, there is no evidence that this has yet occurred, taking into account the performance of the main alternative party.

In these circumstances does spin–doctoring matter? If the truth will always out, if spin is ultimately counter-productive, why bother about the phenomenon, especially when the sheer scale of New Labour's efforts may well have served only to advertise the less attractive nature of a government exceptionally dominated by a single personality? The answer is that it matters a great deal, because the unprecedented nature of New Labour's concentration on presentation has exposed the limitations of our democracy. For the whole of Blair's first five years Cabinet government was effectively in suspense. What Blair wanted Blair got, in a way that Thatcher could never take for granted. About the only blot on the landscape of his unbridled power was his brooding Chancellor, Gordon Brown, whose own erstwhile spin doctor Charlie Whelan revealed the depth of his wilful resentment at having been beaten to No. 10 by Blair.

Parliament was treated with disdain and left to rot, except in so far as it was necessary to secure Blair's ends. To be fair to him, most Labour MPs, many of them astonished to be in Parliament, seemed to be content to behave like ciphers and to have their privileges ridden roughshod over by the executive in the bargain. The opposition parties counted for even less. Betty Boothroyd protested ineffectually until she was succeeded as Speaker by Michael Martin, who was made of less stern stuff, though even he complained about the sidelining of the Commons. Blair had the Commons, if not the Lords (which he proceeded counterproductively to try to emasculate), just where he wanted it.

The senior Civil Service, from Cabinet Secretary downwards, was overwhelmed by the sheer power of a party with a massive 179 majority, next to no experience of government and even less respect for tradition, the constitution and the established ways of doing things. They had to cope with a somewhat anarchic Prime Minister and a government learning on the job, imbued with fanciful notions of what the Conservatives had got up to for eighteen long years and no pressing distractions in the form of economic crises or trade union disruption. In pursuit of office New Labour had also mislaid whatever convictions it had left after Thatcher's handbagging. They chased gimmicks such as 'Cool Britannia' and the 'Third Way' rather than carefully worked-out policies. Their only constant was their determination not to blow their economic legacy too quickly.

Conviction was replaced by spin – the ruthless manipulation of the message and the media, untrammelled by Civil Service ethic and constitutional restraint – and the narrow pursuit of immediate advantage, apparently to the blissful disregard of the longer-term consequences reflected in Blair's standing in the polls in April 2002. The chase for favourable headlines and good impressions, however misleading, removed the top echelon of the GIS. It conjured up, at the cost to the taxpayer of well over £4 million a year, a battalion of special advisers more than twice the size of the previous largest such force under John Major, not all of whom concentrated on seducing or bullying the media, although Jo Moore demonstrated what they were capable of getting up to. Apologists say that eighty-one spin doctors in a Civil Service of some 500,000 are neither here nor there. They are being disingenuous. A fair comparison is not even with the 3,000 in the top strata of the Civil Service – the senior policy makers; it is with the tiny fraction of the Civil Service staffing ministers' private offices.

Spin doctors thus came to exercise inordinate influence at the heart of No. 10 and ministerial teams in a government led by a media-mad Prime Minister. The central power of Campbell was demonstrated by his routine presence at Cabinet meetings (which I never attended), his urge to control and his readiness even to bawl out on paper, for the leaking thereof, ministers such as Harriet Harman and Frank Field at the Social Security Department. But that power was never quite enough to prevent some spin doctors, as Charlie Whelan and Jo Moore showed, from pursuing their mission to the narrow immediate advantage of their ministerial patron instead of the Government's wider reputation. This reinforced the public impression of a government 'spinning out of control', perhaps the most overworked headline of the Blair years.

Britain had never seen the likes of this before. It was the product of a controlling political mindset, lacking serious political conviction, and the unbridled power that Blair demonstrated that a Prime Minister can exercise in our system if Cabinet, Parliament and senior Civil Service all fail to function properly. Our Cabinet system of government is supposed to be the exercise of collective will and responsibility rather than a rubber stamp for an aspiring president. Our Parliament is supposed to hold the executive to account while at the same time securing the legislation that the governing party is entitled to enact by virtue of its manifesto commitments. Our senior Civil Service is supposed to keep the system operating with good order, discipline and integrity.

All failed to a greater or lesser extent for five years, though there are now occasional hints of redemption in Cabinet and Parliament. As a result Blair has, in practice, been more powerful than an American president, whose actions and authority are constitutionally limited by Congress and Senate, with a proper sense of their own rights and responsibilities as lawmakers. Never before in postwar Britain have all three dominoes fallen like this. But perhaps the most crucial collapse was that of the Cabinet domino. Its continued

failure to exercise its collective restraint in the face of evidence of
the damage to the Government facilitated the continuation of the
Mandelson/Campbell ethos and of operations from opposition into
government in a way that was previously unimagined.

Campbell and his spin doctors simply could not have existed
before 1997. Cabinet's failure, and Cabinet ministers' own addiction to spin and to spin doctors, rendered the senior Civil
Service seriously impotent. They would, of course, deny it.
They can reasonably say that nobody knows how much restraint
they have exercised and how much worse it might have been but
for them, since we have little idea what their advice has been or
how it was heeded. We have to judge by results. They are not a
pretty sight.

The devastation wrought on the constitution is arguably worse
because of the performance of the media. I have sought to show
how for centuries the press were at best tolerated and how
working journalists, as distinct from editors, were careful not to
overplay their hand. It was perhaps inevitable, with a change in
society's values in the 1960s and with the growing sense of media
power fuelled by television, that press, radio and television in their
different ways should have become more self-confident, more
demanding, more conscious of their power and, sadly, nastier. That
could help to explain Campbell's urge to subjugate, as distinct
from manage, them. It was not, however, inevitable, given their
innate pride in themselves as independent searchers after truth and
light, that overnight the media should become so tame under Blair
after being so beastly to Major.

That tameness is all the more puzzling because of the brutal
methods employed by Campbell and his ilk to cow the craft of
journalism. In earlier, more robust times they would have earned
him very short shrift indeed. Of course, every self-respecting
editor can dig up examples of a continuing independence of mind
and spirit during Blair's first term. But at least until the Dome
débâcle on the eve of the millennium they were a radically different media from those I had known as a Government press officer
from 1967 to 1990, even allowing for the years of Thatcher admiration. They sharpened their edge after the 2001 election, but all
too often that edge remains blunted, not by the way the press

ignores the twin features of spin and 'sleaze', but by their treatment of stories, by their hiding on inside pages of material that would have had them in a state of front-page hysteria in my time. The Fourth Estate, as the fourth domino to fall, did little to discourage Blair spin.

29

Bottling the genie

A S ALWAYS, the Parliamentary recess in August 2002 brought the Government some relief as it entered its sixth year. It did not, however, stop spinning. Even moving the Labour Party's headquarters from the Millbank Tower to older premises in Old Queen Street, off St James's Park, was portrayed as symbolic, putting behind it the crucible in which the Government's remarkably damaging methods of managing the media had been crystallized. As the summer wore on, the Government was accused of chicanery over its supposed policy to deport 30,000 failed asylum seekers and in claiming to have brought street crime under control. In truth, its problem had become insuperable. So assiduously had it poured itself into a mould that the Government was irrevocably cast as an inveterate spinner. Whatever it did, it was assumed to be bending or twisting the facts. It had become incredible.

The response of some of our liberal so-called élite would be to get rid of the Lobby, as though it were the engine of the Government's fate. This has been their parrot cry for decades, and they often wrongly pronounced the system – 'Ingham's hallelujah chorus', as Jonathan Aitken once described it – dead during my time as No. 10 press secretary. They seem to assume the Lobby is a creature of Government, when in fact it is an independent body for journalists, run by journalists. It is not at the Government's disposal.

None the less, Alastair Campbell has moved steadily away from the Lobby system he inherited, trying to take credit for a more open relationship with journalists. The briefings by the Prime Minister's spokesman were first put on the record and then posted on the internet to circumvent the Lobby middlemen and give it to the internet public 'straight'. The effect was rather spoiled when Nicholas Jones, found evidence that the record was somewhat selective. Then, as relations with the media steadily deteriorated, Campbell produced a new gimmick on 2 May 2002. Morning Lobby briefings were to become press conferences, open to all journalists, including specialists in whatever issue was topical as well as foreign correspondents resident in Britain. Sometimes these briefings would be taken by ministers and, in that event, could be televised and broadcast whereas, when officials took them, cameras and microphones would not be admitted, to preserve the officials' anonymity. If anything, this was a snub to Parliament. At a stroke Campbell, presenting the move as a further release of the Government's stays, had created a regular alternative forum to the Commons in which ministers could perform before the news cameras.

Two further moves brought, first, a monthly American presidential-style televised press conference by the Prime Minister to by-pass the filter of the press and reach the viewing public unedited and uninterpreted, and second, occasional prime ministerial appearances before the Commons' liaison committee, composed of the chairmen of the thirty-five Commons' select committees, no doubt to try to squash the notion that Blair doesn't take Parliament seriously. His performance at the inaugural press conference was described by the *Sun* as 'fudge and flannel from a world-class showman', which would not satisfy the voters. His Commons interrogators were accused by *The Guardian* of 'attacking him with their feather dusters'. It would have been better had he been seen in each case to have been withstanding a savaging. Both forums seemed contrived and unreal. But that is the problem when a government gets a reputation for spinning.

None of these innovations is a substitute for a sensible day-to-day relationship with journalists. They are also a tacit admission that the Government cannot eliminate whatever troublesome specialist groups (such as the Lobby) the media come up with. In a free society the media can organize themselves as they will to facilitate

news-gathering. Their attachment to the group concept was confirmed in a devolved Scotland, which had a chance to start afresh
but found political correspondents insistent on aping the
Westminster model. This is not surprising because groups work to
the advantage of the majority weaker journalists (for example,
those in the provinces) who would otherwise find access to information and ministers more difficult. Helping the weak is not a bad
thing if it contributes to the preservation of a multiplicity of media
outlets. The group therapy involved in any Lobby or collective
briefing does, of course, expose journalists to the risk of a press secretary 'stampeding' their judgement. It also exposes the press secretary not merely to vicious journalists who take delight in playing to
their own sadistic gallery but also, more importantly, to day-to-day
scrutiny by the media, a revealing way of keeping their finger on
the Government's pulse. By admitting journalists generally to
morning briefings, Campbell no doubt hoped to limit the time
available to political correspondents to pursue their unhelpful preoccupation with the latest political difficulty.

The alternative to the Lobby is an individual No. 10 relationship
with journalists. This is fine in theory but probably impractical
because of the sheer volume of inquiries that would result.
Regular collective meetings are at least a convenient way of saving
time. The demise of the Lobby would facilitate one of the worst
aspects of spin-doctoring – playing one journalist off against
another, as has occurred in briefing about the single currency –
and would probably bring a faster breakdown in media relations
than anything else yet devised. Get rid of the Lobby and the
Government would create the conditions for its reinvention, as
Churchill (by ignoring it) and Jo Haines (by ceasing to meet it)
tended to confirm.

In any case, the Lobby is not the real problem. Nor are special
advisers, as such, nor, within reason, their numbers. The problem
is how best to have a sensible, functioning, principled and effective
relationship between the Government and the media, acknowledging all the tensions that arise in a healthy democracy. We shall
not solve it unless we recognize that it arises from the abuse of a
well-established system that worked reasonably well until the Blair
government stamped its hobnailed boots all over Whitehall and

Westminster. That system would have worked much better if the British system of government had been more open, taken communication more seriously and been less disdainful of communicators. In that event it might also have been less open to abuse. It is therefore important to recognize that, for all its violence to the system, New Labour did at least identify some of its failings, even if it went about remedying them the wrong way by sacking the most senior members of the GIS.

While the Government, having substantially created the problem, tries to finesse it, Parliamentarians, the opposition parties, past, present and future Cabinet secretaries, the Civil Service unions and anybody who takes our Parliamentary democracy seriously are cudgelling their brains to find a way forward. The first issue we need to dispose of is whether to preserve a professional, permanent and politically impartial Civil Service, in the sense that it retains its capacity effectively to serve the people's choice of government, or whether to replace it with the American 'spoils' system, which results in a turnover of some 7–8,000 posts when a new president comes in. There can be no question of summarily ditching the Northcote–Trevelyan reforms of the late nineteenth century, which removed the Civil Service 'from the field of political jobbery by the adoption of open competition as the method of entrance', as G.M. Trevelyan put it in 1942. Any such notion is a matter not for the incumbent government but for Parliament after proper public debate. But we need to be on our guard against drifting into a hybrid system through the proliferation of a combination of special advisers and cronies. There are those such as Charlie Whelan who cannot for the life of them think why a government should not bring in whomever it wants to do whatever job it wants done at public expense. The danger is that that is where we shall end up if we are not careful. The taxpayer will then have been hi-jacked for political ends.

If we choose to stick with the existing system, we need to resolve three issues: how many paid special advisers/cronies a government should be allowed; the terms on which they should be employed (that is, what the taxpayer should allow them and not allow them to do); and how to ensure that the political impartiality of the Civil Service is preserved.

The public have a right to limit the number of special advisers since they pay their wages. After all, they limit by law the number of ministers who can be paid from the public purse. However, the abstract case for limitation of numbers is clearer than what that limit should be. Provisionally the Conservatives have suggested it should be 25% below the current tally of eighty-one, of whom some twenty-six are in No 10. At present very few have any real grasp of what is a fair and reasonable number to permit a government to be properly advised or of whether a cap might be circumvented by the appointment of assorted tsars and the likes of Lord Birt, former director-general of the BBC, who seems to be accountable only to the Prime Minister (since he refused to give evidence to a Commons select committee).

Far more important and necessary to determine, if numbers are to be properly regulated, is whether it is legitimate for special advisers to be employed at public expense, not for their policy expertise but for their party political sympathy, in a political role and whether that political role can be defined. In one sense this is a simple issue. There are broadly three kinds of special adviser: those with expert policy input; those, usually young apparatchiks, who aspire to a Parliamentary seat and are learning the ropes; and media specialists who may or may not seek a Parliamentary career. Policy experts are not the subject of controversy, provided they observe the special advisers' code. It is the other two – apparatchiks or apprentice politicians and spin doctors – that cause difficulties. It has been estimated that up to half of New Labour's eighty-one special advisers have a communications role, though the official number is just eleven.

My inclination would be to permit the Prime Minister to have a personal think-tank or policy unit of, say, six special advisers and each Cabinet minister two special advisers, picked for their policy expertise. If any minister wished to employ more, he or she should be required to make a case to the public accounts committee, which is pre-eminently concerned with securing value for money for the taxpayer.

I would also permit each Cabinet minister, including the Prime Minister, a single political secretary at public expense. His job would be to liaise on political issues with the party in Parliament and the country, together with the minister's Parliamentary private secretary – an MP. This would formally recognize the political training role of special adviser posts. Political secretaries would be prohibited from any governmental presentational role and in their political work would be subject to the existing provisions of the code of conduct for special advisers.

That leaves special advisers operating partly or wholly as spin doctors. On the face of it they present an acute difficulty. It has never been possible to divorce presentation from political benefit, as was recognized in the guidance I grew up with on Government publicity which conceded that a well-founded publicity campaign can redound to the political benefit of the party in government. The notion that all Government press officers are therefore working to the Government's political advantage is used to argue that Campbell's position is more honest than mine was or, by implication, than the position of any other No. 10 press secretary. It is, in fact, just as much self-serving nonsense as New Labour's solution to the persistent stories of benefits accruing to Labour Party donors and their businesses – namely, to have the state fund our political parties. Instead, the long-standing recognition that good press officer work can bring a political benefit is an argument not for party political appointees to 'regularize' the matter but for Civil Servants operating under restraints set out in this book to ensure that any benefit is natural and incidental. It is entirely right that the very considerable power of any government and its pub-licity machine, paid for by the taxpayer, should be constrained by rules that are enforceable and enforced.

Accordingly, I would ban, on the basis of this government's per-formance, the appointment of special advisers with a media role and with control over Civil Servants. That would also eliminate Campbell and Jonathan Powell, Blair's chief of staff, in their present form. We should then have a clear, consistent and conse-quently enforceable system across government safeguarding, to some extent, the political impartiality of Civil Servants.

To reinforce it, and the Civil Service press secretaries who would have responsibility for managing the Government's presen-tation, I would require the preparation of a code of practice that laid down details of their access to ministers, meetings and the information required to do their job. The problem of senior Civil Service disdain for communication and communicators may be more acute post–Blair rather than less so, given the damage caused by the excesses of Campbell and his spin doctors.

I would also seek to guard against any recurrence of the New Labour problem arising from ignorance, after effectively a generation in the political wilderness. Opposition parties should understand the constraints and limitations under which Civil Servants and not least Civil Service press officers must operate. There are various ways in which this could be done, but there is no substitute for working experience. Accordingly, I would provide leaders of opposition parties with a qualifying proportion of votes at a general election with an official Civil Service press secretary charged with doing his best, within the Civil Service code, for his temporary employer. Such an arrangement would not preclude the opposition parties, any more than it would the governing party, from a polemical approach to communications with the public through their own party's political apparatus.

The next issue is how to enforce any regime that is instituted. There are three elements in the debate. First there are those who would have a Civil Service Act providing statutory protection for the impartiality of Civil Servants, limiting the role and powers of political appointees − that is, special advisers − and providing for greater prime ministerial and special adviser accountability. Then there are those such as, notably, the immediate past Cabinet Secretary, Sir Richard Wilson, who wish to promote a debate by canvassing the idea of the Civil Service Act. Finally there are those such as Lord Armstrong of Ilminster, another former Cabinet Secretary, who have no urge to legislate, except perhaps to put a statutory limit on the number of special advisers, since legislation encourages a narrow view as to whether behaviour falls on the right side of the line instead of a wider and more restraining view as to whether it is in the public interest. All are, however, desperately concerned to preserve a professional, non–political career Civil Service in the national interest.

This brings us to the crux of the problem, assuming politicians are willing to clarify whether they wish to stick with an impartial Civil Service and whether or not they agree with the new framework of control of numbers, duties and behaviour I have outlined. It is the issue on which spin doctors have focused attention: how rules can be made to stick and why, if existing rules have not been enforced, any new legislation will be, whether primary in the form of a bill or secondary in the form of regulations.

There has been no lack of rules and codes for either ministers or special advisers for the last five years, but there has been a willingness and an ability to ignore them when they might have got in the way of perceived political advantage. Demarcation between impartial Civil Servants and special advisers exercising authority over them has also been blurred. Civil Servants in No. 10 report to one of three political appointees. In view of their performance during what will become known as the Poodle Parliament of 1997–2001, it is impossible to regard the average Parliamentary select committee as the obvious enforcing agent. For this reason thoughts increasingly turn to legislation in the form of a Civil Service Act. Its enforcement remains problematical. Yet if we cannot rely on our established institutions, reinforced as they are today by whole kennels of standards watchdogs, then our democracy is in a parlous state.

The best reason for returning to the order of the pre-1997 watershed, supplemented by iron rules of the kind I have suggested, is the manifest failure of the Blair way of government, with its obsession with media manipulation, to uphold its reputation and that of politics generally. Spin-doctoring as practised in the past five years has proved lethal to political reputations. Rational politicians would recognize this and act on it. It is certainly something that the wider private sector public relations industry has sensed. In March 2002 *PR Week* concluded after its PR and media conference that 'the PR industry must seek to win back its credibility by divorcing itself from spin doctoring'. This damaging phenomenon has flourished because of the failures to varying degrees of the Prime Minister, Cabinet, Parliament, senior Civil Service and the media. The public have registered their protest: fewer than 60% voted in the 2001 election. It is not merely No. 10 or the Government that is spinning out of control: it is our democracy. The wages of spin are disrepute and decay.

Index